FURNITURE STYLES (No

of the Chippendale Gang)

only five really original st
of our modern Western civilization: Queen
Anne in England; Colonial, Shaker, and
American Fancy in the United States; and
Empire in France.

UNITED STATES

COLONIAL
1630-1725

Because it was designed to be used instead of looked at, its simple beauty, gained by indirection, has never been surpassed. The first and most "functionally designed" furniture of all.

SHAKER
1760-1800

Simply unique, a "sport," a wonderful mutation out of the wonderful mind of man.

American Fancy
1790-1840

A joyful, frivolous spree of imaginative imitation that includes, beside the well-known Fancy chairs, also Spool furniture, Boston Rockers, and the Hitchcock chairs.

American Victorian
1840-1910

After Victorian, which was as American in origin as it was English, came an atrocious series of fads that even exceeded Victorian in bad taste. Included were Turkish, Spanish, and French cubism styles.

FRENCH

Renaissance
1502-1643

From here until Empire, the French cabinetmakers followed the English in "borrowing" their ideas from the Greek and Roman ruins—and even went to Egypt at the height of their creative poverty.

Louis XIV	1643-1715
Louis XV	1715-1774
Louis XVI	1774-1793

PROVINCIAL
1730-1810

A country version of Louis XV, made well into the 1800's, and a great improvement, by simplification, over the fussy, sissy stuff French royalty loved so well.

EMPIRE
1804-1815

The most recent of the really original styles coinciding again with the birth of a new society, the Republic of France, born in the blood of revolution.

THE FURNITURE DOCTOR

The FURNITURE DOCTOR

Being practical information for everybody about the care, repair, and refinishing of furniture...with easy to follow directions and tricks of the trade that use commonly available materials...all presented with the author's usual hilarious anecdotes in the Yankee manner and more about his infamous Uncle George.

by GEORGE GROTZ

Garden City, New York
DOUBLEDAY & COMPANY, INC.

Library of Congress Catalog Card Number 62–7640

Printed in the United States of America

This book is fondly
dedicated to
MY INFAMOUS UNCLE GEORGE,
who has always claimed that
anyone who spends even one winter
in Vermont deserves some kind
of a medal

WARNING: PREFACE AHEAD

HOW TO USE THIS BOOK

Now there is a heading to make women weep and strong men cry!

How to use this book, indeed!

Who ever reads a book he has to find out how to use? Not me! Why that's like reading the directions on a can before you have messed everything up. Personally, I always prefer to wade in profoundly uninstructed on the obviously nutty theory that I already know everything. But there is a way of justifying this. I tell myself that I will learn more from my mistakes than I ever could by being a submissive follower of instructions and bowing to the dubious authority of some distant and unknown manufacturer. What can he know sitting in his alternately steam-heated and air-conditioned office? It's us fellows out on the firing line that know what goes on. You have to wear gloves in your shop in the winter and roast in your own sawdust in the summer to really know a thing or two!

Therefore I suggest to all readers like myself that they read no further. Cease and desist. It will only make you neurotic or something.

STOP READING HERE.

Now for those of you who go about things in an adult and intelligent way, let me say that this book is designed to give specific answers to specific questions—on all aspects of furniture care, repair, and refinishing. In other words, you don't have to take a course in cabinetmaking, and then one in wood finishing to find out how to replace a broken rung. The whole process is described in one listing in the section on EASY-TO-MAKE REPAIRS.

That's right, just like a cookbook. Glance through the Contents and you will see.

But there is lots more to it than that, because I wanted to make this a really comprehensive book—the kind I always wished I could find when I first started. That was about fourteen shops ago, but that is another story. Anyway, you will also find many listings that define, describe, or explain.

Let's say you want to find out what tulip poplar looks like, and how to identify it by color, feel, grain, and so forth. And you want to know if it is the same thing as tulipwood, which the fellow down the street says it is. Well, it isn't the same, and you will find both of them listed in the section on ALL ABOUT THE WOODS. You will also find a lot more that I think is interesting and you ought to know if you are going to work with either of them.

But let's get back to your questions that involve a "how-to-do-it" process. If your question is how to refinish a pine table, simply find the listing for *pine* in the section on WOODS. Maybe you already know that you want to make your pine table look like cherry (somebody told you it could be done), and you want a varnish finish on the top. In the section on FINISHES: DECEPTIVE, you will find a listing for *faking cherry*. Reasonable? And the listing for *varnish finish* comes in the section on FINISHES: CLEAR. Not to mention that there are all kinds of cross references back and forth to help you find your answers as quickly as possible.

And so it goes. The best thing to do—as it is with a cookbook—is to spend a few minutes scanning the Contents to orientate yourself to the Grotz brand of logic that underlies the organization of this book. In fact, there is even a mild logic to the order in which the various sections are arranged. This is for people who are tired of reading dictionaries and are looking for a small encyclopedia to read straight through.

Finally, for those who can spare a few minutes, I have gone

to the trouble to write a general introduction to each separate section. I am told by experienced authors that nobody ever reads these either—any more than they read prefaces or instructions on cans. But I have conformed to tradition and done my part by writing them, so anything you feel you could do about reading them will be appreciated.

And that's all. Except, in the words of my dearly beloved sister, when you get old and gray, may you spend all your winters in Florida, and your summers midst the cool, green grasses of Vermont.

Good luck.

GEORGE GROTZ

April 2, 1961
E. Poultney, Vt.

CONTENTS

THE FURNITURE DOCTOR

Section 1

THE GENTLE ART OF ACQUISITION

Or, gold is where you find it—whatever that may mean

Hello, out there! And welcome to the strange but happy world of people who are always fussing around with their furniture.

But do you really care? I mean about acquiring furniture. Isn't it a pretty stuffy subject for a spring day like this. Do you realize that while I am forced to sit here in the house this afternoon, outside the air is like a clear, cold sip of well-water. And this year's brand-new sun is beating down on the hills of Vermont, still soggy from the melting-off of the winter snows. And down in the village this morning everyone was talking about whether it is time to set out tomato plants.

On a day like this all I can think of is that everybody I know already has more furniture than he knows what to do with, anyway. But maybe you are one of the inexcusably young, and are just getting started at gathering the encumbrances of life.

Or maybe your house has just burned down. (I suppose that's a little grim, but we pull no punches in Vermont.)

Or maybe you have just been divorced.

Or maybe you have just run away from home.

Or just migrated to this country.

Or had all your furniture stolen by some robbers with a moving van while you were away on vacation.

Or you sublet your house to a couple with nine small children.

Say, it gets to be quite a lot of people when you stop to think about it, doesn't it? So in the following pages I have tried to tell all the things that I—and quite a few friends—have learned about the advantages and pitfalls of all the sources for furniture we could think of.

Of course, if you have plenty of money, there really isn't any problem. All you have to do is to go to good furniture stores or well-established antique dealers. So most of these sources are places where you can pick up the raw material for furniture. Inexpensively. Then you have to start thinking in terms of what you can do with the "horror" that you have acquired. Can you repair it? Refinish it? Cut down the legs? Decorate it? Or combine it with something else you already have?

But you will have to excuse me now. Through the window I see my wife coming across the lawn (if you can call it that at this time of year) carrying a flat box full of something leafy and green. Obviously the discussion is over, and the elders of our town have decided that indeed it is time to set out our tomato plants. I wonder if she bought any tar paper, or if we will have to cut the bottoms out of tin cans again? And where was it I saw that trowel just a few days ago?

antique shops These cover the United States like the National Broadcasting Company, and believe me, they are all in close contact with each other. This is because some things go better in some parts of the country than others. This results in a degree of transshipment around the country that has led some observers to believe that most dealers make their living by selling to one another.

For instance, Empire is sneered at in New England, but brings a good price in the South. Pine furniture sells best in northern New England. Cherry sells better in Connecticut than it does in the other New England states. Oxbows that go for five dollars in New England or the Middle West bring fifteen dollars in Texas (where, I suppose, they are more useful for proving that one's granddaddy came out by covered wagon).

And, of course, there's a great deal more of this that I don't know about, or have heard and forgotten. The point to the prospective buyer is that you're not likely to get a bargain in an antique shop. On the other hand, the chances of your

getting gypped are also pretty thin. These people are in business to make a living. And—like the rest of us—whether they want to be honest or not, they have to be to keep old customers and get new ones.

The only thing to look out for is that there are quite a few two-price shops. I'd *guess* about 15 per cent. By a two-price shop I mean one in which all the merchandise is marked up 10 or 20 per cent over what the dealer really wants for it.

This isn't really dishonest, it's more of a sales trick. The dealer has simply found that he or she sells more if the customers can feel they have got a bargain. It's just a matter of everything being on sale all the time.

For those who are interested in locating antique shops, the largest national publication in the field is the magazine *Antiques*. While not on all newsstands, it can be found in public libraries, and frequently contains ads and listings for hundreds of good shops all across the country.

But the person who is trying to stretch his money doesn't belong in an antique shop. As I have mentioned before, antique dealers are in business to make a living. Therefore, they use their free time doing their own finishing, repairing, cutting down, etc. The result is that they have few pieces for sale that still have potential for improvement. For such pieces, you have to find auctions, pickers, and junk dealers; or, to some extent, the Good Will and Salvation Army stores. All these are covered in listings below.

attics Naturally, if you have an attic, you've already looked in it before buying this book. The problem is to get into other people's attics. After you have exhausted any friends or country relatives, the best way I know to get into other people's attics is the way the pickers and dealers do it. This is to run an ad in your local paper to the effect that you buy old paper and rags. Then when you get inquiries, you dress in your dirtiest clothes, and go calling in a twenty-five-dollar automobile.

This gets you into the attic, and there you can look around. First you buy the rags, and then the real larceny begins. Let's say you've noticed a chest of drawers that you figure is worth ten dollars. What you do is walk over to a complete wreck of a chair not worth ten cents, and start worrying aloud if it's worth a couple of dollars to you. (Or the dummy can be a jug with the bottom broken out of it, and you make believe you don't see this.) Anyway, once the victim's appetite has been whetted, you say something like, "Well, I guess I could give you a couple of bucks for the chair, if you'll throw in that worthless old chest over there that I can use for storing paint cans in my cellar."

Once home, you throw away the chair, and start to work on your ten-dollar chest that has cost you two. Indirection, it's called. The old con game. If you'd said you'd wanted the chest to refinish for your bedroom, it would have cost you fifteen dollars.

But watch out for the little old ladies in the country. With them you are likely to find that the chest has been eaten to a dusty hollow shell by wood beetles and is worth less than the chair!

auctions Making good buys at auctions isn't really easy. You have to know the tricks of the game. Let me give you an example. About two weeks ago I went down to Bus Mars' regular Tuesday-night auction in Pawlett. Before the sale started I saw an old beat-up table, drop-leaf, that was pure cherry as far as I could see. So I set my top price at $14.50. Well, when the table came up, Bus started it at $5. I bid and finally got it for only $7.50. Joy. Until I got it home and scraped an edge of a leaf, and found it was not cherry, but a wood as light as poplar. Chagrin. Smart boy got fooled. But then when I took the leaves down to the bare wood, the thing turned out to be curly birch, which is better than cherry any day.

So the first rule for buying at an auction is to be lucky. The second is, *always* get there early and inspect the merchandise before the sale starts. When I haven't done this I really have been stung. Like the pine commode I bought that turned out to be oak. And the sea chest with the bottom and back rotted out of it. *Caveat emptor,* for sure!

The third rule is to decide on the price you are willing to pay, and not let the excitement make you go over it. Sure, something might go at $8 when your top bid was $7.50. But that doesn't mean you would have got it for $8. You'd have had to go to $8.50 at least, and if the other bidder really had wanted the thing, you might have been forced up to $12.50 or more before you realized you had auction fever.

borax stores Borax is the trade term for flashy-looking but very cheaply made new furniture. The term probably goes back to the days when the wooden boxes in which borax was shipped made good substitute furniture in mining camps and other outlying districts.

This stuff is so bad, you can hardly believe it. The wood grain is actually printed on composition board and then finished in a murky way with a spray gun. Only enough real wood is used for the frame as is needed to hold the box together. It is then sold at three hundred dollars a set to poor people who are sucked in with a "no money down, only twenty-five cents a day" offer. And of course it falls apart before it's half paid for.

It's the modern version of selling the Brooklyn Bridge to an Irish immigrant. Among others, my great grandfather bought that, but then he turned around and sold it at a profit. (Not really.)

cabinet shops Unknown to most people every major city still has shops where fine furniture and reproductions are made by hand, and made to last. There's not much money in it, but the men who run these shops do it because craftsmanship is in their blood. Most of them are really artists, and their furniture is just as well made as it was in the Golden Century of cabinetmaking—that is, the 1700s.

It's priced a little higher than factory-made things, but the difference is more than worth it. And the same goes for pieces they have found and restored.

Canada This listing is included because it seems that these days Canada is where the antiques are coming from. One wholesaler I know of buys three truckloads a month—except in winter. On the East Coast one of the places this stuff funnels through is the New Bedford area of Massachusetts. Of course, a lot of things are still coming to light in Maine, Vermont, and New Hampshire. These mostly go to Connecticut dealers, and then to New York City or wherever.

But when mechanized farming comes to a rural area the first bumper crop of furniture appears, and this is happening in Canada now. Where you would go on the West Coast I don't know, but you can be sure the same thing is happening. There it must filter down through Washington and Oregon towards the big cities in California.

furniture stores Anything bought at a cheap furniture store is a waste of money. If you don't know of a good old-line furniture store—and they are dying out—go to the furniture department of a department store with a good reputation. Also, don't be surprised when your six-hundred-dollar bedroom set can only be sold for one hundred dollars five years later. Furniture depreciates even faster than automobiles. That is the best reason for buying antiques. They not only don't depreciate, they go up in value over the years because of their constantly increasing scarcity in proportion to the population.

Good Will stores These are stores run by charity groups both to raise funds and to give work to older people, and so on. They get their furniture by donation, and repair it, and often refinish it. Sometimes the refinishing is fine, but at other times it's pretty bad. In that case though, it comes off easily. The prices asked are fairly low, and many dealers make regular calls at such stores to see if an occasional "real buy" has come up. Sometimes it does. I used to go to one place that charged eight dollars for small oak chests of drawers and only four dollars for pine, which are always older and better antiques than any oak.

inheritance Hard as it may seem at times, it is really better to just wait than to try to hurry things along.

junk dealers Don't be disdainful—or as one of my sons says, "snobby"—about junk dealers, for they are a prime source for both antiques and furniture that lends itself to remodeling and decoration. In fact, they usually have drifted into close association with dealers and decorators.

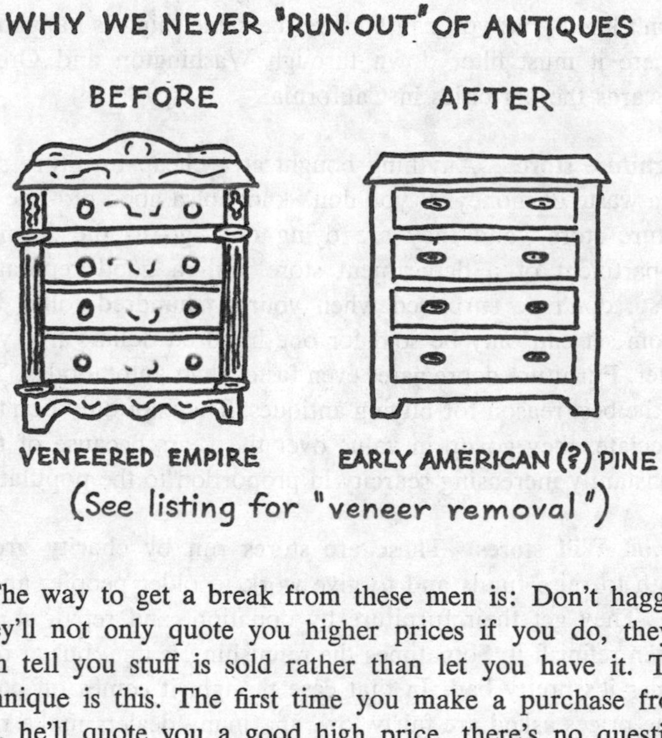

The way to get a break from these men is: Don't haggle. They'll not only quote you higher prices if you do, they'll even tell you stuff is sold rather than let you have it. The technique is this. The first time you make a purchase from one, he'll quote you a good high price, there's no question about it. But instead of objecting, say something like, "Well, that's more than I was going to pay, but I suppose you men have to make a living too." In fact, you can even ham it up by being sympathetic about how high his overhead must be, and how hard it is to get steady help, and like that. He's probably paying fifteen dollars a month for his store, and fifty cents an hour to his stumble-bum help, but it is impossible for you to go too far. Junk dealers are smart, and almost always are secretly rich, but one thing they all have in common is absolutely no sense of humor.

kits (reproductions) Here I have to make a completely unsolicited (and, believe me, unpaid) commercial. The biggest operator in this field is Francis Hagerty, of Cohasset Colonials, Cohasset, Massachusetts. His line is limited to reproductions of Early American pieces, but he has everything from cupboards to cobbler's benches, and they're good. I've assembled and finished a lot of them, and with a little "distressing" you can hardly tell them from the real thing (see section on AGING ANTIQUES).

I suppose the real purpose of making reproductions in kit form is to be able to sell them reasonably by mail. There are many shops making reproductions and selling them unfinished but assembled. These sell in their own local areas. However, there is some sale by mail. See listing for *unfinished furniture* (*reproductions*) at the end of this section.

lumber yards Many people don't realize that most lumber yards not only sell standard lengths of lumber, but will for a small extra charge cut it, plane it, and otherwise work it. Places called "mills" will do all kinds of woodworking for you. These are places that make storm windows and doors, built-ins for kitchens of new houses, and so on. Any carpenter can help you locate one. Often, lumber yards and mills are combined operations.

If you can measure, and make a scale drawing, you can have furniture kits cut out of pine boards, and also trestle tables, shelves, bookcases, record boxes, and things like that. Built-in cupboards are a good trick, too. I once made one which covered the whole end of a room about ten feet wide. First make a sketch to decide what you want the thing to look like. Make it big, or redraw it bigger. Then make your measurements against the wall—you can even draw the setup on the wall—and then mark down the lengths of board needed on your drawing. If you are going to have doors, don't order the wood for them at first. Wait until you have the risers, shelves, and facing pieces all up. Then measure the size of the openings for the doors, and take these measurements down to the mill. The reason for this is that the openings may not turn out the size you expected, and it makes the measuring in the first place easier.

The room-end cupboard with shelves and doors that I made cost about thirty-five dollars for the lumber and another ten dollars for cutting, and took a day to put up and paint white. It could have been stained. Can you imagine how much all that shelf and storage space would cost even in the cheapest unfinished furniture?

pickers They are the bird dogs of the antique business. They came into existence because the areas in and around cities have been literally picked clean of old furniture. So the dealers in those areas—where most of the selling is done—have come to rely on people who live in the hinterlands to do their buying for them.

Sometimes even whole states get picked clean. Dealers from Connecticut, for instance, buy most of their stuff from pickers in upper Vermont, New Hampshire, and Maine. And recently, of course, from Canada, where the pickings are best. Pickers buy a lot of things at auctions in their areas, but many things are brought to them, because everybody has found out that they will give five or ten dollars for a two-hundred-year-old curly-maple table. They then sell it to a dealer from the suburbs of some city for forty dollars. The dealer has it refinished, and sells it to his customers for something over a hundred dollars.

A picker will sell to you as well as to a dealer, and for the same price—especially if you tell him you are furnishing a house and will be back for more. The trouble is finding these pickers with their barns full of treasures.

One of the best ways is to cruise around looking for antique shops that are on back roads off the beaten path of even the summer tourists. The logic of the situation is, How could he be making a living if he wasn't selling to other dealers. Of course, most won't even have signs out. The only way to find them is to marry a newspaper reporter (male or female) who knows how to ask questions in the right places—of the licensed auctioneers in an area, for instance.

Salvation Army stores The same situation as with *Good Will stores*. See listing in this section.

town dumps Many city people will laugh at this, but in many small towns, the town dump is called "the store." I am sitting in a chair, next to a table, both of which came from our dump. A sort of general agreement comes into being that when you have a piece that might be of some use to somebody else, or could possibly be repaired, you don't throw it over the edge of the dump, but place it to one side.

The best times of the year are at spring-cleaning time, and when the summer people are closing up their cottages and houses at the end of the season. Good pickings.

unfinished furniture (modern) It is amazing what a good finish can do for these pieces. See sections on FINISHES.

unfinished furniture (reproductions) Some very good chairs, and sometimes even tables and chests, are offered by mail through the mail-order sections of the "home" magazines, and there are many factories doing local businesses around cities. You find these outlets especially in recently developed suburban areas, as opposed to old-time residential sections. Of course, you don't find them as frequently as places selling unfinished modern.

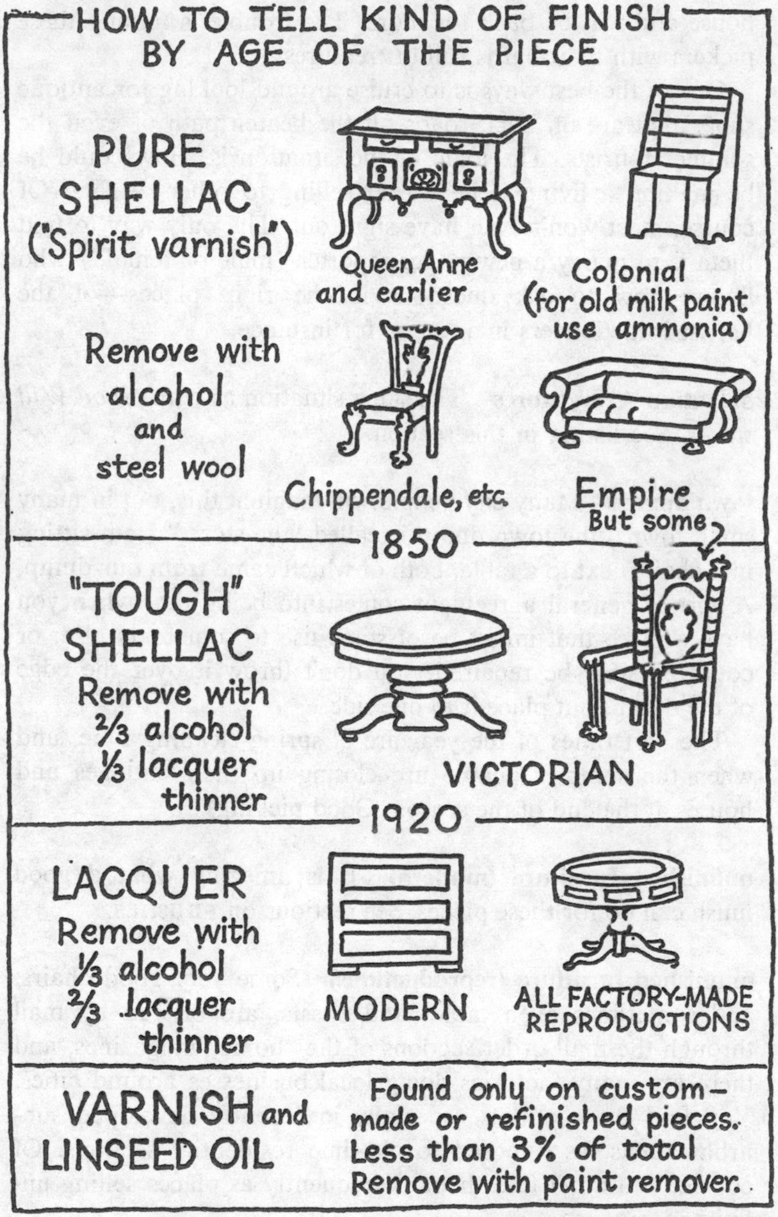
HOW TO TELL KIND OF FINISH
BY AGE OF THE PIECE
PURE
SHELLAC
("Spirit varnish")
Queen Anne
and earlier
Colonial
(for old milk paint
use ammonia)
Remove with
alcohol
and
steel wool
Chippendale, etc.
Empire
But some
1850
"TOUGH"
SHELLAC
Remove with
2/3 alcohol
1/3 lacquer
thinner
VICTORIAN
1920
LACQUER
Remove with
1/3 alcohol
2/3 lacquer
thinner
MODERN
ALL FACTORY-MADE
REPRODUCTIONS
VARNISH and
LINSEED OIL
Found only on custom-
made or refinished pieces.
Less than 3% of total
Remove with paint remover.

Section 2

33 WAYS TO RESTORE OLD FINISHES

Being a scientific survey—of the easiest ways out!

Years ago my little old Irish grandmother told me that there used to be a recipe for rabbit stew that began, "First you catch a rabbit." And I suppose that's funny enough as it stands, but not long ago one of my little old New England ladies told me a different version. According to her it goes, "First you decide if what you have is a rabbit." For the uninitiated, the reference here is to woodchuck. But believe me, woodchuck stew is delicious—so long as you don't know what it is until the meal is over.

Well, anyway, the point is that when trying to restore an old finish, it's the New England recipe that counts: first you have to figure out what kind of a finish it is that you have in hand. And there are two approaches to this problem.

The easiest one is the historical approach. By that I mean that if you know when the piece was made, you can tell even before you see it what the finish will be. This is the sort of information that the old codgers use to impress the innocent. I saw one do it at an auction once. Some summer people had bought an early Victorian table. It was the kind of Victorian with simple curving lines (instead of a lot of fussy machine-carving) that looks like a first cousin to Empire because it is. Well, the summer people were involved in an argument as to whether the finish was varnish or shellac or lacquer or what.

So they appealed to the old codger. He walked up and put his palm on the table and moved it lightly around while he looked off into the distance as if he was a gypsy fortuneteller about to go into a Chinese trance. Finally he announced that it was shellac.

With that and not another word, he walked away while someone in the crowd nodded knowingly and said, "He's never wrong, he's got the touch."

Well, touch indeed. The touch had nothing to do with it. The old joker had simply glanced at the table long enough to see that it hadn't been refinished, and then he knew it had to be shellac because that was all they ever used on that kind of furniture. Varnish and lacquer hadn't been invented at the time the table had been made.

I'll get back to the other historical ways of telling what a finish is in a minute, but first let's not pass by the point of how to tell whether a piece has been refinished. This takes a little practice, but here are some clues to start with: First, look for a crispness to the edges and carving—if any. If a piece has been scraped or resanded by hand, this is easy to see. And even if paint remover has been used, a brush or some steel wool had to get into the process, and the crispness gets softened.

Second, look for any chips or nicks in the finish that may reveal another finish underneath the top one. You can even try to chip some finish off with your fingernail in some hidden spot. Third, look underneath the piece. It's a rare refinisher that will be so careful as not to leave some signs of his work in places no one ever sees. For instance, where a chair leg enters the bottom of a chair, the bottoms of table leaves, and so on.

Another sign to look for is any unevenness in a flat surface—unless the piece is so old or "country" that it may have been hand-planed and sanded. Once you have become used to the idea of looking at furniture like a detective, you won't even know why you have decided a piece has its original finish. They either have an "as made" look, or they don't. If that lovely, aged look is set off by a perfect finish, you figure it out. How can this be the original finish? And incidentally, having the original finish is an important point of value on any fine old treasures you may uncover. You don't splash paint remover on a table George Washington may have used. And even if it was only one of George's friends that used it, you hesitate before turning the piece into just another refinished antique. You may be cutting the value of the piece to less than half of what a collector would pay for it in an "as-found" condition. I guess it's a matter of the scratches and dents being a part of history and all that. In a New Haven museum they even have a chest of drawers with its side crushed in—by a British cannon ball.

Meanwhile, back in Vermont, we were discussing how to tell the kind of finish on a piece of furniture by its age. Here the big point is that all clear finishes were shellac up to the beginning of the Victorian period. Lacquer and varnish hadn't been invented. But then around the time machine-carved oak furniture burst upon a defenseless world, someone began fooling around with shellac to see if he could make a tougher finish. Maybe this experimentation started a little earlier in the Empire period, but the knowledge didn't spread very far. Anyway, shellac was—and is—a very unsatisfactory finish, because water left on it will turn it white, and alcoholic drinks will wash it away. Not beer, maybe, but just try a good martini! So these fellows started putting things into shellac and taking them out, and then throwing the whole mess away and getting things in drums from DuPont, until they came up with lacquer. It is a lot better than shellac, because it won't wash away—though it will white-spot.

And what about varnish? Well, it also was developed in Victorian times, and is far superior to lacquer. Even pure alcohol doesn't bother it. But the trouble with varnish is that it doesn't lend itself to mass-production techniques. It takes hours to dry and days to "cure," or dry thoroughly. And lacquers are dry in a few minutes after they hit the surface—where they are sent with a spray gun. And this keeps the production line moving.

So the only time you run into a real varnish finish is on a hand-crafted piece—modern or reproduction—that is made in a small shop catering to the class trade. Or, of course, you will often find it on a refinished piece.

Now I seem to hear a thousand cries of protest that all begin, "But the man in the furniture store said . . ." And what he told you was that your furniture has a Sooper-Hooper, Magic-Stamina Varnish Finish. Well, it just doesn't. Except in the sense that varnish is anything that coats something else. I have worked on department-store furniture for many years, and once I even had a job where I went around to houses touching up furniture delivered from all the big stores in New York City. I never ran into a single piece with a varnish finish. And I can also assure you that the ethics of the average furniture salesman are about equal to those of the average used-car salesman. But that is another story.

So what all this amounts to is that shellac and lacquer take care of 95 per cent of the furniture that you will ever run into at, say, an auction. Varnish takes care of 3 per cent. What's left for the remaining 2 per cent? Well, you might run into a linseed-oil finish. This will only be found on a piece that has been refinished, and a pretty good piece at that, because of the time and effort this finish takes.

Then there is the penetrating-sealer finish. This is widely used by people who buy unfinished furniture because it is an easy, one-coat, wipe-on operation. But it is also being used on some good modern furniture, especially that with the Scandinavian look. This finish is easily identified, because it has no built-up look, no thickness. The wood still shows its grain, as if it had only been stained and waxed. However, the surface of the wood has been hardened and the stain protected by a sealer that has actually penetrated into the wood fibers.

Finally, there is a wax finish. Often the wood has only been waxed, though sometimes it is stained first. This has the same look as the sealer finish, but isn't, of course, as good. This is the simplest finishing job, and can appear on a piece of any age or value.

And that covers the field as far as historic determination of what a finish is. The other method is the scientific one of seeing what solvents will dissolve the finish.

Here is the simple chemistry of the business:

Test for varnish: Varnish, once it has dried, will not redissolve in anything. It can be destroyed by paint remover—and sometimes by lacquer thinner—but in those cases it crinkles up, and cannot be rebrushed. Varnish is also a tougher film than lacquer or shellac. When you try to penetrate it with your fingernail, you can mark it, but it won't crack the way shellac or lacquer will. Its oil content makes it more pliable.

Test for lacquer finish: Lacquer will dissolve in lacquer thinner only. Wrap a small piece of cloth around your finger, and wet it with lacquer thinner. If a scuffed or worn finish begins to smooth out when wiped with this cloth, then the finish is lacquer. The lacquer thinner penetrates the lacquer and softens it, reliquefies it. Then in a few minutes the lacquer thinner has evaporated, as it is highly volatile, and the lacquer is hard again. Only now the surface is smooth and glossy. The effect to look for is the same as if you had licked a scuffed-up lollipop. Except that the lacquer thinner evaporates faster than water. Nothing else will do this to lacquer. Only lacquer thinner.

Test for shellac finish: Shellac will redissolve in wood alcohol. Sometimes, also, in lacquer thinner, but not always. And besides, dissolving it with lacquer thinner proves nothing. Or at most it proves only that it is either shellac or lacquer. To test for shellac, use the same cloth-wrapped finger, this time dipping it in denatured alcohol. The effect is the same as with lacquer thinner on lacquer.

It should be pointed out here that wood alcohol is the same thing as denatured alcohol. Whatever it is made from, alcohol is alcohol. Except rubbing alcohol, which is about 80 per cent water and is useless in this whole business, so forget it.

However, we have to go on a little more about alcohol, because it isn't sold under that name any more. It is sold under trade names like Quakersol and Solox. There are many more such made-up names, but they always have a "sol" in them—for *sol*vent. And you can be sure you have the right thing if it says on the can or bottle that the contents can be used as a thinner for shellac—which is the main use for alcohol. Usually the label says "shellac solvent." The reason for this perfidy is to avoid having denatured alcohol—which is very poisonous—mistaken for drinking alcohol.

antiques As the introduction to this section points out, how you go about restoring a finish depends on what the finish is: shellac, varnish, etc. So after determining the finish on your antique, refer to the listing for that finish in this section. However there are some special points to be made about the restoration of antiques as opposed to modern furniture or factory-made reproductions.

The main point is that if you like your furniture to have clean, crisp lines, flat surfaces, and an unscarred, flawless look—well, then, you shouldn't have antiques because you don't deserve them. The whole idea of an antique is that it brings the character of times gone by into our time. And the signs of wear and use are part of that character.

Of course, this is a purist's point of view—the point of view that museums take—and you will see a great many compromises made with it. For instance, Windsor chairs were almost always painted—red, green, black, mostly. But their thick pine seats and graceful hickory spokes look awfully good with a clear finish. So people often scrape them down, but leave traces of the original paint to show through the clear finish.

The tops of old cherry tables are another typical example. When oak furniture flooded the country during the early

1900s, these lovely things were demoted to the kitchen, or to the back porch, the basement, or the paint shop in back of the garage. As a result, their tops usually show not only normal wear, but downright abuse. So the compromise made in refinishing them is to try to remove the signs of abuse (they are usually crisscrossed with knife cuts) but to leave signs of wear. You have to sand the knife cuts out, of course, but you leave the edges rounded, with a nick in them here and there, and you let the surface be a little wavy.

Another disputed point about refinished antiques is whether the finish should be dull or glossy. Well, in spite of the fact that you can get rabid opinions on both sides of this question, depending mostly on the section of the country that you live in, it still remains a moot point, and you can decide either way without feeling guilty about it. Those who like the finish dull say that the pieces look older, or show their age this way, and also that antiques should be preserved "as found." Those who like glossy finishes say that is the way the things were finished originally, and that therefore they are really the purists. So far as I'm concerned, both points of view seem entirely valid. And that's what moot means, doesn't it?

See also: listings for *antiques* in section on REPAIRING, and for *dull glow* in section on RUBBING DOWN.

black spots See listing for *rings,* below.

blushing Many old pieces—especially of Empire vintage, but it can happen to a finish of any age—are covered with a white haze. They look as if someone has steamed them, and this, of course, is literally what has happened. At some point in their lives, moisture has condensed on them, and then with a rise in the temperature been slowly "boiled" off. Unheated houses are good for producing this effect. Especially abandoned ones with a couple of broken windows so that the moisture can get in on damp nights, steam up on hot days.

This can happen to any kind of finish, even varnish, and

this haze is really just a gigantic white spot. It is the same as the white ring left by a glass or bowl on which moisture has condensed and run down onto the finish. Except that there is this difference: it is a much milder case, in that the whiteness does not penetrate very deeply into the finish. And therefore the cure is much easier than in the case of *cracking* and *crumbling*. (See listings that follow.)

The first thing to try—especially in the mildest cases—is dipping a piece of 000-grade steel wool in oil. Any oil will do: mineral oil, engine oil, boiled or raw linseed oil. Then, applying the oil freely, rub the steel wool back and forth, following (running with) the grain of the wood. You are actually removing the surface of the finish that has whitened. But you are doing it with such a fine abrasive that you are "polishing" the revealed clear undersurface at the same time.

Of course, you can perform this same operation with pumice (rottenstone is too slow-cutting). If you do use pumice, mix it with water to the consistency of cream. Then take a piece of wood (a six-inch length of one-by-four is about the right size) and wrap three or four layers of soft cotton rag around it. Be sure the bottom of the block of wood is smooth—with no wrinkles. Use this surface to rub the pumice against the finish and grind off the white surface film.

If you want to be really professional about it, cut the block of wood to have sharp, square edges and corners. Then glue a layer of felt on the bottom. Make the felt piece a little bit bigger than the block all the way around, and when the glue is dry, place the block with the felt side down and neatly trim off the excess with a razor blade. Such a block is especially useful for getting into the corners of paneling.

Warning: Never use pumice without a padded block. It is amazing how fast it can cut through the finish and expose the bare wood if the pressure of your rubbing isn't distributed evenly by a flat padded surface. Also watch out for any unevenness in the surface of the piece of furniture. If there is a slight warp or bulge, the pumice will take the finish off it even with a good soft, flat rubbing pad.

In other words, steel wool is always the safest on old pieces, and pumice is rarely used except on machine-planed surfaces. If this sounds as if I am trying to scare you away from pumice, you are following me perfectly. I know that there are old-timers and fine craftsmen who use it all the time on every kind of surface. But they know what they are doing, and have developed a touch that can come only from experience. If you want to develop a touch, go ahead. But be prepared to ruin a couple of finishes while learning.

Returning to our process, when the entire surface is clear of its white film, clean it. In the case of steel wool, just dust it, and then apply wax or polish. In the case of pumice, wash the surface with water, and dry it overnight before waxing or polishing. This will let the moisture dry out of any cracks, such as around paneling, into which it may have seeped.

chipping This is the term used when a small piece of finish flakes off, usually as the result of a blow. It also means that the wood underneath the finish has not been damaged.

The professional cure for this is the use of a *shellac stick*. And for quite small chips a *wax stick* can be used. (See listings for both of these processes further on in this section.) But the easiest and safest way—although it takes longer—is to fill the hole with a plastic varnish.

First make sure the chipped surface is level. If the chip is on a side of the piece, turn it so that side is up. Now, using a fine camel's-hair brush, fill the hole in the surface with a film of quick-drying, plastic or synthetic varnish—one of the modern brands. (See listing for *varnish* in section on SUPPLIES.) Make sure the film wets to the edges of the hole, and then with your finger tip wipe off any varnish that overlaps the surface. Let this dry twenty-four hours in a warm place, and repeat the process until the varnish in the hole is above the surface of the finish. It will take three or four layers, and therefore three or four days. Then cut down the varnish with fine emery paper wrapped around a small flat block of wood. This is done by wetting the surface and the emery paper with a thin lubricating oil, such as "3-in-One," and gently moving the block back and forth over the varnish. The rubbing surface of such a block should never be less than three inches wide and six inches long, regardless of how small the hole was. If you use a smaller block, one of its corners may accidentally cut through the surrounding finish before your varnish fill-in has been cut down until it is flush with the surface. When the patch is flush with the surface, wipe the oil off, and wax or polish.

cigarette burns For the rank amateur, the most practical approach to a cigarette burn is to refinish the whole top of the table, or whatever the piece is. If the top is of solid wood, the best approach to this is to sand the finish off. Then, if necessary, restain the top to match the sides. Seal the stain in with a coat of shellac, and then touch up the blackness of the burn mark in the wood with ordinary enamel paint that you have mixed or tinted to be the same color as the wood.

To do this so that it is hardly noticeable, smudge a bit of paint, just the barest amount, over the blackness with your finger tip. Because you have sealed the surface with shellac, you can do this over and over until you get it right. When it is right, you will be able to see the smudge, but nobody else will ever notice it.

The only difficult part of this process is mixing a paint that is a perfect color-match. And as most people don't have tinting colors around, with which to tint the enamel (starting with a brown, usually), maybe the simplest way is to buy a cheap set of oil paints. Then, after mixing your color, add enough dryer to bring the paint to the best smudging consistency for you. About two drops to a quarter-teaspoon of paint is all you need for twenty tries at getting the proper smudge.

After the smudge has dried, of course, apply a coat of

varnish over the whole top. Use only varnish in this situation. Shellac or lacquer will mess up the smudge.

Of course, cigarette burns also can be eliminated without refinishing the whole top. This is done by the use of shellac sticks or wax sticks. For these processes, see the listings for *shellac-stick patching* and *wax-stick patching* further on in this section.

cracking or crazing This usually occurs on the side of a piece of furniture that has been placed near a sunny window. On a hot summer day, with the window closed, the sun can bring the temperature on the surface of the wood up to a hundred and fifty degrees. Naturally the finish, no matter what it is, can't stand this for any length of time. It's a slow burn that drives out the small percentage of oils that make a finish pliable. Pliable in comparison to slate or glass, that is.

Usually a pattern of very fine lines is called crazing. When the cracks are wider—and I've seen them as wide as an eighth of an inch—the term is *crawling*.

The way to restore such a finish is to redissolve it in its solvent, brush it out even again, and let it dry. Of course, this will only work with a shellac or lacquer finish. But since 90 per cent of all finishes are shellac or lacquer, the odds are with you. So first determine the finish—shellac or lacquer (see the introduction to this section)—and then turn to the appropriate listing further on in this section: either *lacquer finish* (*reamalgamation of*) or *shellac finish* (*reamalgamation of*).

crumbling If a finish actually begins to powder or flake off, it was probably an inferior finish in the beginning. But on the other hand, it may have been exposed to frightful conditions—dampness in the winter and baking in the summer. And after about twenty-five years of this in an abandoned house, even you or I would probably be in pretty bad condition.

As with cracking and crazing, restoration by reamalgamation not only can be done, but it is really a fairly easy job. After determining whether the finish is shellac or lacquer (see the introduction to this section), turn to either *lacquer finish* (*reamalgamation of*) or *shellac finish* (*reamalgamation of*).

dents Wood is built like a hard sponge, and that's why dents can be taken out of the softer woods like pine and mahogany. Harder woods like oak and maple don't really dent. To make an impression in them, you have to hit them with a hammer so that their more brittle, closely packed fibers actually break. So when we are talking about denting, we are really talking about the soft woods.

The way to get the dent out is to fill the fibers—or the spaces between the fibers—with water. This softens the wood, causes it to swell up, and therefore to resume its original shape. It's the same as when you drop a dried-up natural sponge in water.

So the basic approach to dents is to steam them. This is done by placing a wet pad of cloth over the dent, and then holding a hot iron down on the cloth.

In the case of unfinished wood the problem is fairly easy. At first press the iron down hard to drive the steam into the wood. Then just let the iron sit there, turned on low, and wait. Keep wetting the cloth. This treatment may take anywhere from fifteen minutes to four hours. And if you have one of the woods that are in between hard and soft, you may never get the depression all the way up. In that case you can sand around the depression with a flat block of wood—so that the cutting action doesn't reach down into the depression.

In the case of finished wood you have to take the finish off first, and then proceed as above. Unless, of course, you resort to a shellac-stick patch, which is the best, quickest, and easiest way—*if* you have learned how to use a shellac stick. See listing further on in this section for *shellac-stick patching*.

A final tip: in the case of a dent which is difficult to remove—and they get progressively more difficult as the wood gets harder—you can try puncturing the wood with tiny holes to let the steam in. If you don't have a very tiny drill, take a straight pin and hammer it in about a quarter of an inch. Then carefully pull it out with pliers. With large-grained wood such as walnut, mahogany, and oak these holes will never be seen if you make them in the large open pores. But even if they can be seen in the softer woods, the swelling will tend to close them up once the steam is in the wood. So in wood without pores, don't use the drill, but stick to the pin. Also, whatever evidence of the holes remains can be filled in and touched up before applying the new finish. This can be done with Plastic Wood or crack filler. After applying a sealer coat of shellac, use a fine brush to touch the spots with a paint that matches the surrounding wood, then varnish. For more details of this retouching process, see listing in this section for *cigarette burns*.

In the case of an antique you can leave your puncture marks there and say they are worm holes.

flaking Same as *crumbling*.

French polishing This is an amazing process used for many years—hundreds of them—both to apply a finish and to restore one that is mildly scuffed or shopworn. It is the nature of the beast that it gives a very glossy finish, which used to be more popular than it is today. But this can always be dulled by a light rubbing with 000 or 0000 steel wool.

The procedure is to first wash off any wax with mineral spirits or turpentine—nothing else will do it. You then make a small pad of fine, washed cotton (old white shirts) about a quarter of an inch thick. (I can't stop to count how many layers that is.) You wet this pad completely with boiled linseed oil, and then squeeze it out. Now use this pad to rub a thin coat of shellac onto the present finish. The crazy part, I mean, is that it works. Also the pressure of your oiled pad forces shellac into the minute imperfections on the surface of the old finish.

The technique is to rub the surface quite hard, but with a motion that never stops, so the pad will not stick to the shellac. This makes polishing legs easy, but large flat surfaces are harder. For the latter use a figure-eight motion.

As the oil is squeezed out of the pad, keep rewetting it with a few drops of oil at a time, and keep applying about a quarter-teaspoon of shellac at a time to the pad. Sometimes it is desirable to thin the shellac a little with alcohol. This is the kind of process you should try first on some useless piece before attacking the top of your grand piano. It is not a hard skill to learn. Four or five experimental patches on a useless surface will give it to you. You want to get the feel of how much shellac and how much oil you need on the pad. And even an experienced French polisher will get his pad started on a useless piece, or the inside of a leg where it won't show if he has too much shellac on the pad and it piles up.

When the shellac does pile up, or you accidentally stop your motion, which will leave an impression of the cloth in the surface, the whole area you were working on must be cleaned off with another pad that has been dipped in alcohol and squeezed out. Apply more alcohol a little at a time to keep the pad wet enough to pick up the shellac you want to remove.

This process can be used on any finish: shellac, lacquer, varnish, etc.

hazing Same as blushing.

inlays Whenever I see a piece of missing inlay, or even a place where some veneer has been chipped off, a glint comes into my eye and I can't keep a half smile from coming to my face. This is because inlays are the professional refinishers delight. They look hard to repair—so you can charge a good price—but when you get them in the privacy of your shop they are really quite easy to do. And there is also the satisfaction of pulling off a good trick, which makes the job fun.

To begin with, if you've still got the missing pieces, the job is simple. Just scrape the glue off the back of the piece and off the wood in the hole it came from, and then glue it back in. If the piece is only loose, break it out, or off, so you can scrape the old glue and dirt out. You can't just squeeze glue in over the old glue, because there is a fifty-fifty chance that it won't hold.

If the piece is missing, there are five ways of going about the job.

The most obvious is just to scrape the area from which the small piece of veneer is missing, and stain or paint it the color it should be. With dark pieces you can even use ink, and who will notice? Especially if the damage is on the side of a piece or in some other place that isn't likely to be noticed.

If the missing piece is in a more noticeable place, the classic method is to steal a piece of matching veneer where it isn't noticeable, and transfer it to the hole that bothers you. The new hole is then just stained or filled with wax or shellac stick as will be explained in a minute.

When stealing a piece, use a brand-new single-edged razor blade. The sharp cutting corners of such a blade are ruined once they have been put into a holder. With this blade, cut out a piece of veneer just a little bit larger than the hole you have to fill. Then, holding the piece next to the hole, carefully trim it a little at a time until it is the same size and shape. Then glue the piece in. If you have left a small crack, after the glue has dried you can fill this with wax stick or colored crayon.

The wax-stick process is discussed under its own heading elsewhere in this section. But obviously the hole should be filled with wax of the same color as the missing inlay. If the surface isn't subject to wear, all you need to do is scrape and polish the surface smooth, and leave it. On a table top the spot—or the whole top of the table—can be coated over with another finish *after* the wax has been coated with shellac. Wax will bleed into and soften all varnishes and most lacquers, but not shellac.

The shellac-stick process is the same filling technique, and is also discussed further on in this section.

The final method, and the hardest, is to fill the hole with a new piece of veneer. To find out where to obtain veneers, see the section on SUPPLIES. The trick here is to not cut the patching piece out of the veneer until after you have stained and finished the veneer to match the color of your missing piece. Then cut and fit the veneer just as if it were a stolen piece.

Incidentally, when you are patching a place where a piece of veneer has broken off roughly, use a razor blade to trim the hole so that it has straight edges. This way you can get a perfect fit, and the edges of the patch will be less noticeable.

lacquer finish (reamalgamation) One of the charms of lacquer is that it can be dissolved and will dry out again over and over. And you can get away with doing this sometimes several times with a film of lacquer that has already been applied to a surface. This is the cure for a lacquer finish that has *blushed*, *crazed*, or *cracked*.

Here the trick—as so often—is to experiment a little before you plunge in and ruin everything. Start with the back or inside of a leg, a place that won't show. Here is a safe place to find out how wet you are going to have to get the surface. Also, how long and hard you can brush or wipe the surface without creating a bare spot. The thicker the lacquer film is, of course, the safer you are.

Some people prefer to wipe the lacquer thinner on with a small pad of cloth, and this is all that is necessary in the case of a minor decay of the surface such as in *blushing* or *hazing*. When the surface is cracked, it may be necessary to soak the surface with a few applications of lacquer thinner, using the lightest brush stroke possible. Then when the lacquer has softened all the way through, you can gradually increase the pressure of your brush until the finish is spread evenly.

I suppose the big danger point—the part that takes experience, and the reason for experimenting first—is knowing when to stop. Don't try to get the surface absolutely perfect or completely free of brush marks. A lot of these will disappear as the surface dries. And the rest will not be noticeable after you have rubbed the dried surface with fine steel wool and waxed or polished it.

Except in cases of crumbling—where the finish is too loose—the first step is to wash the piece with mineral spirits or turpentine. These alone will dissolve any wax that is on the surface or in the cracks, and the presence of any wax will result in little patches in the reamalgamated finish that won't dry.

Second, plan to work on any large flat surfaces only when they are level. This particularly applies to a bureau or chest of drawers. Take the drawers out and place them with their tops up to work on them. After you have done the top surface and it is reasonably dry, turn it first on one side and then the other, and then on its back.

In the case of a straight- or curved-legged table or chair this is not important. They can be worked in their normal position. Though you may want to put a chair on its back to work the back slats if it has any.

Now, the actual application of the lacquer thinner to the finish. Pour the lacquer thinner into a bowl or cup. Use a good two-and-a-half-inch brush. This can be a varnish brush or a good grade of paint brush. CLEAN.

CLEAN.

Brushes must be REALLY CLEAN at all times. The cleanest are the ones that are new. The only others are those that you have cleaned immediately after previous use with lacquer thinner. Not mineral spirits, not turpentine.

Brushes used in finishing should always be cleaned immediately after using with LACQUER THINNER. This is not a crackpot fixation on my part. It is not an opinion. It is an absolute necessity. See introduction to section on FINISHING.

Now quickly and gently brush the whole surface you are working on with the lacquer thinner. In the case of a large area, start at one edge and, brushing parallel to it, proceed with regular long strokes across to the opposite edge. These brush strokes should be *across* the grain.

Without waiting for the lacquer thinner to sink in completely, brush the surface *with* the grain. In the milder cases of finish decay this will be all that is necessary. Haze and fine cracks will disappear. Then all you have to do is let the finish dry, rub it down with 000 steel wool, and wax or polish.

As the decay of the finish is progressively worse, you are going to have to apply more lacquer thinner, and brush it on the surface more times—alternately across and then with the grain so as not to disturb the distribution of the film on the surface. Always finish with a brushing that goes with the grain. In the case of a crumbled finish it will take quite a lot of soaking with lacquer thinner (it evaporates fast) to get the finish solids back to brushing consistency. When they are, brush them out evenly over the surface and let it dry. Since you can't wash the wax off a loose, crumbling finish, you just pray there wasn't any on it.

With good furniture—either modern or old—this process almost always works, because the top surface of the finish is thick enough and a clear lacquer. You run into difficulty when the finish is either thin or carries a stain in it. In this case, the slightest streakiness in your rebrushing of the lacquer will show up and you may decide just to take the finish off (with rags and more lacquer thinner). To restain such a piece before applying a new finish, the best thing to use is an aniline dye dissolved in alcohol. See section on STAINING.

Opaque lacquer—blacks and greens are common—will react the same way as clear lacquer or lacquer with a transparent stain in it.

A final point: naturally a lacquer finish can be coated over with a coat of fresh lacquer after it has been reamalgamated. So if your restored surface is not even or smooth enough to please you, this is a good idea. That way you can build up a coat of lacquer thick enough so you can cut down any ripples or unevenness with emery paper wrapped around a sanding block—a perfectly flat piece of wood about two inches wide and five inches long. See listing for *sanding finishes* in section on RUBBING DOWN.

linseed-oil finish About the only thing you can do with a shoddy linseed-oil finish is to clean it first with turpentine or mineral spirits and then with soap and water. Then rub the surface well with 000 steel wool until it has a dry scuffed look, and reapply more boiled linseed oil. If none of the imperfections in the old finish penetrate through it, this will do the job. Of course, after cleaning and scuffing the surface, you could apply a coat of varnish instead. See listing for *varnish finish* in section on FINISHES—CLEAR.

Shellac can also be applied over a linseed-oil finish, but not lacquer. Lacquer will act like paint remover and crinkle the oil finish.

milk-paint finish There is really no way to restore the old dry finishes that we roughly call milk-paint finishes. There is nothing that will dissolve them. The only course—if you insist on destroying their character just to have everything neat—is to repaint them with the same kind of paint. See listing for *milk-paint finishes* in section on FINISHES—OPAQUE.

modern finishes The only specific point to be made about modern finishes is that they are almost all lacquer, so see the listing in this section on *lacquer finishes* (*reamalgamation*). Since the better grades of furniture have the thickest coating of lacquer, these are the easiest to restore. In the case of the increasingly popular *sealer finishes*, see listing also in that section.

paint finish There is no way of restoring the ordinary paint or enamel finish, except to sand it smooth, and re-enamel it. It might be noted here, however, that the dullness of a painted finish does not come from using a dull or flat paint, but from using an enamel and buffing it with 000 steel wool when it is good and dry. This is then waxed. Generally speaking, enamel can be thought of as a varnish with an opaque pigment in it.

Of course, good painted finishes are quite rare except on decorated pieces, so it is always well to consider whether what looks like paint isn't really an opaque lacquer. See listing in this section for *lacquer* (*reamalgamation of*).

peeling This is the result of a top layer of finish not sticking to the one under it, or not sticking to the sealer (usually shellac) used to hold the stain in the wood so it won't bleed into the finish. It is caused by the undercoat having wax or oil on the surface when the top coat was applied. If large areas have peeled, or if the peeling is occurring in a number of places, there is nothing you can do about this except remove the finish and apply a new one.

Cases of peeling, incidentally, hardly ever occur except in modern furniture. It is either cheap stuff, or, if good quality, something went wrong in the factory the day the piece went down the finishing line. If you haven't had the piece very long, you can have it replaced if you bought it in a good store. Even a bad store will replace it if you get a lawyer.

rings White rings are the same as *white spots,* so see that listing further on in this section. But many rings are black, and here you are in serious trouble. These rings are caused by water that has penetrated the finish and entered the wood. This, of course, doesn't happen in just a few hours, but usually is the result of a vase with water in it having been left on the surface. It is the water condensing on the vase that finally eats through the finish. It will do this to shellac in a day or two, to lacquer in a somewhat longer time, and while it may take weeks with varnish, it usually happens eventually—before the water in the vase has evaporated.

The only cure is to remove the finish from the whole top. Then the black ring—or other similarly caused black spots—can easily be removed with a saturate solution of oxalic-acid crystals mixed in warm water. Use about a pint of water, and add the crystals—available in paint and drug stores—until no more will dissolve. Brush or wipe this solution on, and as soon as it has soaked into the wood the black will disappear as if by magic. It is best to brush the solution on the whole surface, as the oxalic acid may also bleach the stain out of the wood, and it is better to have an evenly bleached surface. It is easier to restain the whole surface than just the spot.

Incidentally, I know oxalic acid is a frightening name for anything, but it is nothing to worry about. It may be poisonous if you drink it—a lot of things are—but it won't hurt your fingers. In fact, you won't even feel it except in scratches or cuts. However, after it has dried it will leave fine crystals on the bleached surface, and when you wipe them off they get into the air and make you sneeze.

After using the oxalic solution, wash the surface of the wood well with water before restaining. Otherwise the bleaching effect of the oxalic acid will make the stain go on blotchy.

scratches Deep scratches are serious, and unless you want to remove the finish and sand them out, the best resort is *shellac-stick patching* or *wax-stick patching,* both of which are listed in this section.

scuffing Same as blushing, as far as treatment goes.

sealer finish A sealer finish can be restored by additional coats of sealer brushed onto the surface, and then wiped off in five or ten minutes, leaving a trace of the new coat of sealer on the finish. The surface should be cleaned and scuffed with fine steel wool first, of course.

Floor sealers are the same as those used on furniture, and they are widely available. If the piece is scratched at all you will want to use a sealer of the same color as the finish. For this purpose the sealer is easily tinted with colors ground in oil—the kind you use to tint paint, and available in almost any paint store in tubes or small cans. The colors you will want are burnt umber and burnt sienna—also raw umber and raw sienna for a complete pallet of browns and tans.

You may want to apply several coats of sealer twenty-four hours apart. Lightly scuff the last coat with 000 steel wool and wax the surface.

Voilà. Like new!

sealing-wax repairs In many sections of the country shellac stick is called, and sold as, sealing wax—because they are the same thing.

shellac finish (reamalgamation) Because dried shellac will readily dissolve in denatured alcohol, it is quite easy to restore a worn, scuffed, crazed, or blushed finish. The technique is the same as that described in *lacquer* (*reamalgamation*), a listing that will be found in this section. However, there are some special points to be made about shellac.

The first is that some shellacs are tougher than others, and can be reworked better with a mixture of three parts of alcohol to one part of lacquer thinner. This is especially true with shellacs of the Victorian period, when improvements were being made. For shellacs before that period, alcohol is sufficient by itself. It is also sufficient with shellac that has been applied in the last twenty years, as there has been a return to manufacturing pure shellac.

The second point is the danger of shellac blushing if it is applied in damp weather. Alcohol is anhydrous, meaning that it absorbs water out of the air. This causes the formation of an opaque white film on the surface of the shellac as it dries. The solution for this, of course, is to apply more alcohol in a dry atmosphere. In line with this, whenever you use alcohol try to have a fresh bottle, or at least keep a tight stopper on the bottle or can at all times. The same goes for shellac, which will also absorb moisture from the air. Buy it in as small quantities as possible, and always keep it tightly stoppered.

As shellac coatings are usually quite thin, it is advisable to give a restored finish at least one extra coat of fresh shellac before doing any rubbing with 000 steel wool. This is the only difference in technique in restoring a shellac finish or a lacquer finish.

shellac-stick patching Shellac sticks bring us into the realm of magic. With them it is possible—and in just a few minutes—to "cure" a cigarette burn so that the patch cannot be seen unless you know where it is and look for it with a magnifying glass. The same is true for scratches, dents, and any other marks on a finished surface.

The only trouble is that not by the wildest flight of the imagination can you conceive of an amateur being able to use shellac sticks. By the time you've learned to use them you have a profession—or at least a highly skilled trade. And unless you know what you are doing, it will only take about thirty seconds to make the smallest imperfection in a surface into a historic mess. At least it will become historic in the annals of your family. For that reason, the amateur should stick to wax sticks and colored crayons, where every time you bungle you can just wipe the wax away and try again until you get it right. For the use of wax sticks see *wax-stick patching* further on in this section.

However, a natural-born craftsman who likes to do fine work with his fingers is not going to be discouraged by this—and shouldn't be. If you like to fix watches and clocks, or do fine carving, or if you really understand oil painting, this is a craft you can master in about fifty trys. Which is a lot better than water colors, where the old saying is that the first five hundred don't count!

For such people, here is the technique. First assemble the following:

(1) An alcohol lamp.

(2) A burn-in knife—which is exactly the same thing as a good-grade grapefruit-cutting knife.

(3) A shellac stick that is a perfect match for the color of the damaged surface. Shellac sticks come in a hundred different standard colors, and even these, of course, can be blended when in their hot liquid state.

(4) A piece of very fine emery paper wrapped around a perfectly flat block, with rounded edges, about three-quarters of an inch thick, an inch and a half wide, and four inches long.

(5) A small bottle of light mineral oil or thinned linseed oil.

The procedure then is to heat the knife over the flame of the alcohol lamp. Also heat the end of the shellac stick, and pick up a small amount of the liquid shellac onto the hot knife.

The molten shellac is then forced with the knife into the hole in the finish. (In the case of a cigarette burn, scrape it out with a razor blade so that there is a hole to fill.)

With your hot knife, smooth the surface of the shellac in the hole—it hardens as soon as it is cool. Then wet the patch and the area around it with oil, and using the emery block, very carefully grind the patch down until it is level with the rest of the surface.

If there is any sign at all of the patch, there are about a hundred shades of dry colors that can be smudged over it to conceal it perfectly. But this is a technique that absolutely cannot be described in words, and must be demonstrated. If you want to see it done, all large furniture stores employ men who do this kind of work. They either work steadily for one store, or service a number of them.

Finally the patch is *French polished* (see listing in this section) and then brought to match the degree of gloss or dullness of the rest of the surface with steel wool.

Well, that's how it's done, and if I've made it sound easy, don't believe me. But once you learn the delicate touches it takes, it's a lot of fun. Satisfies the Jehovah complex, or something.

varnish finish Unlike shellac and lacquer, varnish cannot be redissolved in any liquid, and therefore it is difficult to restore a shabby varnish finish. About the best that can be done is to clean off any wax with mineral spirits or turpentine, and then scuff the surface thoroughly with 000 steel wool. Always have your rubbing stroke follow the grain of the wood. Then you can build up the surface with a linseed-oil finish over the varnish. Three or four applications of linseed oil will be enough in this case. For directions on how to do this, see listing for *linseed-oil finish* in section on FINISHES—CLEAR.

veneers The techniques here are the same as for inlays, which are themselves, of course, small pieces of veneer. So see listing for *inlays* elsewhere in this section. See also listing for *veneers* in section on REPAIRS.

watermarks Black spots caused by water getting into the wood. See listing in this section for *rings*.

wax finish The so-called wax finish is simply a coat of ordinary furniture wax on bare wood. It is best, of course, to use one of the harder grades, such as Simoniz. That's the Simoniz for cars—*not* the product for furniture—if you are trying to build up a finish. To restore such a finish, of course, it is simply a matter of applying more wax. Or in bad cases you may want to wipe the old wax off with mineral spirits or turpentine, and start fresh by building up coats of wax. Leave about four hours' drying time between applications of wax. For reference, see listing for *wax finish* in section on FINISHES—CLEAR.

wax-stick patching When it comes to patching deep scratches, digs, cigarette burns, etc., colored wax can be made to perform wonders. And if you have the right information, it doesn't take any particular skill, just a little patience.

To begin with, let's discuss the material. Any colored wax can be used. This includes common crayons, which are simply pure paraffin softened with a little oil. If you buy one of the larger assortments, you will get several good browns and reds. Add the black, the yellow, and the white to these and you can mix up a match to almost any color of stain or finish. There are directions for doing that below.

Companies that sell refinishing supplies are another source for colored wax sticks. These are especially designed for patching and come in many colors. See section on SUPPLIES.

Finally there is an excellent product for just this purpose that is distributed—somewhat spottily—through hardware and paint stores. This is a set of five sticks in good furniture colors. These have some beeswax in them, and that makes them just the right hardness to work well.

In addition to the wax you will need, if you want to be fancy, a curved grapefruit-cutting knife, but a common table knife will do as well. You will also need a single-edged razor blade, and a source of smokeless heat. An alcohol lamp is the handiest, but the flame of a gas stove will also do. Candles and matches will not do because their smoke gets into the wax and blackens it.

The procedure is simple.

First, clean the hole you are going to fill. In the case of a cigarette burn, scratch out the burned wood and finish so that the injured area is below the level of the surface of the finish. For this use your knife and razor blade.

Then, using spoons or jar caps, mix some wax to match the color of the finish. Each time you mix some, you are going to have to let the wax cool to see what color it will really be, but this happens fairly fast. When you have arrived at a good color match, heat the wax again, and dribble it into the hole. Now with the dull blade of the table knife, scrape the wax until it is level with the surface of the finish. When the wax is level, it sometimes helps to stroke it lightly with your finger tip to smooth it.

And here's the beauty of using wax: if you don't get it right the first time, just pry the wax out and try again.

If the patch is in a place where it doesn't receive any wear, you don't really have to do any more. But for a good job, on the top of a table or bureau, it is best to coat the area of the patch with thin shellac—two parts alcohol to one part shellac. In fact, you might as well coat the whole surface. Shellac must be used over wax, as wax will bleed into either varnish or lacquer and make a gummy mess that will never really dry.

Finally—after the shellac is dry—don't rub it down or scuff it with steel wool, but apply a coat of varnish over the whole top of whatever it is you are working on. When this is dry, you may scuff it with steel wool to get the proper degree of dullness, and then wax the surface.

This is really a very easy process. The only critical part of the operation is mixing the wax to the proper color. So it should be pointed out here that either beeswax or paraffin can be used (or a mixture of them), and that they can be colored with aniline dyes of the kind that mix with mineral spirits or turpentine—as opposed to the kind that mix with alcohol and water. With these materials it is easy to manufacture your own wax sticks. Dry colors that are sold in paint stores may also be used to color the wax.

white spots White spots, like blushing, occur when water gets into the surface of shellac or lacquer. The commonest cause is a wet glass, but any water left on an unwaxed surface will do it. A good coating of wax, of course, is the best protection—other than a coat of varnish, which will not turn white.

As very few white spots go deeply into the surface, they can be removed in a number of ways. The most obvious is to polish them off with an abrasive such as steel wool or pumice mixed to a paste with turpentine or a light oil, or mineral spirits. Even some of the common, kitchen scouring powders will do it.

Once a spot has been removed this way, it is best to treat the whole surface with the same abrasive, and then wax it so that the degree of shine or glow is even across the whole area.

In minor cases, some cigar ash rubbed in with saliva and the tip of your finger sometimes will do the trick.

In serious cases, where the whiteness has penetrated all the way down through the finish, abrasion is not the right answer, because you will end by cutting right through the finish to the wood. In such a case you have to resort to the use of lacquer thinner. The perfect way to apply this is in a fine spray. But if you don't have a spray gun or dry brush, such as commercial artists use, the best technique is to wipe the spot lightly with a small pad held between your thumb and forefinger.

This pad should be about an inch and a half square, and consist of about six or seven layers of soft cotton. First wet the pad completely, then wring it out as hard as you can. Then with light strokes start brushing the white-spot area. If nothing happens, gradually add a little more lacquer thinner to the pad, a few drops at a time. When the surface is wet enough, the spot will disappear.

The only trouble with this is that it creates a shiny area and the rest of the finish may be dull. This, of course, is quite simply remedied once the area has been allowed to dry thoroughly—say, for four hours, to be perfectly safe. You simply dull the area by rubbing or scuffing it with 000-grade steel wool, and then steel-wool the rest of the surface evenly.

Then apply wax or polish again, and that's it.

worn edges If only the finish is worn off an edge, and the color is still all right, the best way to put finish back on is by *French polishing* (see listing elsewhere in this section). But the usual problem is that a rather sharp edge is worn, and the corner of the wood shows through lighter than the rest of the finish.

In this case you can use black ink, and French-polish over it if the piece is of a dark enough color. But barring such luck, you can buy a set of water colors—the kind that come in little tubes—or some approximately matching single tubes at an art-supply store. Mix the color to match, using the least amount of water necessary, and retouch the edge, using the side of a small camel's-hair brush. Wipe off any false tries with a damp rag until you get it right.

The water paint will lighten as it dries, but don't worry about that; it will return to its wet color as soon as you coat it with shellac by *French polishing*. Or, of course, you can use a spray can of clear lacquer, shellac, or fixative. Build up a few coats and then very carefully scuff the glossy surface with 0000-grade steel wool. Then wax or polish.

Oil paints can be used instead of water colors. In that case, thin them with a mixture of half linseed oil and half drier. The trouble with oil colors is that they may take a week or more to dry, and you cannot apply lacquer—even from a spray can—over them. Only shellac or varnish.

Section 3

HOW TO LOVE YOUR FURNITURE

In which the polish versus wax controversy is settled for once and for all, and Uncle George cuts down a swing tree

As my dear old Uncle George used to say, "When you can make something for a dime, and sell it for a dollar, there's bound to be a lot of liars in the business." Of course, my Uncle George lived back in the days when there was no control over advertising claims at all. And people used to be a lot more naïve than they are today. It is no longer possible to advertise a "guaranteed" fly killer that consists of two one-inch cubes of wood, and the printed instructions: "Place fly on block marked *A* and squash with block marked *B*."

Even so, there's a lot of profit in waxes and polishes, with the result that the manufacturers of them have managed to maintain a pretty high degree of confusion. So the purpose of the entries in this section is to set the record straight about what the various waxes and polishes will do, and won't do.

Of course, the question I am asked most often is, "Which is best, a wax or a polish?" Well, I used to hem and haw about that, because I didn't want to hurt anybody's feelings. I guess I was afraid somebody might sue me, too. But now that I am an old man, what can they do to me? If I must spend my few remaining days in jail, I will use them to meditate on the folly of man. My blood has cooled for the lustier pleasures of life, and the fires of my ambition have long ago flickered and died in the blackness of the night.

(So if I don't dramatize myself, who will?)

Getting down to cases—though that old-man fantasy is one of my favorites—the answer is that oil and oil-base polishes are technically better than waxes. And by waxes I mean paste waxes, liquid waxes, beeswax, and the silicone preparations, which are alternately called waxes or polishes but actually belong to the wax family.

By oil polishes I mean mineral oil, which comes out of the ground the same as automobile oil, and the creamy white polishes that are made by emulsifying this oil with water.

The reason for this preference of mine is the same one that museums and piano manufacturers have. Namely, that a film of oil on a finish provides a better moisture seal than a coat of wax does. I don't mean that it keeps water-moisture in the air away from the finish, but that it keeps the essential oils in the finish from "steaming" out over the years. This prevents the cracking, crazing, or crumbling of a finish.

Why then, are waxes so popular? Well, in the first place the American people have been sold on them—the same way they were sold on big automobiles with "stabilizing" tail fins. A cousin of mine, who is an engineer, has told me that he and his friends have calculated that even the largest of these fins wouldn't have any real stabilizing effect until the automobile reached about 250 miles an hour.

Well, when it comes to all the fancy new kinds of waxes, the American woman has been sold on the idea that she owes it to herself to do the quickest and easiest thing. And I don't expect to reverse the trend.

Of course, a good coat of paste wax does have its advantages, because not only will it offer the best resistance to spilled water and drinks, but it also offers the best resistance to scuffing in a case where a surface gets a lot of use.

The only trouble is that it's hard to find a good paste wax these days. Even the ones left on the mass market have been made "easier" by loading them with soft, cheap paraffin and taking out the hard waxes, such as carnauba, that made them good. The only really good waxes generally available are the hard ones in the flat cans that are used for automobiles. And these are the very best waxes you can get to use on furniture. They are difficult to apply, of course. You really have to rub. But that's because they contain hard waxes that will last ten times as long as the others.

All that seems perfectly clear to me, but I still hear a plaintive cry from the back row: "But that still doesn't answer my question. Which is the best for my good furniture or antiques? Which should I use? Which do you use?" And that pins me down—a position I hate to be in because now somebody's feelings have to get hurt. However, here goes.

For use in the home, it's wax. Only an idiot would use an oil-base or lemon-oil polish, even if museums do. Wax is much easier to maintain and keep looking nice. And the fact that oil will preserve the finish isn't that important. The finish is going to get worn out by normal use long before it deteriorates from not having an oil-seal on it. And in fact, for furniture that is going to get normal use, wax is a better protection against scuff and wear than oil is.

What do I mean by wax being easier to maintain? I mean that if you wax your furniture, you only have to do it once a year. Or for frequently-used pieces like dining-room tables, perhaps four times a year. Before each application you only have to wipe it clean with a moist rag. This will take off the water-soluble dirt. The mineral-spirits thinner in the new application of wax will remove the grease or oil-based dirt—transferring it to your application cloth, of course. Over the years these wax coats will build up to the point where you will want to wash them all off with mineral spirits and start from scratch—about once in every five or ten years.

On the other hand, if you use an oil-base polish, you are going to have to apply it at least once a week to remove smudges and finger marks. You are also going to have to dust it much more frequently (depending on how dusty your house gets), because oil holds any dust that falls on it, while the slightest draft will blow dust off wax. Wax is slippery. As far as cleaning an oil polish goes, oil never really has to be cleaned off because it doesn't "pile up" the way wax will over the years. This is also another count against oil, because repeated applications will tend to darken the finish by working the grime that accumulates on the surface right into the finish so that it can never be washed off. Wax, too, tends to get gradually darker over the years, but this darkness disappears when the wax is washed off with mineral spirits.

Another question we always hear—in spite of the directions on all the cans—is, "What is the best way to apply wax or polish?"

Well, there isn't any particular trick that will make any difference in applying wax. It's just about as hard to polish if you start right away as it is if you let it dry a few minutes. What makes it harder to polish is applying too thick a coat. The thinner the coat, the easier it will be to polish. And after the first coat, a thin one is just as good as a thick one. It does the same protective job, and will look nice just as long as a thick coat will.

In applying an oil polish it is always good to use a cloth previously dampened with water. The polish will go on easier, and you get a cleaning effect thrown in gratis.

So what about beeswax, and "feeding the finish," and cleaning finishes, and that fellow down the street who swears by shoe polish? Well, those and as many other oddities as I can think of are covered in the following pages. And I have also included detailed entries on the preparations I've already mentioned. In fact, I even give some formulas, so all you need are the bottles or jars and some labels to put yourself in business for yourself.

Of course, you'll have to make up your own lies, and that is the part that counts.

Which reminds me of the polish my Uncle George got up. He called it "Rosewood Polish," because rosewood was one of the popular fine woods of his day, and he wanted a name with connotations of quality. After all, he charged a dollar for it, and that was a lot of money in his day. And even if it did only cost him a dime to make—bottle, contents, label, and all—it was still perfectly legitimate. Except that he got carried away when he wrote the label. I wish I still had a copy of it, but I remember clearly that when you finished reading it, you were left with the unmistakable impression that the contents would turn any wood you used it on *into* rosewood.

There weren't any laws to stop him in those days, but needless to say, he never sold the same person twice. And he soon ran out of customers in and around Coxsackie, which is a place near the Headless Horseman country of the Hudson River Valley.

I suppose that sounds as if I am calling my Uncle George dishonest, and actually he was one of the most honest men I've ever known. In his own mind anyway. Maybe not in some of his actions—he knew the things he did weren't honest. But he didn't lie to himself, and after all, isn't that the kind of honesty that counts? I mean, doesn't everybody have to lie some of the time? Otherwise you'd never have any friends, and probably get punched in the nose at least once a day.

For instance, my Uncle George was the only man I ever knew who was honest enough to admit that he hated children. They were always messing things up in his shop. If you can mess up a place that is already messed up. And every time he heard their joyful shouts at play, he would wince. So he was always chasing them away or telling them horror stories about his days in Alaska that gave them nightmares.

One boy got his revenge, though. That was little Billy Eddy. The way it started was that the Eddys lived in a house about a hundred feet from my Uncle George's shop. Well, there was a tree about halfway between the two buildings, and Billy's father hung a swing on one of the limbs. Billy thought this was great, and every afternoon he used to play airplane in the swing—with appropriate and loud sound effects, of course.

After a couple of months of this Uncle George was getting desperate. It wasn't just when the racket was going on. He'd anticipate it all day while Billy was at school. So one day he hit on the happy thought of checking the boundary line between the two properties. The result was great. It was perfectly clear that while the limb extended into the Eddy's yard, the base of the tree was on my Uncle George's property. So he had the tree cut down, and eventually used it for firewood.

Thus originated the expression: "a man mean enough to cut down a swing tree." Naturally you've heard that before, but what very few people know is the story of Billy Eddy's revenge. Mainly because it took him thirty years to get even.

Believe me, this is a true story.

The way it happened was that near the end of his life my Uncle George was living mainly on the income from a few houses that he owned and rented out. Well, one of these fell into the hands of some Hudson Valley hillbillies. It was one of those families that have eleven or twelve children (even the parents lose count) and the father only manages to find work during the summer months. Which leads to a lot of nonpayment of rent.

So naturally Uncle George started eviction proceedings. And to his aggravation and downright rage these took three years, because it turned out that little Billy Eddy had grown up to be a very good lawyer, and he gave his devious and procrastinating services free to Uncle George's tenants.

Young Billy—William now—managed to keep the case going until it reached the Superior Court of the Southern District of the State of New York. There he finally got a dressing down from the judge for wasting so much judicial time over the preceding three years. But that didn't really hurt him any, and he had the enormous satisfaction of being able to lean over and whisper to Uncle George as he left the courtroom, "Mighty expensive firewood, wasn't it."

Of course, Uncle George almost blew up right in his seat, but a couple of months later I caught him smiling out the window, and asked him what was so funny. After a little while he grinned and said, "Mighty expensive firewood, wasn't it?"

almond sticks Almond sticks are tight rolls of felt saturated with a thin mineral oil that are a holdover from my Uncle George's day—back before there was any supervising of advertising at all. As advertised—mostly by mail—this device is supposed to remove scratches, but all it actually does is wet down any dry particles of finish in them. You get better results with *colored polish* or *shoe polish,* for which see listings further on in this section. For real repair of *scratches,* see section on RESTORING OLD FINISHES.

beeswax polish Beeswax will give a tough dull coat to a furniture finish. The trouble is that in a pure state it can hardly be polished at all, and is duller and more nonslip than you would want. So it is usually used as an extra ingredient. See listing for *wax* (*paste*) below. A basic mixture would be half paraffin and half beeswax dissolved (with heat) in enough mineral spirits to make it a soft paste, or even a liquid. Actually, the commercially marketed products have considerably less beeswax than that, and are mostly paraffin, the basis of all waxes.

Beeswax can also be emulsified in water, which makes it a creamy white liquid. Other waxes or oils are usually present. This is done the same way you make soap, or at least the principle is the same. Water and wax or oil are held in suspension by the addition of an alkali or other emulsifying agent. Ammonia does it, too.

So, generally speaking, the use of beeswax in the name or label of a product will indicate a dullness or antique glow, or whatever you want to call it, in a wax. Or to put it another way, beeswax is added to a wax or polish mixture to cut the gloss or shine.

black spots The cure for these is treated in the section on RESTORING OLD FINISHES. See listing for *rings*. But perhaps there are those who are especially interested in preventing them, because they get them without knowing where they come from. The answer is that water has penetrated the finish and soaked into the fibers of the wood. Most often they are caused by a sweating vase, and usually the finish is broken.

But not always. Sometimes water or moisture gets through a pinhole imperfection in the finish without noticeably damaging the finish.

The best way to prevent this, of course, is a coat of hard paste wax. Not to mention putting plates under sweating vases. Doilies are not enough.

candelilla wax This is one of the very hard waxes—the other is *carnauba*—used in paste and liquid waxes to give the coating more durability. See *wax* (*paste*) and *wax* (*liquid*) further on in this section. It is obtained from a Mexican plant, and has a melting point of around 156 degrees Fahrenheit.

carnauba wax In its pure state, this is a slate-hard wax that you have to hit with a hammer to break, but it will dissolve in mineral spirits (paint thinner), and is considered the best of the hard waxes. Its melting point is 185 degrees Fahrenheit. For what it's worth to you, it's scraped from the leaves of a palm tree that grows mostly in Brazil. See *wax* (*paste*) and *wax* (*liquid*) further on in this section.

cleaning finishes There is no one best way to clean a dirty finish, because it depends on what kind of dirt is on it. The safest thing to use, and always the first to try, is mineral spirits, which is usually sold as paint thinner. This will dissolve both wax and oily or greasy dirt. If this doesn't work on some of the dirt, then try plain water, rubbing with a rag. As a final resort, soap and water with a brush.

But even if you have had to go as far as soap and water, give the piece a final hard wiping with the mineral spirits. Soap and water won't touch wax, and there may be spots that still have a film of wax on them. This is only important, of course, when you are going to apply a coating of varnish over the cleaned finish, as any traces of wax will prevent the varnish from drying.

The danger in using water is that it may cause a shellac or

lacquer finish to develop a film or whitish haze. If this does happen, it's not tragic, but you will have to go to the trouble of rubbing down the surface with 000-grade or finer steel wool. Use strokes that follow the grain of the wood, and rub only hard enough to remove the haze. Then either apply a new coat of finish, if that's what you were planning to do, or just wax or polish, which is usually all that is necessary.

colored polishes These can make an amazing improvement in scuffed and scratched pieces of furniture. They are simply mineral oil that has been colored a dark brown with aniline dyes. The best procedure is to clean the piece first. Then let it dry thoroughly so that the colored oil can penetrate into the imperfections of the finish. For the best job of all, scuff the piece with 000-grade steel wool first. Even after you have applied the polish, scuffed areas that persist can be given further rubbings with the steel wool, and this often improves matters. Just be careful not to rub all the way through the finish.

cracking (prevention) This is caused by excessive heat, when a finish is left in direct sunlight or next to a radiator. Cracking is caused by the shrinking of a finish due to the loss of essential oils. Over a period of time they "steam out." The best protection against this is an oil or oil-base polish, which provides a much better moisture seal than a wax. For cure of this condition, see listing for *colored polish,* above, and listing for *cracking* in section on RESTORING OLD FINISHES.

fading (prevention) Certain aniline dyes will fade when exposed to sunlight over any extended period. There is no prevention for this other than keeping the piece out of direct sunlight. The better grade of dyes is sunfast, but there is, of course, no way of telling what quality was used in staining a particular piece of furniture.

feeding the finish Along with "feeding thirsty wood fibers," this is one of the greatest pieces of malarky ever invented by the mind of man. How can you "feed" something without penetrating into it? And no wax or oil polish actually penetrates into shellac, lacquer, or varnish—much less through it to those poor "thirsty wood fibers." Really, now. When this particular advertising claim is used, all you're likely to get is overcharged.

Besides, what are those thirsty fibers and finishes supposed to be fed? They're dead now, you know. Pieces of wood have come out of Egyptian tombs where they lasted three thousand years in perfect condition without a drink. In fact, the dryness is what preserved them. When moisture got in a tomb, all the wood rotted.

French polishing An ancient technique, this is the application of a thin coat of shellac by brisk rubbing with an oiled pad of cloth. As such, it is not a dressing or protective coating for a finish, but a permanent surface. For details of the method, see the listing for *French polishing* in the section on RESTORING OLD FINISHES.

hazing (prevention) Since hazing is caused by moisture in the air—to the degree where it condenses on the finish—the best protection is probably a good coat of wax. Now, I know I have recommended an oil polish as best for preserving a finish. But we have to be realistic. This hazing usually occurs on the sides of bureaus and chests for the very reason that people don't get around to polishing or waxing them very often. So if you go over all parts of your furniture two times a year, an oil polish would be best, but if you can't be bothered with this, a wax will stand up and keep repelling moisture much longer—say three or four years.

lemon-oil polish I hate to sound like a reactionary old crank, but to my knowledge all of modern science has yet to come up with a better protective dressing for a furniture finish—shellac, lacquer, or varnish—than plain old mineral oil, which has been bubbling out of the ground here and there since long before man achieved any importance on this planet. And scented mineral oil is all that lemon-oil polish is.

Oil not only keeps moisture in the air away from the finish, it also keeps the essential oils in the finish from drying out. This prevents hazing in the first instance, and fine cracks from appearing in the second.

It should be pointed out here that the lemon scent along with a pale-yellow coloring is only the one most commonly and traditionally used. Almond scent and blue, green, or no coloring occur in many locally distributed brands. Sometimes a small amount of drier is used, which floats on top of the oil. This actually stays in the fibers of your polishing pad, simply stiffening them so that the surface polishes to a higher gloss.

linseed-oil polish Linseed oil differs from mineral oil in that it has the ability to absorb oxygen from the air and in so doing to dry out to a tough, hard film. This makes it the basis of most paints and varnishes—except, of course, the new plastic varnishes. So when a finish is wiped with linseed oil (thinned with mineral spirits or turpentine) it doen't simply dress the surface, it actually adds a permanent protective film. To use a linseed-oil polish is the same as applying a linseed-oil finish over the present finish.

The advantage of this is that the linseed-oil film is far more resistant to alcohol and the acids in vegetable juices, etc., than a shellac or lacquer.

The disadvantage is that each coating of oil will gather dust and smoke particles from the air, which are incorporated into it as it dries. This gradually darkens the finish—very considerably over a period of ten or fifteen years.

Therefore the best use for linseed-oil polish is to apply it to new finishes twice a year for a couple of years—or every other month for a year—and then revert to an oil polish or wax. See also *linseed-oil finish* in section on FINISHES.

mineral oil Any nondrying oil derived from a petroleum base—that is, coming from the earth. Except that it contains no additives, mineral oil is the same as the oil used to lubricate machinery and automobile engines. It is the basis of *lemon-oil polishes, oil-base polishes,* and some of the *white polishes,* for which see separate listings elsewhere in this section.

oil-base polishes These are the *lemon-oil polishes* and some of the *white polishes,* for which see separate listings elsewhere in this section.

plastic polishes Although they are not common, occasionally you will come across a polish that bills itself as a miracle worker because it has a plastic base. These are about the same as the plastic preparations used to polish kitchen floors. They work the same way, and there is certainly nothing the matter with them except that they result in a higher gloss than most people want on their furniture. It is the same as the gloss of a *French polish,* for which see listing under RESTORING OLD FINISHES. The principle involved is the same except that a plastic is used instead of shellac, and the plastic redissolves and is redistributed with the next application.

shoe polish Jones In almost every town or neighborhood there is someone who swears by shoe polish for use on furniture. And for my money, these people are not the jokers that they sound like at first blush. I have tried shoe polish, and it works fine, especially on a scuffed and worn piece.

The reason for this is that shoe polish is simply colored wax. And the better brands are of just as good hardness and quality as the commonly available furniture waxes. They also have the advantage of coloring and filling minor imperfections in the surface of a finish. They do not penetrate as well as a *colored oil polish* (see listing above) but they fill better. A good schedule for faking is first to use the colored oil. After wiping it off good and hard, apply the right color of shoe polish several times, and finally use a clear paste wax.

silicone polish Silicone is a chemically manufactured substance that is practically the same as wax. It has the advantage of being very easy to apply and polish—much easier than a natural wax preparation. However, you cannot build up a thickness of it by repeated application the way you can with wax. At least not noticeably.

Another disadvantage—for refinishers at least—is that silicone penetrates into some finishes—especially lacquers. And this makes the finish repel additional coats. There was a big to-do about this in the automobile-painting business, because automobile paint is actually lacquer, and silicone is used in many automobile polishes. But the problem was solved by adding a small amount of silicone to the lacquer that was to be applied.

This comes up in refinishing furniture only when you are spraying a reconditioning coat of lacquer on a piece that has been polished with silicone, or brushing on a coat of certain plastic varnishes. The solution is to scuff the old finish well with steel wool, and brush on a sealer coat of shellac, rubbing it right in with the brush, before applying the lacquer or varnish.

wax (liquid) These are usually a creamy white liquid, although some are quite thin, and others almost a semipaste. In any case they are an emulsion of wax in water. A typical formula would be 5 per cent carnauba, or candelilla, or some other hard wax, 10 or 15 per cent paraffin, about 10 per cent mineral spirits, and the rest water. The two waxes are dissolved in the mineral spirits, and this is mixed under heat with scientific accuracy and the addition of a few drops of an emulsifying agent. Special commercial agents are used, but you can do the same thing with soda ash, wood ashes, lye, or ammonia. It's a parallel process to making soap, only in this case fine droplets of wax are suspended in the water instead of fat.

In using them, there isn't any difference between a liquid wax and a paste wax. Except that in the liquid wax, the water evaporates to leave a solid film of wax, and in the case of paste wax the mineral spirits evaporates. See listing for *wax (paste)* below.

wax (paste) A typical formula for paste wax is 10 per cent carnauba or other hard wax, 15 per cent pure paraffin, and the rest mineral spirits. The percentages can vary a great deal. The more mineral spirits, the softer the product. The more hard wax, the better, or harder, the final polish will be, but it will also be to the same degree harder to polish. It will take harder, brisker rubbing. The more paraffin, of course, the easier it is to polish the coating. And incidentally, we are talking about pure paraffin, which is less oily than the kind used to seal jelly jars.

The manufacturing process, and anybody can do it at home, is to heat the waxes and mineral spirits over a low heat until the wax dissolves. Then let it cool, and you have paste wax.

For a duller sheen to the final polished coating, beeswax is substituted for some of either or both of the other waxes. Not more than 5 per cent of the total can be beeswax or the product becomes too sticky to polish well.

white polish Originally, white polish referred to an emulsion of about 50 per cent water and 50 per cent mineral oil (see *oil-base polishes*, above). And this is still preferred by the same kind of purist who prefers lemon oil (see listings above for *lemon-oil polishes* and *mineral oil*).

The advantage of mixing mineral oil with water in an emulsion is that the water has a cleaning action. The oil dissolves greasy dirt, and the water removes anything that is water soluble, thereby covering the field as far as surface dirt is concerned. That is why these polishes are still used in institutions and offices. They are quick and easy, and perform the needed cleaning job while giving the same protection as a lemon-oil polish.

However, there are now many other white polishes on the market. These are the silicones and liquid waxes, and various combinations of same.

Section 4

EASY-TO-MAKE REPAIRS

Or, Patch it up, wear it out,
Make it do, or do without

Sometimes, I feel like a voice crying in the wilderness. My wife says that the wilderness wouldn't have me, but that's another story. What I'm getting at is that repairing furniture would be easy for reasonably handy people if they would only heed my lonely cry as I wend my way across the desert and through the barren forest: "No nails," I wail, "No nails!"

But no one pays any attention—in spite of the fact that it has been well established for five or six centuries that the only way to hold furniture together is with glue. Also, you can't use screws, iron angles, or metal plates. That way lies, if not madness, at least the town dump. No fastening device made of metal is ever one-tenth as good as a joint of wood glued to wood.

The only excuse for a screw in wooden furniture is to hold two pieces together while the glue dries. Of course, in most cases the screw is then left there after it has served its purpose, which is where most people get their bad thoughts on this subject.

So this is rule number one: abandon hope, all ye who have recourse to screws or nails.

Rule number two is based on another understandable but totally wrong belief: that glue is glue, and that therefore one kind of glue will stick to another as well as it will to raw wood.

In fact, there are even some sadly misguided souls who believe that glue will stick better to glue than it will to wood. Nothing could be less true. Not only will one kind of glue not stick very well to another kind, but fresh glue will not stick well to dried glue of the same kind, or even out of the same bottle. They look like they are going to stick. They even seem to be pretty firm when you try the joint after it is dry. But under the stress and strain of use, such joinings will give quite easily compared to the use of the same glue between two raw surfaces of wood.

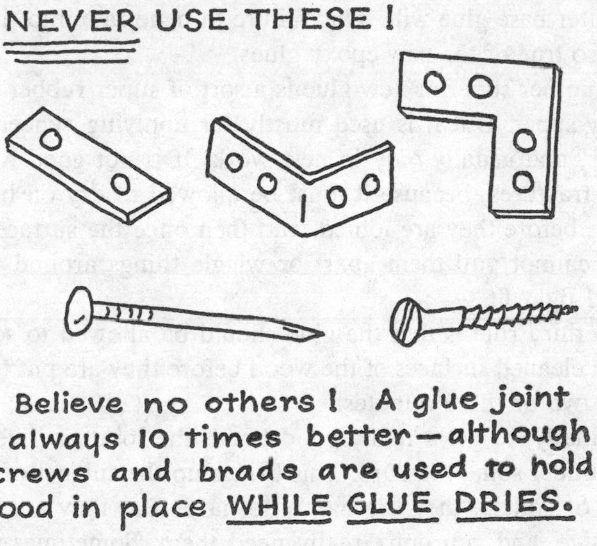
NEVER USE THESE !
Believe no others ! A glue joint is always 10 times better—although screws and brads are used to hold wood in place WHILE GLUE DRIES.

The rule here, of course, is: when a glued joint gives, clean the old glue off all surfaces before regluing.

When it comes to which glue to use, the answer is to use one of the many new brands of creamy white glue, such as Borden's Elmer's Glue, to name one widely distributed brand, or the cabinetmaker's stand-by, Weldwood, which is a pale, tannish powder that you mix with water to the consistency of heavy cream. The general practice in a cabinetmaker's shop is to use the white glue for run-of-the-mill jobs, but to mix up a small amount of Weldwood when he wants to be extra sure, or the joint must be extra strong.

These glues are now preferred to the old brown glues—hot glue and fish glue—because as they dry, a chemical change takes place so that they cannot be redissolved in water. This is important because moisture in the air, which softens the old-fashioned glues, causes loose joints.

The plastic, clear glues of the airplane-cement type are pretty resistant to moisture, too, but they are not good on wood because they do not penetrate into wood fibers the way a water-base glue will. This failure to penetrate into the wood is also true of the new epoxy glues.

Another superior new glue is a sort of super rubber cement. Very super. But it is used mostly for applying veneer to surfaces, and usually only in new work. It is not good for joints and fractures, because it must be allowed to dry on both surfaces before they are joined, and then once the surfaces touch you cannot pull them apart or wiggle things around to get a good tight fit.

A third rule is that the glue should be allowed to soak into both cleaned surfaces of the wood before they are put together. For two or three minutes.

Finally, to get a really good bond, the joint or glue should dry under some pressure. This brings up the subject of clamps, and of course, they are handy to have. But they are also expensive, and you don't really need them. Sometimes you can get pressure by using the weight of some heavy books. And you can always get pressure by using a couple of loops of clothesline and twisting them tight with a stick the same way you do a tourniquet. This is especially useful for regluing chair rungs and legs. Of course, if you are going to save ten dollars on a repair job, it is certainly worthwhile to buy a couple of C-clamps at any good hardware store for fifty cents apiece. You may need to use them again, you know, for lots of things. To hold down a jiggling sewing machine, for instance. At least

GLUING
without
pressure
is
a
waste
of
time

that's where I always find mine when they are missing from my workbench.

So the tools you need for repairing are really very simple: glue, a sharp knife, and some clothesline—and, when necessary, a couple of C-clamps.

For easier reference, we have divided this section into five parts. These separately cover all the things that can go wrong with chairs, chests, tables, and upholstered pieces. There is also a final part covering surface defects such as dents and blistered veneers.

And, oh yes—heat. Don't try to glue wood in a cold room. It doesn't have to go down to freezing to cause the glue to crystallize and crumble. I know, because I once had fourteen tables fall apart on me. There were fourteen of them, because I had a scheme for making a fortune by manufacturing television tables. The barn was warm when I glued them, but later that night it went down to ten degrees. It was sometime late in August as I remember it. But if that sounds like the winters are bad in Vermont, they're nothing to what they are over in New Hampshire.

Clem Weatherbee's father got off a good one about that once. They were living on a farm just over the border in New Hampshire. One summer a gang of young surveyors came through and told him that they had just discovered there had been a mistake in the old survey of the line between the states. They said that he wasn't in New Hampshire, but in Vermont.

The old man allowed a small smile to crack his old Yankee face, and said, "Well, that's good for sure, boys. I don't think I could have stood another one of those New Hampshire winters."

arms broken When an arm is broken, the joints on each end of it are usually loosened too. For that part of the problem, see immediately above. As to the break itself, first take the whole arm off, and refasten the ends, again as in listing above. At this time you also reglue the break spot, clamping it together with a C-clamp if possible. If a C-clamp will not fit or stay on due to the curve, apply pressure with clothesline tourniquets. (See illustration.) Do not try to repair the break without regluing the ends of the arm at the same time. If the ends are loose, the arm will only break again.

arms loose This refers to a wooden arm on a wooden chair. Upholstered arms are taken care of further on in this section. This is about the only exception to the rule that you can't hold furniture together with screws. But on the other hand, these are the joints that give most often. The only remedy takes a little nerve, because the heads of these screws are covered with either little wooden buttons, or flush-set wooden plugs. The former can be pried out with a knife or chisel, and saved to put back, but the flush plugs have to be dug out with something sharp and pointed. When you finally find the head of the screw, clean the slot carefully so you can get a good grip, and unscrew it. You'll have to do this at both ends of the arm—where it joins the side of the seat as well as where it joins the back. When you have the arm off, plug the chewed-up screw holes with pieces of matchstick or toothpicks. Let this plug dry in the hole. Then scrape off all the old glue, and glue the piece back on with Weldwood, drawing the joint tight by re-inserting and tightening the screws. Wipe off excess glue that squeezes out right away with a wet rag.

If button plugs were used to cover the screw heads, just push these back in with a little glue to hold them. Where flush plugs were used, fill the holes with colored wax (an ordinary brown crayon is good) or shellac stick. (See listings for *shellac stick* and *wax stick* in section on RESTORING OLD FINISHES.)

falling apart When a chair is really loose and rickety, it is easier to take the whole thing apart and start over again. To do this in a hurry, make a padded hammer by taking a pad of felt or any heavy rags and tying this onto the head of a hammer with some more strips of rag and some wire. With this device you can knock rungs and legs loose from their sockets without leaving hammer marks even on finished surfaces.

GOT A SOFT HAMMER
IN YOUR HOUSE?
Just strips
of heavy rag
For knocking
furniture apart
without bruising it, of course.

When you have the pieces lying around you on the floor, scrape off all old glue, and then go out to the store and buy a package of toothpicks. Now glue the whole chair together at one time, *not* piecemeal. When you have it together again, stand it on a level floor or table so that the bottoms of all legs are touching the level surface. *In this position,* insert the toothpicks wherever they will fit into loose joints. Push as many as will fit into each joint, and then cut the protruding ends off with a single-edged razor blade.

When a socket is really chewed up, you will want to cut larger pieces of wood to use instead of the toothpicks.

If other repairs are needed—such as a split seat—do all your gluing at the same time. This is to avoid some joint going askew so that two previously glued sections won't fit together, or one leg lifts a cockeyed inch and a half off the floor.

legs broken Chair legs break either where the rungs go into them, or at the top where they join the seat. In both cases the best answer is a whole new leg. However, you can *try* to glue back a piece broken off at a rung joint. Use Weldwood for sure on this. Stand the chair upright and place the heaviest weight you can get on the corner of the seat over the leg. A whole set of the *Encyclopaedia Britannica* is good. Also a garbage can full of water, or an old locomotive.

If the break is at the top of a leg that goes into a hole in a wooden seat, you can try the same thing. In both cases, though, if there is any looseness in the rest of the leg structure, the whole business must be reglued at the same time to minimize strain on the break.

In the case of cushioned chairs, the sides of the frame holding the cushion are tongued into the top of the leg. It's called a mortise-and-tenon joint, the mortise being the hole, the tenon the tongue. Here again the problem is to get sufficient pressure on the joint after it has been cleaned and reglued. Cabinetmakers use pipe clamps which are adjustable to any length, but they cost about five dollars apiece. Sufficient pressure can really be applied with a clothesline tourniquet that goes all around the outside edge of the seat. Be sure to pad the corners with several layers of heavy rag, because soft as it is, even clothesline may damage the finish on the corners. (See illustration.)

legs loose See general instructions under *falling apart*.

rungs broken It is foolish to try to reglue a broken rung—unless you are going to put the chair in a museum where no one will be allowed to put his big foot on the rung. Instead, take a piece of the rung to a hardware store and buy a length of dowling of the same size. Cut this to length, and whittle the ends to the same size as the old rung. If the rung you are duplicating had a taper, the best way to reproduce this in your dowl is with a piece of very rough garnet paper. This costs more than ordinary sandpaper, but cuts ten times as well. It may take a couple of hours to sand, but if you don't have a couple of hours to waste of an evening, repairing furniture isn't your line anyway. After you have achieved the shape you want, smooth the surface with a medium and finally a fine sandpaper.

Then glue your new rung back into the chair, and stain it to match. The easiest way to do this is with "colors ground in stain," which can be bought in small tubes in a paint store. Bring a piece of the rung to the store with you to help you pick out the color you want. See *colors ground in oil* in section on STAINING.

Finally, two or three coats of shellac, rubbed down with 000 steel wool after each application will be enough of a finish.

rungs loose See general instructions under *falling apart*.

rungs missing See instructions under *rungs broken*.

slats loose Whether they run crosswise or vertically, the slats in the back of a chair are usually supposed to "float"—that is, rest loosely in the slots they fit into. And when they are glued, this is only to keep them from rattling around. However, the usual trouble with slats is a looseness caused by the wall of the containing slot being broken. Well, here is a perfect excuse to try to talk you into buying a couple of C-clamps at your hardware store. They usually run about forty-five-cents apiece, and once you own them, you'll wonder how you ever ran a house without them. You can use them to hold small pieces of wood for sawing, all kinds of small glue jobs, for holding down jiggling sewing machines, a hundred things around the house.

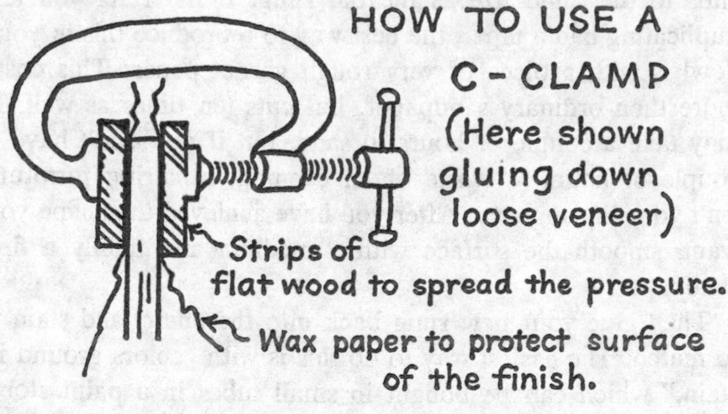
HOW TO USE A
C-CLAMP
(Here shown
gluing down
loose veneer)
Strips of
flat wood to spread the pressure.
Wax paper to protect surface
of the finish.

The illustration above shows how these are used with small blocks of wood to prevent indentations in the surface. The wax paper will prevent one of the blocks being accidentally glued to the chair.

If the piece broken out from the wall of the slot has been lost, the first thing to do is to glue the end of the slat firmly into its slot. Do not glue the other end, as looseness at the other end will put less strain on the glued end. After the glue is dry (Weldwood), fill the hole remaining with *shellac stick* or *wax stick,* for which see listings in section on RESTORING OLD FINISHES.

If the piece that has been lost is large—say, over two inches long—this is a job for a cabinetmaker, who will put in a new piece of wood.

brasses It is almost impossible to find an exact match for a missing drawer pull, but many good hardware stores carry lines from which you can get a complete set—both in modern and traditional designs. Also, one of the tricks of the trade is to substitute brasses for knobs on old pine chests, or even on unfinished modern ones that have aged a little. (For some of the nefarious methods used to do this, see the section on FAKING ANTIQUES.)

For this purpose, the best source of brasses is Horton Brasses, Berlin, Connecticut. This brand is far superior to anything you can buy in a hardware store. In the first place, they are solid brass. They are also perfect reproductions of old brasses that were hand-struck from steel dies. Even the nuts used to attach them look as if they were cast in an open mold, and then tapped. Maybe they are, for all I know. They also have knobs, finials, bed bolts—the whole works in antique hardware. The last time I sent for a catalogue the price was thirty-five cents.

Incidentally, the best way to get an antique pine chest cheap is to buy a battered Empire chest and soak the veneer off in a lake. See *veneer removing* in section on FAKING ANTIQUES.

drawers loose The first cause of loose drawers is a broken or missing guide inside the chest. These are easily replaced with scrap-wood strips and a few brads. But sometimes the bottom of the drawer is worn down so that you have to lift the front of the drawer to get it all the way in. Do *not* try to add wood to the bottoms of the drawer sides. Not unless you are a cabinetmaker, that is. Instead, look at the track the drawer slides on. If it has been gouged by the in-and-out passage of the drawer, fill the indentation with Plastic Wood. Or if the track is all right, and the wear really is on the bottom of the drawer sides, raise the level of the track by gluing thin pieces of wood onto it. Pieces from bushel baskets are good for this.

drawers sticking The problem, of course, is that the drawer is too large for the hole it fits in. But do not start recklessly planing away on the bottom or top edge of the drawer, or you will have a drawer that still sticks, but which in addition will now have to be lifted up to get the front all the way into its hole. The reason for this is that the sticking is caused by a warping, however slight, of the sides of the drawer. So you have to plane, scrape, or sand some wood from the top and/or bottom of the sides.

Of course, before going into surgery of this sort, you should try soaping the sides and bottom edge of the drawer—there may be two or three people left in the world who don't know about that trick.

falling apart Completely regluing a chest of drawers takes a little time, but is really very easy, since it is only a box with a few boxes fitted into it. However, here are a few hints on how to go about it.

(1) Use a padded hammer (see illustration) to knock the loose pieces apart.

(2) Scrape off all dried glue so that the new glue can sink into the wood and get a good grip.

(3) Glue the drawers back together first, keeping them as square as possible. Clamps aren't necessary, but you may want to use a few brads to tack pieces together while the glue dries.

(4) After the drawers are dry, glue the chest together, and immediately put the drawers in it, to make sure they are going to fit after their case is dry. You will often find that you've got the chest a little askew, and the time to correct this is before the glue dries. The preglued drawers make it possible for you to get things straight—or if not straight, at least crooked in

the right way so that the drawers will fit. Of course, you have to be sure to wipe off any excess glue so that you don't glue one of the drawers into the case permanently.

knobs Plain wooden knobs are available in good hardware stores. No one seems to reproduce the turned Victorian type, but you can get a carved wooden drawer pull in a simple Victorian leaf pattern (either cherry or walnut) from Albert Constantine & Son, 2050 Eastchester Road, New York 61, New York.

Loose knobs of the kind that have their own wooden screws should be made tight when regluing them by using strips of glue-saturated cloth. Enough cloth so that they stuff in tightly.

legs broken Sometimes the leg of a chest will be smashed in moving it around, or the glue loosens and a piece breaks off. What most people need in this case isn't information but encouragement to start the job. The big obstacle is laziness about taking all the drawers out of the chest and turning it upside down on a rug or blanket. When that is done, glue the pieces back together, using brads to hold them while the glue dries if necessary. After they are dry, try to reinforce the structure by gluing a small square block of wood inside the back of the corner. This is almost always possible.

panels split Whether they are in the sides of chests or cupboard doors, panels should "float" free in their slots so that expansion and contraction caused by moisture will not cause them to crack or split. One way to prevent split panels is to varnish or shellac the inside of the panel as well as the outside. This helps maintain a stable moisture content in the wood.

Once such a crack has occurred, it is sometimes possible to close it up by soaking the inside of the panel with water by leaving wet rags lie on it for anywhere from four hours to three days. Then you can glue a thin piece of wood over the whole length of the crack on the unfinished side to prevent the crack from opening up again. At the same time, use a pointed knife to loosen the edges of the panel from the slots containing it.

If the split or crack has been established for a long time, this water treatment may not work. But by using a sharp, pointed knife, you can probably loosen at least one half of the panel and force it toward the other half to close the crack. And again, batten it from behind. Trying to fill such a crack with shellac stick or anything else is a mistake, because this doesn't cure the cause of the problem, and the crack will only open up again.

top split Splits in large pieces of wood are caused by their not being thoroughly dried before they were fastened down. And, of course, bringing an old piece into a steam-heated house or apartment may provoke a situation that was latent. In the case of a bureau or chest of drawers, the procedure is to take out the drawers, turn the case over, and take off the top by either unscrewing, if screws were used, or knocking out the small triangular strips that were used to glue it to the top of the frame. A hammer and chisel are the best tools to use for doing this. Then the two pieces of the top are reglued under pressure, and the top is refastened to its frame.

The technique for holding these pieces together under pressure is the same as that used for regluing a split table leaf, and is given a few pages further on in the section on table repairs under the heading *leaf split*.

top warped The method for removing a warp from the top of a chest or bureau is the same as the one for *leaf warped* a few pages further on. A special point can be made, however, about the tops of bureaus and chests of drawers. Many people don't realize that these are fairly easy to remove from their cases. This is because most people aren't used to seeing the case minus its drawers and turned upside down. When this is done, you will see that the top is held onto the frame by screws. Sometimes it is glued on with little triangular strips of wood.

In that case, knock the blocks out with a hammer and chisel, and the top will come the rest of the way off quite easily, preparatory to the unwarping procedure.

wooden pulls When loose, these are best glued back on rather than fastened with screws from the inside of the drawer. Scrape off all old glue and use Weldwood powdered glue, mixed to a creamy consistency with water. It is good to use screws from inside the drawer to tighten the pulls while drying, but this involves drilling holes if screws weren't previously used. For a source for Victorian wood pulls, see listing for *knobs,* above.

falling apart (drop leaf) For some reason or other, the bigger the piece, the less likely the amateur is to tackle the job. And that is wrong. Many a small chair is harder to fix than a big table. You will find that the construction of a table is incredibly simple when you take the time to examine it. And also, all leaf-bearing tables are built the same way. (The same is true of pedestal tables, treated in the next listing.)

I guess it all goes back to the tongue-and-groove joint. Once that was invented, everybody realized—from China to Italy—that this was the best way to make a table. Four pieces of wood are fitted into slots in the tops of the legs, and that's it. The top is fastened to this frame by screws coming up from underneath, and the leaves hang on hinges from the edges of the top.

So the proper way to reglue one is to *first* turn the table upside down on the floor. Then you will be able to see the heads of the screws that hold the top on. Unscrew these, and the leg structure comes off. Then it is easy to knock any loose corners of the frame apart with a hammer. Scrape the crumbling old glue out of these joints, and reglue them, pushing in toothpicks, matches, or small wedges of wood to fill any loose spaces.

And here's the trick that avoids trouble later on: wipe off

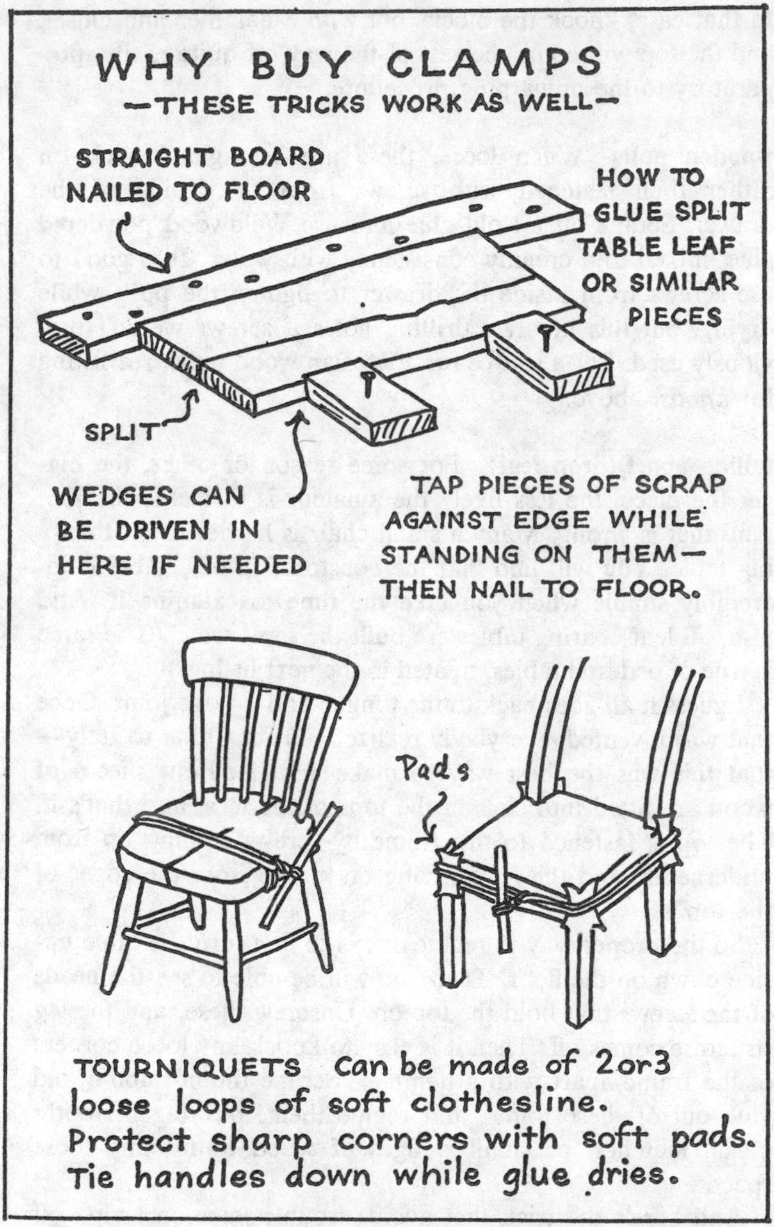
WHY BUY CLAMPS
—THESE TRICKS WORK AS WELL—
STRAIGHT BOARD NAILED TO FLOOR
HOW TO GLUE SPLIT TABLE LEAF OR SIMILAR PIECES
SPLIT
WEDGES CAN BE DRIVEN IN HERE IF NEEDED
TAP PIECES OF SCRAP AGAINST EDGE WHILE STANDING ON THEM—THEN NAIL TO FLOOR.
Pads
TOURNIQUETS Can be made of 2or3 loose loops of soft clothesline.
Protect sharp corners with soft pads.
Tie handles down while glue dries.

any excess glue, and screw the leg structure loosely back onto the top. This will insure that the frame will be a perfectly square rectangle. Clamps aren't really necessary for this kind of joint—tongue and groove—if you have taken up any looseness with your toothpicks and little wedges of wood.

As to fastening the frame permanently to the top, be careful to save the screws you take out. If part of your trouble is that the holes they come out of are loose, force Plastic Wood into the holes and screw the screws into them—and the frame to the top—while the Plastic Wood is still wet. This will cause some of the Plastic Wood to squish out. Don't let the Plastic Wood dry in the holes first, because the screws are too likely to push it right on through the top of the table. Same goes for wood plugs.

And that's all there is to it. Troubles with hinges, tops, and leaves are treated in some following listings.

falling apart (pedestal) The commonest pedestal tables are the Victorian oak dining tables. Others are small tables, usually tilt-top from the Early American period. In any case, the hardest part in repairing a wobbly one is to get it turned upside down so you can see how it was put together. The central leg always goes into a frame, to which in turn the top is screwed from underneath. For what to do next, see listing immediately above.

If the looseness is where one of the three or four small legs come into the central post, you really have a problem. What almost always has happened is that the bottom of the central post has split, and this is one of the few times in this book that I am going to have to say: take it to a cabinetmaker. These legs never come out of the end of the central post without breaking it apart, and then you need very good clamps to get the thing glued back tight again.

hinges broken As always, first turn the table upside down on a carpet so you can get a good look at what is the matter.

Just like many moral issues, these problems are a lot less discouraging once you bring matters out into the light. If the only problem is that the pin in the hinge has broken, you are in luck. All you have to do is get a finishing nail (the kind with a very small head) of the same diameter as the pin. They and sold by hardware stores and lumber yards. Using the nail and a hammer, knock the old pin out and replace it with a section of nail cut to the right length with a hacksaw. The man in the hardware store will do this for you, too, if you are reasonably polite or a good customer.

If the hinge itself is broken—or more likely rusted away—you have to replace it with one of exactly the same size and shape. No fooling around. Try no almost-the-same-size substitutes. The leverage is such that the slightest variation in size will cause the end of the leaf to bind or, when the leaf is up, make a crack wider at one end than the other. So take the hinge off and carry it around with you in your pocket the next time you are in the city, and make a tour of hardware stores.

To replace the old hinge, you must, of course, remove the top from its frame. For this process see listing above on *falling apart (drop leaf)*. Then proceed as common sense would indicate.

hinges loose When table leaves become rattly, the screws holding the hinges to the leaves have become loose. Turn the table upside down on the floor (on a soft rug, of course), take the loose hinge screws out, and reset them into some wet Plastic Wood that you have forced into the holes. If the holes are very loose, put in a few short pieces of toothpick first.

If any of the screws are missing, take out one of the good ones, and take it to a hardware store to get an exact match. The point of the screw will often have been cut off, so have them do that for you at the hardware store, too. Do not get fatter screws, but duplicate the old screws exactly, and take up the looseness by stuffing the hole. This is the only way to be sure of not pushing through the top of the table, which is to be avoided at all cost.

If the leaf has been loosened by dirt between the edge of the top and the edge of the leaf, clean it out, of course. Often you can also relieve pressure against the leaf by trimming the edge of the table. Use some rough garnet paper from any good hardware store for this.

leaf broken When a piece of a leaf has been split entirely off, there are two solutions to the problem. The least satisfactory is to cut the other leaf off to an equal length. And believe me, I have seen this done—especially when the broken-off piece has been lost.

The other solution is to glue it back, and this will work only if the glue is allowed to set under pressure. The method for doing this is shown under the illustration headed "Why Buy Clamps?" And why indeed?

Obviously, the leaf must first be removed from the table, and placed flat on the floor, against either the wall or a board nailed to the floor. Lay a piece of wax paper on the floor to prevent gluing the leaf to it. Work with the finished side of the leaf up so that when glue comes out under pressure, you will be able to wipe it off. Mix your Weldwood powder to a creamy paste, and apply it to both edges to be joined. Now push them together fairly firmly to squeeze out the really excess glue. Wipe this up with a wet rag.

Now start the nails in the two pieces of board you are going to use to push the two pieces of leaf together against the wall. Have a helper push against these two pieces, one at a time, while you nail them down. This may take a couple of tries to get both ends tight. And if you expect to be doing this frequently, you can even make two long thin wedges to drive between the edge of the leaf and the two pieces of wood that you have nailed to the floor. By driving these in with a hammer, you eliminate the need for a helper.

leaf split This may be a little hard to accept at first, but the only way to fix a leaf that has split from one end but not completely broken off, is to go ahead and break it the rest of the way off. Then proceed as in listing above. At least that's the only right way, because it is the only way you can get glue into the split.

The other way, which I'm obviously against, is to put a batten across the back of the leaf—after squeezing as much glue as possible into the crack, of course. The batten is then glued and screwed on. Such a job will last, all right, but it just doesn't do any good to the looks or value of the table.

leaf warped Here's the place to go into a general discussion of warps—because table leaves are the commonest victims. To

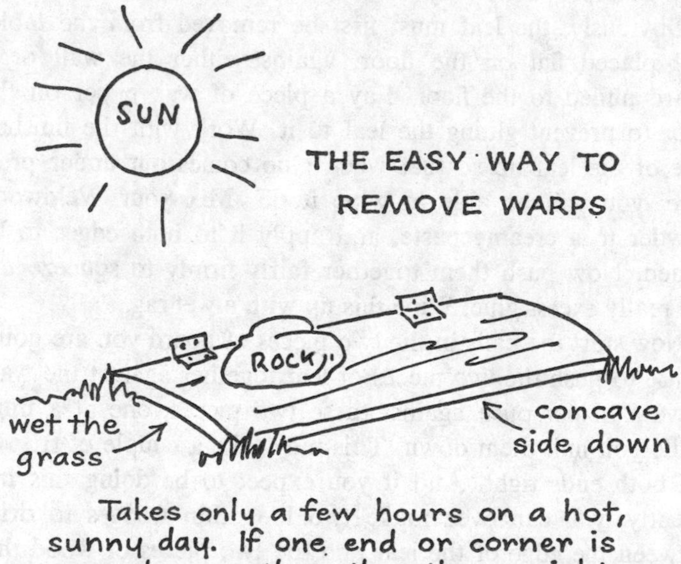
SUN
THE EASY WAY TO REMOVE WARPS
ROCK
wet the grass
concave side down
Takes only a few hours on a hot, sunny day. If one end or corner is warped more than the other, weight it down with a heavy rock.

begin with, warp is caused by moisture which gets into one side of a board without being able to get into the other because of some kind of waterproof finish. If this suggests to you that the way to prevent warping is to finish the undersides of tables and bureau tops, you are absolutely right. In fact, in a good custom-finishing or refinishing job, this is always done.

Returning to the situation of a leaf that's already warped, the cure is to wet the dried-out side. This is always the concave (hollow) side. Happily, any wood that will warp in the first place will unwarp when this is done—regardless of the age of the piece or the duration of the warp.

The easiest method to get moisture content back into the hollow side of a warped board is illustrated. You put the hollow or concave side down on the grass, and let the sun heat the other side. This may take anywhere from four hours to four long sunny days. When the board looks straight, take it into the house, and let it stand around in an even-temperatured room for a few days. Sometimes a little of the warp returns after a few days. If this happens, take it out on the grass again for further therapy. In fact, this time you can leave it until the side facing the sun begins to get a little concave. It is not a job to fuss or worry about, because wood is incredibly pliable. You can make a board warp first one way and then the other, over and over without hurting the wood.

Now here's another point. If you have a complex warp—that is to say, if the board is not only warped, but also twisted—the trick is to put two twenty-pound rocks on the high corners, the ones that don't come down to the grass.

Grass and hot sun are not, of course, available in the winters or in an apartment house. In that situation, make some sort of frame that will suspend the leaf (or whatever you have that is warped) over a radiator—about six inches above it. But this time, have the concave or hollow side up, and on it place five or six layers of rags, and keep them wet by pouring water on them.

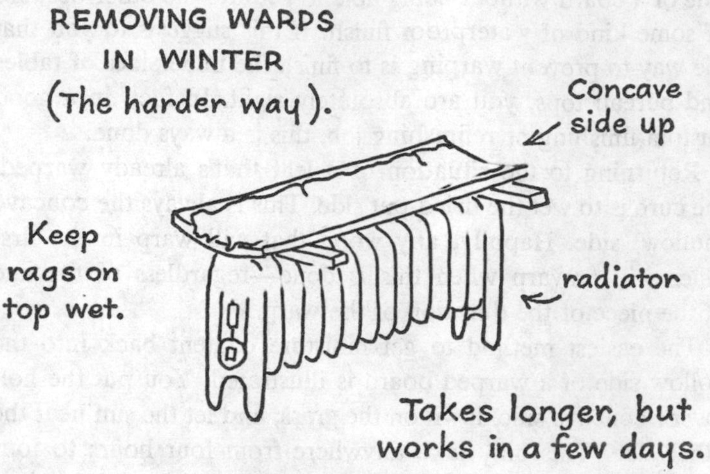
REMOVING WARPS
IN WINTER
(The harder way).
Concave
side up
Keep
rags on
top wet.
radiator
Takes longer, but
works in a few days.

marble-top tables Now here's a gumdrop of information that people have been waiting to hear about for years! Namely, how to clean marble. Up to a year ago I had asked hundreds of people, and the best answer I ever got was to grind it down. Well, that just isn't practical. But finally my Uncle George was messing around in his "laboratory" and came up with this: first, dissolve a cake of any ordinary hand soap in an equal amount of water by cutting it up in small pieces and boiling it gently. When this is slurpy, add equal amounts by volume of quicklime and caustic potash, both of which can be bought at a drugstore. This mixture is brushed on and left for several days, and then wiped off.

Finally, you have to repolish the marble. And this can be done with any furniture cream polish or wax. However, if you want to whiten the marble, make an equal-parts mixture of ordinary washing soda, pumice (from the hardware store), and white chalk (from pounding some pieces of white chalk to a powder).

It used to be the fashion to cut Victorian marble-top tables down to cocktail-table height. But lately the prices of these tables have skyrocketed to $65, $75, and up, even at back-country auctions, so they are now considered too "priceless" for this kind of hanky-panky. At any rate, such cutting down is a job for a cabinetmaker or some other skilled woodworker.

top split When a crack appears in the top of a table, it is caused by the piece of wood drying out and shrinking while its long edges are held down to the frame it rests on. It is a situation where something has to give, and it is usually the top. It splits right down the middle. The method for repairing this is the same as that given above under *leaf broken,* but there is another special problem. After the top has been glued back together, it isn't wide enough any more. At least, not in the case of a drop-leaf table. When the leaves are put down they no longer go all the way, with the result that the table looks something like a butterfly about to flap its wings. Of course, you can settle for this, and call it a new kind of butterfly table. The more reasonable approach is to get a disc sander—the kind that goes with a quarter-inch drill—and sand out the backs of the leaves where they are hitting against the frame of the table. Use the coarsest grade of paper you can find. The point of contact is usually at the tops of the four legs, and you can remove a quarter of an inch or more from the insides of the leaves without anybody ever noticing. Then they will hang straight.

In the long run this is much easier and a far better-looking job than trying to fill the split in the top with wood or anything else. If you put new wood in, it never stains the same color as the old wood of the top, and it takes a real expert to fill such a crack with shellac stick.

top warped Turn the table upside down so that you can find the screws holding the top on. Remove the top, and proceed according to the directions given for *leaf warped,* above.

arm loose Repairing upholstered pieces is one of those jobs that looks hard just because you've never done it before. Actually, there's no mystery about upholstery. Padding is stretched over a rather crude frame of wood, and a covering is tacked and sewed over that. Obviously, to get at a loose joint you are going to have to reveal it to the light of day. To do this, you will have to peel back the top covering and then the padding. There is no arguing about the fact that this will involve prying out some tacks and ripping out some stitching. For those who have the nerve to do this—and it undeniably takes a little—the rest of the game is easy. Reglue the broken joint with Weldwood, using C-clamps for pressure. You don't even have to bother wiping off the excess glue, or to worry about how the job looks. Usually you can use extra pieces of wood as battens over your glued joints for extra strength.

Finally, replace the padding, and tack and sew back the top covering. Of course, your job won't look as good as one done by a professional upholsterer, but it will be a lot cheaper.

bottom sagging The best repair job on a sagging bottom that I ever saw was one done on a Morris chair Old Tom Whetherbee relaxed in for about fifty years of his misspent life. (Misspent according to the standard of values of personnel directors, bill collectors, and status-seekers generally, that is.) Calling him *Old* Tom was an old joke he had worn for years. He encouraged it. He used to say, "Call me 'Old Tom.' It's not that I'm really so old, but it makes me seem more likable."

Anyway, when the springs in Old Tom's Morris chair were finally touching the floor, he turned it upside down, resting the seat on an old wooden box of the right height so that the bottom was more or less level. Then he took a piece of heavy brown paper and made a pattern the same size as the bottom of the chair. He then took this down to the lumber yard and had the boys there cut a piece of plywood the same size as the pattern. Then he drilled about twenty holes in the edges of the plywood, and using three-quarter-inch #7 screws, screwed it to the bottom of the frame of the chair. By the time I saw it, this job had lasted eighteen years, and I can't understand why chairs aren't made that way in the first place. Why webbing should be used to hold springs from the bottom as well as the top is beyond me. And as a repairing technique, this is a lot easier than trying to tie springs and stretch new webbing.

leg broken When the leg of an upholstered chair is actually smashed, the break usually comes where the leg joins the bottom of the frame, which is the weakest spot because the frame is mortised into the leg at this point. And this makes such a messy break that the only cure is to splice in a whole new section of leg—from the bottom to about six inches above the joint. Needless to say, this is a job for a professional.

However, if the break is such that it looks like it might be worth trying to mend, the important point is this: after soaking glue into the raw wood, jam the pieces together to get a tight fit rather than for surface appearance. Then let the joint dry with the chair in an upright position and a couple of thousand books piled in the corner of the seat over the leg. Then, after the joint is dry, it is time to worry about how things look. Cut down any pieces that stick out, with a sharp knife, chisel, or piece of rough sandpaper wrapped around a small block of wood. In fact, scrape or sand the old finish off the whole leg. Then restain, shellac, fill any holes with colored wax (see *wax-stick patching* in Section 3), shellac again, rub lightly with 000 steel wool, and wax or polish.

leg loose In an upholstered chair one loose joint is very like another, so see listing above for *arm loose*. The special point to be made is that a loose leg is a lot easier to fix, because by turning the chair upside down and removing the black ticking on the bottom of the chair, it is easier to get a look at what is the matter. Also, after working as much glue as you can into the loose joint, it is easy enough to glue a couple of bracing blocks into the corners where the sides of the frame join the leg. These should be about an inch square and two or three inches long. The glue you've worked into the joint isn't likely to hold, but these will.

dents Dents can usually be removed by steaming the area. This works best with the softer woods. For detailed directions see listing for *dents* in section on RESTORING FINISHES. Naturally, steaming will ruin a finish, and so is usually only done at the time of refinishing. To fix a dent without refinishing is possible, but takes more skill. For this technique, see listing for *shellac-stick patching,* also in section on RESTORING FINISHES.

dry rot This is the term used when wood powders and crumbles as a result of an attack by a fungus, which gets a foothold at some time when the wood was moist. That's why it is most often found in the feet and legs of furniture. Old tavern tables were especially susceptible because they stood on dirt floors. The old-fashioned cure for this condition was to soak the piece in gasoline or benzine, and they used to try to dissolve different poisons in the liquid. But nowadays there is a widely distributed product on the market called Cuprinol, which everyone in the trade uses. If you can't get it at your local hardware store, try a boatyard or a hardware store with a line of marine supplies. They will have a variation of the product for use on boats, but which is just as good for furniture. You just soak it into the wood.

That will stop the rot from continuing. If you want to strengthen a leg, say, that is half rotted away, scrape out the rotten wood, treat it with Cuprinol, and let it dry out for a week. Then fill the area with a putty made by mixing sawdust into Weldwood glue. Mix the powder to a fairly thin paste with water first, of course. When this is dry, sand smooth, and stain to match the rest of the wood with *colors ground in oil* (see Staining section), as they are about the only thing that will work on the Weldwood putty. They are opaque, but the best you can do under the circumstances.

Of course, dry rot doesn't occur just in legs. If it is in a part of the piece where there is no stress or strain, the filling needn't be with Weldwood putty, but can be done with *shellac stick* or *wax stick*, for which see listings in section on RESTORING FINISHES.

inlays Restoring inlays is the kind of work that should only be tried by the kind of people who used to make airplane or boat models when they were kids—or to keep busy during 1933. To begin with, you need a couple of single-edged razor blades. These cannot have been used previously, but must be freshly unwrapped. Once they have been put into a holder, they are ruined, because their sharp corners break off. You can see this with a magnifying glass if you don't believe me. Obviously, these blades are for cutting veneer. Where you cut will be dealt with in a minute.

Next you need a metal ruler to help you make straight cuts; some old razor blades—that you can already have shaved with—to use for scraping out old glue, and finally, some of the white glue that usually comes in plastic squeeze-me bottles, such as Elmer's Glue.

If the veneer is simply loose (inlays are just small pieces of veneer), the problem is fairly easy, but it often takes a little nerve. Don't just try to squish the glue into the cracks. You have to take one of your old razor blades and pry the piece up until it either comes out as a whole section or breaks off. The breaking of it is quite unimportant. Scrape the old glue and dirt and wax and grease and candy off the back of the piece of inlay, and also out of the hole it was resting in. Then glue it back in.

After the glue is dry, there may be fine cracks around the piece. These can be filled by dripping an ordinary wax crayon into the crack, and then scraping off the excess with a dull table knife. Then wax the whole area, and you are finished.

If the veneer is missing—the small piece of inlay—the first approach to the problem is to try to steal a piece from some place on the furniture where it won't be noticed. If some inlay work is loose, often other pieces of veneer or inlay are loose in places where they are not likely to be noticed. In such a case, carefully and a little bit at a time trim the stolen piece to fit the empty hole. The hole where you stole the patch can be stained—sometimes a little black ink will do—or filled with colored crayon.

If stealing isn't practical, what you need are some pieces of veneer. The best place I know to get these by mail is from Albert Constantine, 2050 Eastchester Road, New York City, 61. Send twenty-five cents for a catalogue and tell him I sent you. (This won't help you, but it might help me. I doubt it, but these things are always worth a try.) Besides veneers of all kinds, he also has sample sets, which are perfect for patching work.

Now here's the trick. First select a piece of veneer that matches the color you want when wet—because that's the color it will be when finished. Or you can stain a lighter piece of wood to the color you want, of course. Then finish the piece of veneer *before* you cut it to the shape needed to fill the empty hole. Sand one side of the veneer piece smooth and apply two or three coats of shellac as needed to match the heaviness of the finish on the rest of the piece you are working on. Now you have all the raw material for patching. Simply cut your pieces to shape, and glue in. If the veneer you have is too thick for the hole, you can either scrape out the hole, or sand the veneer from the back to make it thinner. To do this, wrap a small piece of medium-grade garnet paper (from any good hardware store) around a small block of wood.

Missing inlay repairs are also made with a shellac stick, which is faster if you know how to use one. But such repairs aren't as good. However, see listing for *shellac-stick patching* in section on RESTORING FINISHES. See also *veneer missing*, below.

scratches These come in two varieties: the kind that are only in the finish, and the kind that penetrate the finish and are also in the wood.

Scratches in the finish only can be eliminated by reamalgamation of the finish if it is either lacquer or shellac—which actually covers 90 per cent of all finishes. To find out how to identify the nature of the finish, see the introduction to the section on RESTORING FINISHES. Also see listing in that section for *lacquer finish* or *shellac finish.*

If the scratch has penetrated into the wood, one approach is to sand it out. This is all right at the time of refinishing a piece, but if the scratch is the only fault in an otherwise satisfactory surface, it seems rather drastic.

The simplest thing to do (though not the *best* job) is to stain the raw wood the same color as that around it, and then fill the scratch with colored wax stick. For this, see listing *wax-stick repairs* in section on RESTORING FINISHES. You can also use ordinary colored wax crayons, dripping the wax into the scratch, then scraping the excess off with a dull-edged table knife. The wax can then be shellacked over, but do not use lacquer or varnish directly on wax as they will prevent these two from drying. They can, however, be used over a first coat of shellac.

The finest job, of course, can be done with *shellac-stick patching,* for which see also listing in section of RESTORING FINISHES. But the use of this material takes a real expert.

spots These, of course, come in all sizes, shapes, and colors. Those that have not penetrated all the way through the finish can often be removed by fine abrasion of the finish with 000-grade steel wool from a good hardware store. If this method is used—and works—then scuff the whole surface with the steel wool before rewaxing so that you will have an even sheen. Always rub with the grain.

Some very stubborn white spots will respond to being lightly rubbed with lacquer thinner on a small pad of soft cloth.

Start with the cloth just moist. When the area treated has dried, scuff the whole surface evenly with 000-grade steel wool for the same reason given just above.

Some black spots that penetrate into the wood can be removed with a liquid laundry bleach such as Clorox, applied full strength. Others respond to a saturate solution of oxalic-acid crystals in water. These are obtained at any drugstore. See listings for *white marks* and *watermarks* in section on RESTORING FINISHES.

veneer blistered Blisters can usually be pressed down with an ordinary clothes iron. This is because the glues used in furniture manufacturing have traditionally been inferior. They are the gooey brown liquids that get soft when exposed to either moisture or heat. The only difficulty is that the veneer has swelled in the process of blistering. The trick is to slit the blister with the grain. If the blister is large, you should make a slit—with a brand-new, single-edged razor—that runs the whole length of the blister. Then give it a first or preliminary application of heat. To prepare for this, first place a layer of wax paper over the blister, then three thicknesses of dish towel or an equivalent padding. Now apply the iron hard at medium heat, taking a look every few seconds to see what is happening. What you want is for one or more of the sliced edges of the veener to lap over another under the pressure. When this happens, take a brand-new single-edged razor blade and carefully slice off the amount of veneer that has lapped. Then apply the iron again, and when the veneer is flat, remove the iron and apply the weight of ten or twenty stacked-up books while the glue cools.

veneer loose The term *loose*, as opposed to *blistered*, implies that the veneer has separated at the edge of a board and is more or less flapping. Here the best first approach is that described in the listing immediately above. However, this sometimes doesn't work because the glue may have powdered and fallen out. Or a lot of dirt may have got in. In the case of the space under the veneer being clean, the best thing to do is to work in some of the same kind of glue—in other words mucilage or fish glue, which is commonly available in stationery stores. Then cover the area with wax paper, and weight down the veneer with a pile of books. If the veneer bumps up, resort to the slicing technique described in the listing immediately above.

Where too much dirt has gotten under the veneer, the best thing to do is to pry it up until it breaks off at some point. Then you can scrape the dirt and old glue off both surfaces—the core wood and the back of the veneer—and start with fresh glue on clean wood. The veneer should be broken off because such a break is less noticeable on regluing than a cut made with a razor blade. The raggedness is self-concealing, compared to a straight-line cut.

veneer missing This is similar to inlay missing, so you might read the listing for *inlays,* above. The first thing to do is to prepare the surface, by squaring up your hole. For this you need a steel straight-edge and a brand-new single-edged razor blade. The point is that you can't make a patch to fill a ragged-edged hole. When you are done trimming the edges of the hole, it need not have any regular shape—such as square or rectangular or a triangle. It can have five or six sides, and none of them even parallel to another. But each must be a straight line.

When your hole is trimmed up to have straight edges, and the old glue has been scraped out, make a tracing of it on thin paper, and transfer this shape with carbon paper to the veneer you are going to use to make the patch. To learn where to get the veneer, see listing on *inlays.*

Cutting such a patch is not something to rush through. Work slowly and carefully. Take a whole half hour on the first attempt before you throw it away. Then start all over, and this time you'll get it right.

The real problem in this kind of work is to get a good color match. So just as with inlay work, you should first stain and finish the veneer you are going to cut the patch from, and then cut it on the finished side.

Finally, it is always smart to consider removing the veneer from a whole panel or section, and then replacing the whole area with one piece of veneer. Veneer is quite cheap, most kinds running around twenty to thirty cents a square foot. To remove larger areas of veneer, scrape off the finish, then soak with vinegar. When this penetrates to the glue, in five or six hours, it will soften and loosen it.

When replacing a large area of veneer, it is easier to stain and finish after the piece is glued on. But you will want to experiment first on small scrap pieces to get the right mixture of stain. To hold the larger pieces of veneer flat while the glue is drying, use flat boards that cover the whole surface, and then pile your heavy books on the boards.

worm holes On almost any piece of furniture these are badges of merit. They are like dueling scars. And so they are never plugged up. In fact, I wouldn't be surprised if more than half the worm holes you see are faked. According to one story there are special high-priced worm-hole drills, but I doubt it. It's too easy to make them with a finishing nail. And of course, the other story is that you load a shotgun with bird shot and fire away at ten paces. That's not true either, because the bird shot doesn't go in far enough.

Now I suppose you're wondering how an honest Yankee like myself would know about such nefarious practices. Well, let's just say I heard some of the boys down at the hotel talking about them. Maybe that's where my Uncle George heard about them, too. That's certainly where I heard about an old fellow up here that almost got rich by stealing from a big wheelbarrow factory over in Rutland. He got a job as sweeper, and after a couple of weeks asked his foreman if he could take home scrap lumber to burn in his stove. So after that every few nights they would let him through the gate with a wheelbarrow full. Soon it became common knowledge that he was spending a lot more money than he was earning, and the obvious thought was that he must be smuggling tools out under the scrap lumber. But time after time the guards searched and found nothing. Finally, they found some excuse to fire him anyway, because they were sure he was stealing even if they couldn't figure out what it was.

It took about two years until the secret came out. A couple of the guards got him drunk one night, and convinced him that the statute of limitations expired in two years for men over sixty. "Come on, Clem," one of them said, "just to satisfy our curiosity, what was it you were taking?"

Clem looked down in his beer and smiled for a few seconds. Then he said, "Wheelbarrows."

He'd got away with eighty-four of them, but everybody thought it was so funny that the company never did prosecute.

In case your worms are going too far, you can stop them with Cuprinol, same as dry rot. You buy it in hardware stores, and just soak it on with a brush. Won't hurt the finish.

Grotz's Own Guaranteed and Tried and Proven TABLE OF REMOVERS

This table is designed to give you the over-all picture so that you don't get off on too wrong a foot. Or feet. For details about what the things are, where to get them, and how to use them, see the separate listings that follow these pages.

SHELLAC	Denatured alcohol. (Sold as "shellac solvent".) For the gummier shellacs used in the Victorian era, add roughly 1 part lacquer thinner to 4 parts of the alcohol. No rinse necessary.
LACQUER	Lacquer thinner will dissolve this quite easily. Job will go faster if you add one part of denatured alcohol to every four parts of lacquer thinner. No rinse necessary before staining or applying new finish.
VARNISH	Best thing is a water-rinse paint and varnish remover of the *TM-4* or *Strypeeze* type. Then the less expensive liquid removers. *Some* varnishes are quickly and cleanly removed with a mixture of half lacquer thinner and half wood alcohol. Lye, ammonia and t.s.p. will eat varnish but also darken and chew up the wood underneath, so are not usually used on a single layer or two of clear finish.

PAINT (*ordinaire*)	For a single coat of ordinary paint, read as above for varnish. Enamel paint is just varnish with ground pigment in it. (The "enamel" on kitchen stoves, etc. is actually a thin coat of baked-on glass.)
PAINT (*many layers*)	Here we resort to the strong chemicals. Lye is first. Turns wood brown, will raise fibers on the surface, and must have a final rinse with vinegar to stop the action of the lye in the wood. Also t.s.p. (trisodium phosphate), a milder version of lye.
MILK PAINT (*the dry, dull, old paints that are hard to remove*)	Ammonia works better than anything else on these, regardless of cost. Unpleasant fumes. Turns wood dark, but oxalic acid solution will bleach quickly. Then just rinse with water.
LINSEED OIL	Read here the same as for varnish.

All of the removers mentioned above are commonly available through paint, hardware or grocery stores. And this covers the field. There aren't any secret chemicals. It's just knowing what to use when.

Section 5

REMOVIN' MADE LESS CONFUSIN'

Including some secret formulas
that can save you plenty of pesos

The best way to remove paint I ever heard of was Thomas Tuttle's tank of lye. It didn't last long, but it was a "dinger" while it worked. A real seven-day sensation. Of course, it's not hard to make a sensation in Wells, which is a wide spot in the road about twenty miles south of Rutland. Well, it's not quite that bad. They have a post office and a filling station combined with a general store, which is open most of the day when the tourists are going by in the summer. Last summer two or three stopped. In fact, it's so quiet that the people in surrounding towns have a saying that the last time anything happened in Wells was the big dogfight in 1927. With the exception, of course, of Thomas Tuttle's Wonderful Tank. That was only about five or six years ago.

Most of the time Tom was a respectable farmer, but somehow or other he got interested in fixing old furniture and selling it to a couple of dealers from Connecticut. Well, like anyone who does much refinishing, Tom got tired of scraping off seven layers of paint, and was always looking for a better way. And being a Vermonter, a better way to him had considerable overtones of being a cheaper way. So naturally he had quickly gravitated from seven-dollar-a-gallon paint remover to lye for twenty-two cents a can.

But as anyone who has ever tried it knows, this is pretty

messy work. So he got the idea that if he built a large tank out of sheet metal he could dip small tables and chairs into a lye solution, haul them out, and then just wash them off with a garden hose. I assume that after that he brushed them with vinegar to neutralize any traces of lye left in the surface fibers of the wood.

So Tom built his tank under an old apple tree about a hundred yards back of his barn. It was raised about three feet from the ground on iron legs so that he could build a good fire under it to heat the solution. Except on a warm summer day, lye water won't work without being heated, and summer usually comes on a Wednesday down in Wells. (It gets to East Poultney on the following Thursday.)

Well, the first piece went fine. It was just an old kitchen chair that he thought he'd experiment on. The paint peeled right off, and he ran up to the house with it and washed it off with the garden hose. But the second time disaster struck. This time it was a pretty good chair that he'd paid five dollars for. The trouble was, he'd been lowering these chairs into the tank by means of a rope thrown over a limb of the old apple tree. And by the time he started to haul this chair out, the lye had got a lot hotter, and during the ten-minute dunking he'd given the chair the lye had eaten through the rope. Well, first he had to run and get a pitchfork. Then he had to pile some boxes up so he could stand on them to reach down into the tank. All in all, it took him about fifteen minutes to get the thing out, and by that time the lye had eaten so deeply into the wood that the chair was worthless.

That wasn't all. The next day he thought he had the problem solved by using a chain. This time he tested again with an old kitchen chair. Everything was fine. So he decided to try his pride and joy—an old comb-back Windsor chair that he was counting on to buy him a couple of tons of coal that winter. Down into the bubbling lye it went. In about ten minutes he decided to pull it up to have a look. He pulled. And up came the chain holding only the top piece from the back of the chair. And that was all it held. The heated water had loosened the glue, and the chair had fallen apart.

Up he went on the boxes, and started fishing around with the pitchfork. After five minutes all he had was a leg and one rung, and he realized that the chair was now just a mass of separate pieces. This made him so mad that he scrambled down from his boxes, grabbed a heavy bean pole, and charged the tank like Sir Lancelot. Or more like Don Quixote, in this case. The tank spilled over and Tom ruined a pair of shoes, by sloshing in the lye-soaked grass kicking the pieces of his chair to safety. Then he almost ruined his fingers juggling the pieces as he rushed them over to the garden hose.

And that was the end of the biggest thing that's happened in Wells since the big dogfight of 1927. The tank still lies there on its side underneath the old apple tree. Tom won't go near it. He just avoids the area as he tries to push all memory of the horror from his mind. Spilling from the mouth of the tumbled tank is a patch of brown where in six years not a blade of grass has grown—and may never grow again.

Poor Tom's plight is a little extreme, but typical. Removing old paint—or even some clear finishes—is the hardest part of redoing any old piece of furniture. Every year some new product comes on the market that is supposed to make the job clean or easy or quick or something. And like little children in search of the Bluebird of Happiness, everybody who refinishes furniture tries it. But two eternal truths seem to remain: (1) It's still a messy job. (2) The best removers cost the most money.

The best ones are the new semipaste removers that wash off with water, and leave the wood ready for staining or finishing without any further rinsing or neutralizing.

Then come the paste removers with wax in them that have to be cleaned off carefully with benzine, gasoline, or lacquer thinner.

Then come the liquid removers. These are a little more

trouble than the pastes and also have to be carefully rinsed off with benzine, etc.

When you come to the cheap substitutes such as lye and ammonia, you have proportionately more trouble or mess. When removing lacquer and shellac, the job can be fairly clean if you know about using wood alcohol and lacquer thinner. See listings that follow.

alcohol See *denatured alcohol,* below.

ammonia Used full-strength, as it comes from the bottle, this is an excellent remover. Widely avoided because of the fumes, it does have the special advantage of being the only thing that will cut into the old milk-base paints found on antiques, often as the bottom coat of seven or eight layers of paint. Often lye will take numerous layers, but won't touch the final coat. This is one place where in spite of the fumes, ammonia is the thing. Wear rubber gloves, and rub the ammonia on with 0- or 00-grade steel wool for fastest results. When done, rinse or wipe off any traces of the dissolved paint with water and a stiff brush or rag. No neutralizing is necessary. After the wood is thoroughly dry, it is ready to stain or finish.

Another important thing about ammonia is that it will not raise the fibers of the wood very much, and not at all on harder woods. This makes it excellent for floors if you are off in the country someplace and can't find any trisodium phosphate, which is better, but available only in the larger paint stores.

Ammonia will turn some woods very dark. In fact, ammonia is sometimes used instead of a stain. But if you don't like the darkness, the wood can be returned to its original color by first letting the piece dry, then applying an *oxalic-acid* solution, which is easy to do. See listing in Section 6, on bleaches.

black streaks One of the real headaches of refinishing is the deep black streaks that are often found on light chairs, usually those with cane seats. These streaks are caused by lampblack, which was originally brushed into the wood as the first step in a fake-graining finish. They are found mostly in Victorian pieces, but also in some earlier than that. Getting this stain out of the wood seems to be impossible. I have never heard of anyone who had any success at doing it. You can't sand these streaks out either. They run too deep. The only practical thing to do is to resign yourself to staining the wood a dark color such as walnut. Or you can restore the surface to the original fake graining. What was originally intended was a rosewood finish. Or rather, what was originally intended was to make the wood look like rosewood, which is a dark red with black streaks. So stain the wood with red-mahogany stain. Then varnish over this with a glaze made by tinting a pint of varnish with a rounded tablespoonful of burnt umber color-ground-in-oil (from a paint store). Stir in well, and let the sediment settle. Then brush on without stirring.

Or you can paint the piece dark black and decorate it.

blowtorches These are great for removing a lot of paint—say, seven layers from a paneled room. The fire danger is, of course, just another one of these neurotic bugaboos. Naturally, you don't use a blowtorch without having a garden hose handy. And to be extra safe, don't leave the job for a couple of hours after you've finished work. It's the only possible way to take paint off the outside of a house. The technique is to have a blowtorch in one hand, and the widest scraper you can find in the other. As the paint blisters, scrape it off in a continuous process.

carving People are always asking me the secret of getting paint and varnish out of the crevices in carving. But the only secret I know is patience and persistence. Naturally, you get a stiff brush. Old toothbrushes are the best. Also something sharp like an ice pick, to speed the job by prying out chunks. A good paste paint remover is the best thing to use on carving, because any of the stronger chemicals (lye, ammonia, trisodium phosphate) would be on the wood too long and therefore have time to chew up the surface fibers.

caustic soda This is simply lye in chunks instead of small granules. Instead of this, use the regular flake lye that is sold in grocery stores for cleaning sink drains. They are all the same thing, just as all liquid laundry bleaches are sodium-hypochlorite crystals dissolved in water. Look at the really fine print on the labels if you think I'm making it up.

denatured alcohol Here we have one of the basic elements of the whole refinishing business. Primarily, alcohol is the solvent for shellac—a solid. So its first use is to thin shellac for application. But it will also dissolve shellac in the same way water will dissolve sugar—and faster. That makes it a remover for dirty old shellac, and a reamalgamator for restoring an old dry, cracked, or powdery shellac finish that isn't dirty. You just brush it on, the solid shellac dissolves, and you brush it out evenly. Presto!

Alcohol will not touch a real varnish finish, but will turn a lacquer finish white, because any moisture in the air immediately incorporates itself into the alcohol. (Alcohol is anhydrous, to get technical about it.)

Pertinently, here is a trick you can use. Let's say you've washed a brush out in soap and water as a final step in cleaning it, which is a good practice. Want to use the brush two minutes later to apply varnish? It's easy. Just rinse the brush in about a cup of alcohol. Then shake the brush and blow on it. The alcohol evaporates in about a minute, and the brush is ready to use. Any traces of water in the brush have gone into the alcohol. It's a method used in many manufacturing processes where quick-drying is needed to keep the production line going.

The fumes of denatured alcohol in a closed room will give

you a bad headache. Concentrated in a cellar, for instance, they definitely will kill.

Because it absorbs water from the moisture in the air, alcohol spoils unless kept in a tightly stoppered container. The alcohol in all shellac causes it to spoil in the same way. Therefore, both should be bought in small quantities, enough for the job on hand, and thrown away if there is the slightest doubt. If there is too much water in the alcohol or shellac, it hazes or fogs over as it dries after you have brushed it on.

Denatured alcohol is pure alcohol with a trace of chemical in it to make it unfit for drinking.

electrical devices Every once in a while someone repromotes the idea of removing paint with heat generated by electricity. These devices usually combine a flat heating surface, which gets about as hot as an ordinary flatiron, with some sort of attached scraper to remove the paint after it has been softened by the heated surface moving over it.

This is one of those ideas that looks awfully good on paper, but when you come right down to it, it just doesn't work out. I've tried these devices, but I have found that they are too slow. There isn't enough heat, as there is with a blowtorch. And when you have finished, there is still a lot of burned paint left on the wood that has to be scraped off or softened with paint remover.

end grain Getting paint out of the end grain of a board is sometimes impossible. It depends on how soft or porous the wood is. With a dense wood like maple, the paint doesn't go in far, and you can scrape any traces of paint off with a sharp kitchen knife, a paint scraper, or a chisel. But when the paint is in deep—it often goes in an eighth of an inch—even the best paint remover won't get it out. The only solution is to sand the surface smooth with fine sandpaper (or preferably, the orangish garnet paper), and then obscure the paint with opaque coloring. The usual coloring used is colors-ground-in-oil,

which may be obtained at any paint store. Look first at the umbers and siennas, which are close to the colors wood is usually stained. You may want to buy two colors and mix them. They are a little softer than the consistency of artists oil colors, so do not dilute them or thin them. Dip your thumb in some of the goo, and wipe it on the edge as thinly as you can and still conceal the paint. After drying twenty-four hours, the pigment should be sealed with one thin coat of shellac before applying any other finish.

If you have a set of them around the house, artists' oil paints will work just as well. Apply and seal in the same way.

fake graining This is often called a lost art, and most people say, "Amen, to that. May it rest in peace!" However, there are a few of us who think it is just the greatest—either because it was such an odd thing to do, or because it was such a delicate craft. And as the years go by, more and more people are beginning to feel that it is a mistake to remove fake graining—unless it is battered and scarred beyond being presentable.

The application of this kind of finish is discussed in the section on FINISHES: DECEPTIVE. About the only special thing to say in respect to removing them is that ammonia is often the most effective thing on the undercoats. The top finish was almost always shellac. In the case of a dirty piece, the dirt often comes off with the shellac when you wipe the surface with denatured alcohol, thus restoring the original appearance. If you do this, it is best to then apply a fresh coat of clear shellac.

floors I know that floors are not furniture, but on the other hand, people who are interested in their furniture often have problems with refinishing floors, too. The two best things to use are ammonia and trisodium phosphate. These are both better than lye, because they do not need to be neutralized with vinegar as does lye. Ammonia has the disadvantage of

fumes, but you can leave the windows open and put an electric fan in one so that you can work without too much discomfort. It is the best for floors that were painted with the old milk-base paints—roughly speaking, in any house built before 1800.

Trisodium phosphate is best for the oil-base paints and varnishes. It is a powder, and you dissolve one pound in each six quarts of hot water, then mop it on. This should be done on a warm day—say, seventy degrees or over—because the stuff works better when it is warm.

Both the ammonia and t.s.p. are mopped on and allowed to soak until the paint has dissolved. Then the sludge has to be mopped or scraped up. In many an old house it is feasible to wash the sludge off with a garden hose, letting it drip through to a dirt-floored cellar.

No neutralizing is necessary with these two, though the cleaning-up job is tedious. And, of course, the wood should be allowed to dry for a week of reasonably warm weather—to be sure it is really dry before applying a new finish.

lacquer removing The term *lacquer* now covers a wide range of products. But 90 per cent of them can best be removed with lacquer thinner, not only because it is cheaper than paint remover, but also because it will make the least mess of the surface of the wood beneath the lacquer coating. For an even faster, cleaner job, add one part denatured alcohol to every three parts of lacquer thinner. To give you an idea of the quantities needed, two quarts of this mixture is generally enough to remove the finish from the average dining-room table. Even so, your total cost should be about $1.75, which is still a lot cheaper than the paint remover it would take to do such a job (a little more than a quart).

Do about two square feet at a time. Pour the lacquer thinner on, scrub it in with 00 steel wool, using a stroke that goes with the grain of the wood, and as the lacquer dissolves, wipe it up with rags. After the whole piece has been done,

wipe it off once again with a cloth wet with lacquer thinner. This will pick up any traces of lacquer between the separate areas that you removed previously.

If you remove the finish this way, the wood will dry out in ten minutes or less, and you can immediately restain or apply a new finish—or bleach the wood, if that is what you had in mind.

At the beginning I said that this worked on 90 per cent of all lacquer finishes. On the other 10 per cent you will have to use paint-and-varnish remover. Do not use lye, ammonia, or trisodium phosphate on any clear finish. They tend to raise the fibers of the wood.

lacquer thinner This is the solvent for lacquer. But it also happens to contain a high percentage of acetone, which is the basis of many paint removers. It cuts right into shellac, most lacquers, and more than half of the varnishes. It is usually used with one part of denatured alcohol to every four parts of lacquer thinner for the fastest results. See listings in this section on removing various finishes.

linseed-oil finish When it comes to removing one, a linseed-oil finish is the same as varnish. Their chemical make-up is similar, and they react in the same way to the various removers. Therefore, see the listing further on in this section for *varnish removing*.

lye and all that In the whole field of repairing and refinishing furniture, no subject interests more people than lye. And most people take sides. It's either awful or it's wonderful. I'm one of the people that's for it. And I have some frightful things to say about people who are against it. In the first place, I think that people who are against it are people who like to be scared. These are the Gloomy Guses who are always sure that the worst will happen. There is no point in trying to reason with *them*.

Another group of the against people comprises those who have heard horror tales like the one I was guilty of telling in the introduction to this section. Well, sure, lye will eat wood. In time it will dissolve it into a pulpy mass. But that's no reason for not using lye. We don't give up using kitchen knives because idiots can cut themselves with them.

People don't understand that lye is perfectly safe if it is handled by someone who knows what he's doing. I have used lye for years without any trouble, and I know many other finishers who have, too. It is the only economical and reasonably fast way to get rid of five or six layers of old paint.

Here's how you do it.

To begin with, put three quarts of water in a pail or dishpan. The water should not fill the container more than halfway. Into this, dump three cans of lye. This is the ordinary lye that you buy under a variety of trade names for cleaning drains in plumbing. If the label says the product will clean drains, then it's lye. Do not use less lye or more water than this in an attempt to play it safe. That's one place where lots of people go wrong. The solution simply won't work if it is weaker. Using a dull knife doesn't make peeling apples any safer, it makes it more dangerous. The same goes for lye.

Oh, yes. Don't use an aluminum pan. Lye reacts with aluminum to form a poison gas. It also ruins the aluminum.

You will notice that when you dump the lye in the water, it boils up like the river Styx. And it's about as hot! Next, stir in a cup of wallpaper paste—the kind that is made of wheat. This will give the liquid body, so that it won't run off flat surfaces and will stick to vertical ones. These three quarts are enough to remove thick paint from a drop-leaf table, or three or four chairs.

All this preparation of your solution must be done just before you use it. Also, you should work out in the sun on a warm day—say, over sixty-five degrees in the shade. Lye doesn't work when it is cold.

In applying the lye, I never wear rubber gloves. Just old

clothes. But I do keep a pail of water with a washrag in it nearby. If I spatter any of the solution on my hands, arms, or face, I wipe it off right away, and no harm done. Left on the skin more than ten seconds, lye will burn.

For an applicator, most people tie some rag strips to the end of a thin, two-foot-long stick. The rag strips should extend about six inches beyond the end of the stick. With this homemade mop, you then spread the lye mixture on the paint.

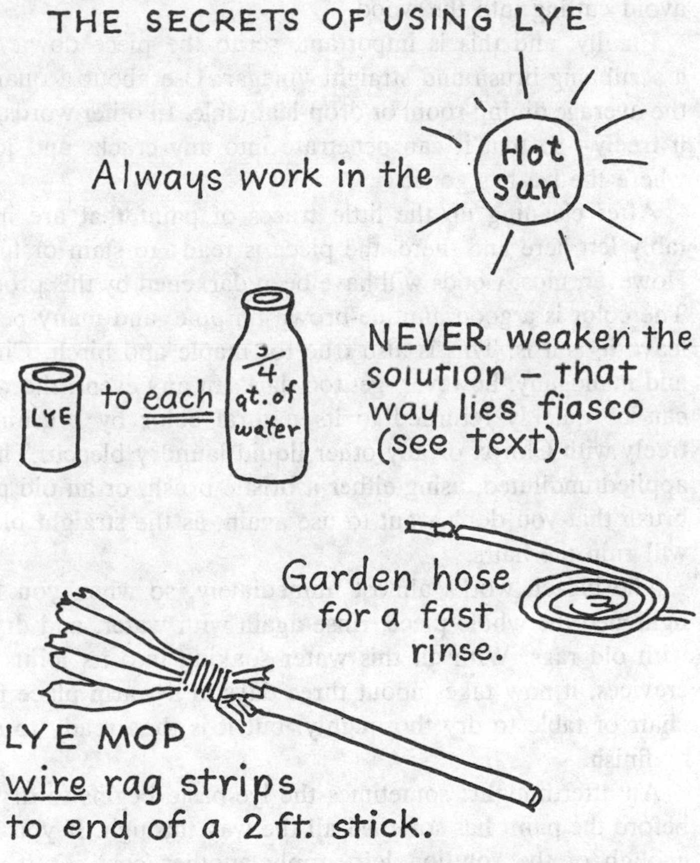

THE SECRETS OF USING LYE
Always work in the
Hot Sun
LYE
to each
3/4 qt. of water
NEVER weaken the solution – that way lies fiasco (see text).
Garden hose for a fast rinse.
LYE MOP
wire rag strips to end of a 2 ft. stick.

How long you leave it there depends on how many layers of paint there are, and how tough each one is. Sometimes lye will go through three thick coats in five minutes, especially on a good hot day. Check every few minutes with a scraper to see how far down the paint has softened.

When the paint is soft all the way down to the wood, the quickest thing to do is to wash off the lye—most of the paint will come, too—with a garden hose. Or buckets of water and a scrubbing brush can be used. Then scrape or push the rest of the paint off with a dull-edged scraper or other blade to avoid cutting into the wood.

Finally, and this is important, scrub the piece down with a scrubbing brush and straight vinegar. Use about a quart to the average dining-room or drop-leaf table. In other words, use it freely—so that it can penetrate into any cracks and joints where the lye has gone.

After cleaning up the little traces of paint that are inevitably left here and there, the piece is ready to stain or finish. However, most woods will have been darkened by this process. The color is a good antique-brown on pine, and many people leave it as it is. This is also true for maple and birch. Cherry and mahogany, however, get too dark. In any event, the wood can be quickly returned to its natural color by brushing it freely with Clorox or any other liquid laundry bleach. This is applied undiluted, using either a bristle brush, or an old paint brush that you don't want to use again, as the straight bleach will ruin the hairs.

The bleach works almost immediately, so when you have lightened the whole piece, rinse again with water, and dry off with old rags. With all this water soaking into its joints and crevices, it now takes about three days in a warm place for a chair or table to dry thoroughly, but it is then ready to stain or finish.

An afterthought: sometimes the lye-paste begins to dry out before the paint has softened all the way through. If you have enough of the solution left, apply another coat. Or simply keep sprinkling the piece with water to keep the paste wet. This often happens when you are working in the direct sunlight on a hot dry day—which is the best kind of day. Of course, you can use lye in a warm cellar, too, in the winter, and get just as good results. Naturally the cellar has to have a drain to carry off all the rinse water, and you can't care about how the floor looks. In fact, when using lye outside, you should work on a piece of ground where you don't care if grass ever grows again. It's not likely to.

Finally, let's lay this bugaboo about the danger of lye for once and for all. I know that there have been other books published that tell you that lye is impossible. I will not say anything about the amount of experience these people have had. But I have personally used the above process at least fifty times without the slightest amount of trouble. And I know a half-dozen other professionals who use it all the time without any trouble. That's all. Grotz knows. Believe no others. They will even lead you to believe that once lye has turned wood dark, the condition is permanent. Nothing could be easier—or more satisfying—than turning the wood back to its natural color with Clorox, and that's available at any grocery store. As a matter of fact, you don't even need to use a neutralizing vinegar bath if you are going to use Clorox right away. It does the neutralizing job at the same time it bleaches the darkness out.

milk paints These are the stubbornnest paints of all to remove, and if you want to be pretentious about it, you can call them "refractory" paints. But if you just say milk paint, everybody will know what you mean. The trouble with these paints is that they are glue, or at least very similar to the casein glues (such as Weldwood) that are also made of leftover milk.

Lye will hardly bother this "paint." Nor will trisodium phosphate, nor any of the paint removers on the market. The only thing that cuts it is ammonia. There is no point in mixing the ammonia with anything else, because that just dilutes and slows it.

Of course, ammonia is rough on your hands, so most people wear rubber gloves. I prefer to wade in barehanded, and keep rinsing my hands in a handy bucket of water. Also the fumes are strong, so it is best to work outdoors. But with cross ventilation it is possible to work in the house.

The procedure is to pour about a cup of ammonia at a time in a pan. Then scrub this into the surface of the paint with half a pad of 0- or 00-grade steel wool, or Brillo if you have it around. The soap won't hurt. Wet the whole piece this way first, and keep wetting the surface down for five or ten minutes. Then go at it with the steel wool again, and this time the paint will come right off. It doesn't peel. It softens, and just "goos" off.

Finally, rinse the piece with clean water, and you are finished. As soon as the piece is thoroughly dry, you are ready to stain or apply a new finish.

Quantities of ammonia needed? About a quart to one drop-leaf table or two chairs. You waste a lot doing chairs.

Now, do not be terrified if the ammonia turns the wood dark. A solution of *oxalic-acid* crystals (see listing under BLEACHING) will bring the original color right back. It's easy. Or, as with lye, you can leave the wood dark if you like the color. This darkening occurs most noticeably on cherry and oak.

oil finish See listing above for *linseed-oil finish.*

paint in pores This is a problem that comes up when someone has been crude enough to apply paint as the first coat on large-pored oak, walnut, or mahogany. Oak is the wood it happens most frequently on. "Dear Furniture Doctor," people write me, "you tell everything except how to get the paint out of the large pores on some woods." That was after I wrote my first book on this subject.

Well, I still don't know.

The only answer I have is the same one that would occur to anybody. Get a stiff brush with small bristles, and keep soaking the piece with paint remover. It could take days. It has for me. Anybody with a better answer, please advise. Use air mail.

paint remover For paint *ordinaire,* the best thing is either a paste or liquid paint remover. There are hundreds of brands, and all work well. Personally, I use old-fashioned liquid removers, which you usually have to buy by the gallon, because they are the cheapest. I get mine from The Staminite Corporation, 109 Water Street, New Haven, Connecticut. Tell Dick Davis I sent you. That won't make the remover any cheaper, but he's a nice guy to meet.

The disadvantage of liquid remover is that it's a little messier to use. Also, because it evaporates faster, you have to do a section at a time—say, an area about as big as a table leaf. But it works fast. You also have to wash the piece down with lacquer thinner after you have finished. This will remove any waxes in the crevices, which prevent the coming coats of finish from drying.

The best removers on the market are the ones that rinse off with water: the Strypeeze and TM-4 kinds. These are two of the most widely distributed brands. There are many others. Of course, this kind is the most expensive.

What else is there to say? Try not to make a mess. The directions on the cans are always detailed and good. Personally, whenever I'm faced with a couple of coats of paint to remove, I always try anything that's standing around, just to see if it will work. Sometimes, lacquer thinner will crinkle it right off. Sometimes ammonia. Or trisodium phosphate, which is like lye, only not as strong. See listing further on in this section. This isn't really an exact science, you know. Besides, you'll have a lot more fun if you experiment. It's like cooking. People who follow the recipes all their lives are missing half the fun.

paint removing Here we are referring to one or two coats of ordinary paint. For many heavy coats, see the listing above for *lye and all that*. For the hard, dry, very old paints, see listing above for *milk paints*.

paneling For removing paint from paneling, see listing for *blowtorch*, above, and for *trisodium phosphate* further on in this section.

plaster of Paris No, plaster of Paris isn't a finish—though some finishes seem to think they are plaster of Paris. You run into it most often in old frames where it was molded to imitate wood turnings or carving. You also find spool furniture and other turned pieces, where plaster was obviously rubbed onto a rough wood surface to smooth it. All such pieces are cheap imitations, and if they weren't given to you, you were stuck.

There is no way to remove this plaster from the wood underneath, because it was always used on a very rough surface. So even if you discovered some way to get the plaster off, you wouldn't have anything when you got there.

Of course, the use of plaster of Paris is legitimate on ornate golden or gilded frames. Much of their carvings and figures are plaster, often with a wooden core. This got started because polished plaster makes a much smoother and therefore better surface for applying gold leaf than does any wood that is reasonably easy to carve. This sort of thing is dealt with further in the section on DECORATION.

red stains Pesky. Now, there's a good old-fashioned word, and these darn things are something it fits. I'm not talking about stains from ink, or paint, or even any sensible furniture stain. And anyone who has ever been afflicted knows what I'm talking about. They can occur on anything made up to 1800, and after you have taken the wood down and sanded and bleached and sanded all over again, there they are—mocking you. The consensus among all the experienced cabinetmakers and refinishers that I know, is that they were made by berry juice applied to the raw wood as a substain before finishing. Early Americans just hated maple and pine and even cherry. Everything had to look like mahogany—as if they were back in the "old country," which they'd either run away from or left by request.

All of which is an interesting dissertation, but I still don't know how to get the stains out with any of the "easily available materials" I'm always talking about.

The only answer is the one-and-two bleaches, which will also bleach the wood to a pale cream color. Of course, you can then stain the whole piece back to any color you want. See entry on one-and-two stains in the section on BLEACHING.

sal soda This is a sort of strong sodium bicarbonate. It is good for cleaning anything, and has some effect on milk paints, but is not much good on anything else. A cup of it in two quarts of hot water is good for washing off the remains of paint remover. This will cut down on the amount of paint remover you have to use to clean a given piece because, once the paint has been softened by the remover, you can finish the job with a sal-soda solution instead of more paint remover. Use a scrubbing brush and rags.

Of course, I'm assuming that you know that sal soda is a common alternate name for washing soda, the kind that is available in grocery stores.

sand blasting This is one of the three great dreams of anyone who has ever had to muck through refinishing jobs to make a living. The other two are to have a lye tank and a machine that blasts hot steam.

Of the three ideas, sand blasting is the least. Besides the expense of the equipment and having a special little house to work in, the result of sand blasting is to make all the wood look new. Of course, sometimes this is desirable, but not very often. It is mainly used by people who are modernizing old furniture—for instance, to make over a hotelful of it.

scraping I hate to. Of course, it is one way to get out of buying any kind of paint remover whatsoever, so therefore quite popular here in Vermont. In fact, most people get out of buying scrapers by using small pieces of broken glass. This really works very well, in fact, better than any metal scraper that you can buy. Just smash some pieces of useless window glass in a pail. Use small pieces, with the longest edge about three inches. Sit out in the sun, out of the wind on a nice fall day, turn your portable radio to *Monitor,* and it's a fine way to spend an afternoon taking an old chair down to raw wood.

Then after a light sanding with fairly fine sandpaper the job will be ready for staining or finishing. Of course, scraping —like sanding—is in disrepute with the purist type of antique lover, because this destroys the aged surface of the wood. This is usually called the patina, meaning simply an aged surface, and is valued as much on wood as it is on a finish. It doesn't show much on small spoked chairs, so scraping is most often done on these.

shellac removing A true shellac finish will simply wash off with *denatured alcohol*, for which see listing at the beginning of this section. For the record, however, any of the removers listed in this section will also take off shellac, which has the least resistance to removal of all finishes.

Around the beginning of the Victorian period shellac was often "doctored" to make it tougher. These shellacs "ball up" when you try to remove them with just alcohol. The problem is quickly solved by adding one part of lacquer thinner to every four parts of the alcohol. It should take about two quarts of such a mixture to remove the finish from a dining table.

Because of the rapid evaporation of both denatured alcohol and lacquer thinner, you work on a small area at a time. Sop the liquid on about two square feet of the surface with a half pad of 00-grade steel wool. The finish will soften in from ten seconds to a minute. Scrub the area with the steel wool, and wipe up the gunk or goo with an old rag. When the whole piece has been cleaned, go over the whole surface again, with a wet rag in one hand and a dry one in the other, wetting and wiping dry as you go.

Besides preserving the patina of the wood, this leaves a sealer coat of shellac in the wood, and it won't raise the grain as water-base removers will. When cleaned with alcohol this way, the piece may be immediately stained or finished with any finish.

This is about the only removing job which you can really say is pleasant work. The alcohol and lacquer thinner won't hurt your hands, and are easily cleaned off with a wet rag in either of them.

To do legs with this removing technique, put a couple of cups of the liquid in a saucepan or pot. Then stand the leg right in the pan so that as you sop the alcohol on the leg, it drips and runs back into the pan for reuse.

spool furniture This particular kind of furniture deserves a special listing because it presents a real problem in how to go about the job, regardless of what finish is on it or what remover you are using.

The first problem is the time it takes to get the finish out of all the indentations between the "spools." The other problem is the exposure of end grain at the side of each spool. Often, little specks of paint are imbedded in this. And in other cases, a stain has been sucked into this end grain, making it much darker than the rest of the wood. Trying to scrape or sand all this end grain by hand is like trying to bail out a lake with a teaspoon. It can go on for years.

As to bleaching the stain out of the end grain, a bleach won't penetrate into the wood until the surface has been sanded.

Discouraging? More than a little bit, as we say in East Poultney. But I know at least one Yankee who has solved the problem. He knocks all the pieces apart with a padded hammer. This only takes about fifteen minutes for, say, a spool bed. Then he puts them one at a time into a home-made lathe. By holding sandpaper and a chisel to them as they spin, he sands the end grain down an eighth of an inch in no time at all. He can do a whole bed in less than two hours, and there are many cabinetmakers who will do the job for less than ten dollars.

I know that not many people have lathes kicking around the house, but this is the only reasonable solution to the spool-furniture problem.

steam If you own a public garage, or know somebody who does, find out if he has a boiler that produces live steam—used for cleaning the undersides of automobiles. Live steam is excellent for removing heavy coats of paint. Of course, there's a slight disadvantage in that the steam will melt all the glue, and the piece will fall apart. So glue it back together. The thing probably needed regluing anyway.

The steam will also raise the grain of the wood considerably, so that all the outside surfaces will have to be sanded smooth. But it's still not a bad way to remove paint from big heavy corner-cupboards and things like that.

trisodium phosphate This stuff really is a trade secret. There's no reason for this. It just is. Nobody tries to make a secret out of it, but nobody seems to have informed the public about it either. This is probably because it is so cheap that there isn't as much profit in informing the public about it as there is in informing them about the high-priced paint removers. Anyway, this stuff is sold by the big paint stores, the kind that supply house painters, and it is the poor man's paint-and-varnish remover.

To begin with, it costs about fifteen cents a pound, and you mix a pound with six quarts of water. For floors, just mop the liquid on. When the paint has softened, loosen it with a stiff brush and wash it off with water. No neutralizer is needed.

When using this chemical on furniture, add a cup or ordinary wheat wallpaper paste to the six quarts to make a paste that will stick to vertical surfaces.

The strength of either of these mixtures is equivalent to the usual liquid or paste removers. They work at about the same speed—slower at temperatures below seventy degrees—and need only to be washed off well before you go ahead with staining and finishing. Of course, the wood gets fairly wet, and the piece of furniture should be allowed to dry for twenty-four hours in a warm, dry place.

Why, then, doesn't everybody use it? Well, in addition to not knowing about it, there is another difficulty. Like lye, it will darken some woods and turn others black, because, practically speaking, it is a sort of weaker version of lye.

The solution to this problem, of course, is that like lye, it will also bleach out—the darkness will, that is—when you apply either an oxalic-acid solution or a liquid laundry bleach like Clorox. See listings for both of these bleaches in section on BLEACHING.

Trisodium phosphate—or t.s.p., as it is usually called—will also burn your skin and ruin any brush the same way lye will. But it is milder, and doesn't do it as fast. The degree that it will burn into wood, in the event that some idiot walks away and leaves the stuff soaking, is so much less than with lye that this is not a real danger.

T.S.P. is also used in cleaning clothes, especially work clothes, and in professional laundries, where a weaker solution is used. If you read the fine print on some well-known cleaners such as Spic 'n Span you will see that they contain from 17 to 22 per cent of the stuff. This is not a strong enough solution for paint or varnish removing.

Getting t.s.p., however, is something of a problem. The fellow at the local paint store probably never heard of it. They've rarely ever heard of much. You have to buy it in a major city. There you usually find it in a paint store that lists itself under "Paints—wholesale" in the Yellow Pages of the telephone book. This means that they sell mainly to large painting contractors. You can also get it from companies that sell cleaning supplies and waxes to institutions.

If you ask a small store or most house painters about this stuff, you will probably get the same kind of old wives' horror tale that you get about lye. All I can say is that if you are going to believe them instead of me, I cannot help you. No hard feelings or anything like that. In fact, good luck. You will be traveling the hard road of the fearful and misinformed, and you will need it.

varnish removing The first thing to try is a half-and-half mixture of lacquer thinner and denatured alcohol, both of which are available at your hardware store or paint store. A total of two quarts—one quart of each—will be plenty for the average dining table.

The reason for trying this first is that if the mixture works, you don't have to worry about the piece drying out or having to wash off traces of paint remover. Both these liquids evaporate rapidly, and any traces left in crevices won't matter. They won't interfere with staining or the drying of whatever finish you put on. And you can stain or finish in five minutes after using these liquids.

For the technique of using this mixture, see listing above for *lacquer removing*, and work the same way.

For tougher varnishes, your best bet is one of the water-rinse, paste paint removers such as TM-4 and Strypeeze. The directions on their cans are explicit, and there is nothing more to say.

Varnish can also be removed with ammonia, trisodium phosphate, and lye, but for reasons given under the listings for these solutions, they are not to be preferred.

wax-finish removing This is harder than it seems. Sure, the solvent for wax is mineral spirits or turpentine, and they will dissolve and wash away any wax. So sop the mineral spirits on and scrub the wax off with half a pad of 00 steel wool. Do this twice. Then finally go over the piece with mineral spirits again, wiping it dry with a cloth before it evaporates.

The trouble is that if the wax was originally applied to raw wood, it will have sunk into the crevices of joints and the end grain of the boards. Any such wax will cause varnish to remain sticky and never dry. The answer here is to first give the piece a coat of shellac, thinned with an equal amount of denatured alcohol. Shellac is not affected by traces of wax that may remain in the wood. Over this sealer coat of shellac, you can then apply varnish without danger.

Section 6

BLEACHING—THE BLONDS I HAVE KNOWN

Or, when Clorox is a man's best friend

Bleaching isn't as hard as it sounds. In fact, if you have the right materials, it is easier than applying a decent shellac or varnish finish. The main problem is a widespread confusion about terms.

To begin with, there are two entirely different kinds of bleaching. The first is bleaching stain out of wood. This is the job run into most often, because almost all wood in furniture is stained to one degree or another. Sometimes a light wood like maple or poplar has been stained quite heavily to make it look like cherry or mahogany. But light woods are also often given a pale stain, not to change their appearance, but to bring out the figure in the wood. Dark woods such as mahogany, walnut, and cherry are also stained for the same reason. Both mahogany and cherry tend to finish with too reddish a tint unless some brown stain is used on them. When walnut is finished naturally, without a darkening stain, it is much lighter than we usually think of it as being.

For this kind of bleaching—the removal of stain from the fibers of the raw wood—there is nothing better than common, ordinary liquid laundry bleach. For its use, see listing for *laundry bleach,* which follows.

The other kind of bleaching is used to remove the natural color of the wood, which is a modern practice. These are the amber, wheat, honey-tone, and driftwood type of finishes.

For this kind of bleaching, many formulas are used commercially, but the best and most available are the one-and-two bleaches such as the popular Blanchit. These are two-solution treatments that are not at all tricky to use. For details see listing for *one-and-two bleach*.

On the next point confusion often exists. These light finishes are not always a result of bleach. Sometimes a light-colored paint has simply been wiped on and off the sanded surface of the wood. This is called lightening with pigment, as opposed to bleaching. Sometimes the two processes are combined.

There is also a third situation, when the stain was mixed into the finish before it was sprayed on. This cannot be bleached, of course, but the wood underneath the finish is exposed as much lighter when such a colored or stain-bearing finish is removed.

A final bleaching situation comes up where wood had been darkened by the action of a finish remover such as lye, ammonia or trisodium phosphate. These solutions turn many woods a dark brown. If this is a desired color, it can be left in the wood. All you have to do is neutralize any traces of the chemicals in the surface of the wood with a wash of straight vinegar. But the wood may also be quickly brought back to its natural color with a solution of oxalic-acid crystals in water. See listing for *oxalic acid*, which follows.

To round out this section, I have included entries on the troublesome *black streaks* and *red stains* that we often run across.

black stains The commonest of these is caused by water that gets into the grain of the wood, and then dries out slowly. It happens to wood stacked in lumber yards, to the decks of boats, and to furniture. It cannot happen unless the water penetrates the finish. This is usually quite obvious. On table tops these marks are often in rings, or other definite shapes, and should not be confused with burns, which they sometimes resemble.

The cure for these water-caused black marks is a saturate solution of oxalic-acid crystals in water, which is easy enough to obtain from a paint store or drugstore. The stuff costs you about seventy cents a pound in a paint store, or a quarter an ounce in a drugstore. Don't be alarmed by the term *acid*. It's just a technical matter. The saturate solution you are going to prepare won't hurt your skin, though if it gets into any cuts or scratches, it will burn like iodine. Or, at least, like iodine used to burn before modern science got hold of it and took the character out of it.

I use oxalic crystals by putting a half pound in a milk bottle and adding warm water to fill the bottle. This does not dissolve all the crystals, but that way I know I've got a saturate solution, and as I use the solution, I keep adding water to the bottle until there are only a few crystals in the bottom still undissolved. For a small job, dissolve an ounce in a cup of warm water.

I should point out, however, that there aren't very many small jobs, because besides clearing up black marks, the oxalic solution will also bleach out any toning stain in the wood, and also slightly lighten wood that has darkened from age. So you usually have to do the whole top of a piece to have an even tone. For a good-sized table top you will need a couple of cups of the solution. It is common to bleach tops without bothering about the legs or sides. The tops are then stained to bring them back to the color of whatever is under them.

On soft woods the solution works in seconds. On hard woods you may have to keep the surface wet with the solution for an hour to give it time to penetrate. You will notice that as the solution dries, a fine white dust forms on the surface of the wood. If this dust gets into the air, it is very irritating to breathe, and will make you sneeze. So it is better to wash it off than to dust it off.

Usually it isn't important to neutralize the oxalic acid if you have washed it off well. In fact, you don't have to bother at all if you are not going to stain the piece before applying a finish, or if you are going to use a dark stain. But in the case of a light stain on a soft wood—a pale antique-brown on pine, for instance—I have found that the oxalic will cause a pink cast or streaks by its action on the stain. This can be avoided by washing the piece first with water. When it is dry, wash it again with two quarts of water in which you have put a cup of sudsless ammonia. This will neutralize any traces of the oxalic. After all this water, let the piece dry two days in a warm place.

Another kind of black stain is the streaks, supposedly imitation "figure," that are found in the wood under a false-grain finish. These were made with lampblack, and to date, I have found nothing that will bleach them out. You have to sand or scrape.

Clorox See listing below for *laundry bleach.*

commercial bleaches It used to be that every shop had its own trade secret about bleaching. But now the patented one-and-two solutions such as Blanchit are almost universally used, because the product is standard and you always get the same results.

The one-and-two solutions are used for bleaching natural color out of the darker woods such as mahogany and walnut. To bleach out a stain, commercial shops use the commercial equivalent of Clorox or other liquid laundry bleach. They buy the sodium-hypochlorite crystals and dissolve them in water. This is what our great grandmothers used to do before someone got the brilliant idea of bottling the solution so that the American housewife wouldn't have to dissolve the crystals herself. Now all she has to do is carry home the heavy bottles from the store. This is progress?

For those who are interested, or who want to avoid the higher cost of the prepared one-and-two solutions, here are some of the other chemicals that can be bought in bulk, and are therefore much cheaper if you have a lot of work to do.

Two cups of chlorinated lime to each quart of water. Allow the white powder to settle on the bottom after stirring. Then use the clear solution. Mix at about eighty degrees Fahrenheit. This works well on the darker woods such as walnut. Neutralize with borax or vinegar.

A 10 per cent solution of hydrosulphite of soda is a good all-around bleach. Neutralize with vinegar—always undiluted in all these formulas.

Sodium perborate is a good bleach. Neutralize with vinegar.

A very effective and cheap bleach for mass production is to first wash the wood with potassium permanganate. Let dry. Then apply a saturate solution of sodium bisulphite.

Solutions are always "saturate," unless otherwise specified. Saturate solution means as much of the chemical as will dissolve in water at normal room temperature. The way most people arrive at such a solution is to start with a gallon jug three-quarters full of water, and then add the powder or crystal until even after shaking, some of the chemical remains undissolved in the bottom of the jug.

To avoid any possible confusion, please bear with me while I spell this out once more: All these bleaches are used for bleaching the *natural* color out of wood. To remove stain from wood—stain that was put onto the wood—use oxalic acid or a liquid laundry bleach such as Clorox. There's an exception to this, but it would only confuse you. Pretend that I never mentioned it.

laundry bleach This is the mainstay bleach used in refinishing furniture. It works with 100 per cent efficiency on all wood stains with the exception of antique berry juice and lampblack, which nothing will bleach.

To use it, all finish must first be removed from the surface. Stain seeps into the surface fibers of the wood, and you have to follow it there with Clorox, which is the commonest trade name for this bleach in my part of the country. I understand there are many trade names, but they are all solutions of sodium hypochlorite in water. This information is always in very small print somewhere on the label.

The liquid is used as it comes out of the bottle. Do not dilute. It can be mopped on with a rag, brushed on with a stiff brush, or scrubbed on with 000 steel wool. What bleaching action is going to take place will take place in a minute. Any color that remains is the natural color of the wood. If this isn't light enough for you, see listings elsewhere in this section for *one-and-two bleach* and *commercial bleaches.*

After the Clorox has done its work, rinse the piece with water, and wipe dry with rags. No neutralizing is needed. When the piece is dry—after two days in a warm place—it is ready to restain or finish.

You will note, however, that when dry the wood has a white or gray cast to it. This is not important. It is caused by a loosening of the fibers in the surface of the wood. You will see that as soon as the surface is wet with shellac, or stain, or varnish, this effect disappears. Of course, in some soft woods this loosening of the surface fibers is quite noticeable. In such cases simply remove the fiber by a brisk, hard rubbing with 00-grade steel wool. Do not use sandpaper if you are refinishing an antique, because this will destroy the patina or soft appearance of the wood. When finished, it will look new—like a reproduction instead of the real thing.

Clorox will also remove inkstains. They are made from the same kind of dyes used to make wood stains.

lye stains When lye is used to remove paint from wood, it usually turns the wood a dark brown. The wood can be returned to its natural color by applying a wash of a saturate solution of oxalic-acid crystals dissolved in water. See listing below for *oxalic acid.*

marble tops See listing for cleaning and bleaching these in section on REPAIRING.

one-and-two bleach This is a two-solution bleach designed to totally remove the natural color of wood. The brand that I have seen most often is called Blanchit, and comes in two bottles plainly labeled "1" and "2." There are other brand names that work the same way. Sometimes the bottles are labeled "A" and "B." First one solution and then the other is put on the wood, and no neutralizer is necessary. Naturally, it will help if you make at least a minor effort to follow the directions on the labels.

This bleach will really remove the natural color from wood. A dark walnut, for instance, will become a light tan color, though sometimes it is necessary to give the wood two complete treatments.

To find this bleach—Blanchit or some similar brand—you have to go to a supplier who deals with wood-finishing companies. A local cabinetmaker can tell you whether it is available in your city or area. You can get it by mail from Albert Constantine and Son, Inc., 2050 Eastchester Road, New York City, 61, New York. At this writing it costs four dollars for a quart of each of the solutions, and can be shipped only by express.

oxalic acid In spite of its frightening name, oxalic acid is not particularly dangerous. You can't drink it, of course, but it will not hurt your hands unless you have cuts or scratches in them. You can get small quantities from drugstores. You can get it much cheaper—about seventy-five cents a pound—from large paint stores. It has two main uses. The first is to remove black watermarks from wood, and to lighten wood that has been turned dark by the use of lye to remove paint. It will also lighten wood darkened by any other remover, such as ammonia. For details, see listings above for *black stains* and *lye stains*.

It will usually bleach out stain the same way Clorox does, but not always, so stick to Clorox or a similar liquid laundry bleach for that purpose.

red stains The reference isn't to red mahogany or cherry stains, but to a pinkish-red stain that is often found to have penetrated deep into the wood of antique furniture. It is a real nuisance, because it will often not bleach out, whatever you use. And it penetrates too deeply in some spots to be sanded out.

These stains were caused by various berry juices that were used to color the wood in olden times. The easiest solution to the problem they present is to stain the whole piece dark enough so that they will not be noticed. If you want to finish the wood in its natural light color, the trick is to give it a first coat of shellac to "wet" the wood down, so that you can see the color the wood is going to be when it is completely finished. Then mix up some regular flat wall paint to an exact match of the color of the wood and smudge this over the pink stain with your fingertip. Believe me, this way of putting the paint on works far better than any brush or spray method. After the paint has dried twenty-four hours, proceed with an additional coat of shellac, and a final one of varnish.

For details on mixing such a paint, see the listing for *colors ground in oil* in the section on STAINING.

stain bleach To bleach out stain—as opposed to bleaching out the natural color of the wood—see listing above for *liquid laundry bleach.*

watermarks See listing at beginning of this section for *black stains.* Also, listing for *oxalic acid.*

white spots See listing in section on RESTORING FINISHES.

wood bleach To bleach out the natural color of wood—as opposed to just bleaching out any stain that may have been applied to it—see listings above for *one-and-two bleaches* and *commercial bleaches.*

Section 7

HOW TO STAIN—IF YOU INSIST

Where we separate the men from the boys, and caution is strongly advised

The first reason woods are stained is to emphasize their figure or grain. Typical woods to which this is done are cherry, mahogany, walnut, and maple. These woods can be finished with just a clear finish, and this will bring out the figure to some extent. But if the wood is soaked with a pale-brown stain first, the figure will be even more definite—you get the illusion that you are looking into the wood. This effect is probably the strongest on cherry, where you can get the illusion that you are looking into swirling colored glass.

The other reason for staining wood is to make it look like something else. Raw pine wood doesn't look like much. But a pale brown stain will at least make it look like aged pine. Pine can also be stained to match any wood that is darker than it is—almost everything except holly. Another wood that is frequently stained is poplar. You can make poplar look like almost anything. On the other hand, some woods are too hard to take stain well. Oak is one. It is hard to make oak look like anything but oak—unless you resort to real trickery. For such trickery in general, see the sections on FINISHES: OPAQUE and FINISHES: DECEPTIVE. As to how each wood takes stain, see the section on WOODS, which gives the characteristics of the commonly used cabinet woods.

The best stains to use are aniline dyes. You can get these

from *large* paint stores or wholesalers, who sell them in small envelopes of powder that will dissolve in either denatured alcohol or water. Alcohol is better, because it will not raise the grain of the wood the way water will. For other sources, see section on SUPPLIES in the back of the book.

This does not mean that there is anything the matter with clear oil stains, sealer stains, or Minwax if a convenient dealer happens to carry them. Their use is discussed in the following listings. The advantage of aniline dyes is that they come in the widest range of colors and intensities. You can do the most with them.

Some of the stains you will find have a lot of opaque pigment ground up in them. These can be useful if you let the pigment settle to the bottom of the can, and use the clear, colored liquid on the top as your stain.

When you *want* pigment in your stain—usually to help obscure what the wood you are using really is—you can get opaque colors in any paint store. See listing for *colors ground in oil.*

Now for some generalities on how to go about staining something regardless of which stain you are using.

The basic problem that most people run into is getting just the right color. If the stain you buy happens to be exactly the color you want, I couldn't be happier for you. But I know from hundreds of letters I've received that people are very fussy and particular about this. Therefore the only answer is to learn to blend two or more stains to get the *right color*. Then you thin it to get just the degree of *darkness* of that color that you want.

This is not as hard as it sounds, as you can see from the accompanying chart. This chart shows how you can mix any color or shade you want from five basic stains. In fact, you can easily get along with four stains. The black isn't really necessary except for modern, offbeat shades.

Walnut is the basic brown. Always try it first. Try a small daub on the underside of a leaf or the back of a leg or on a

How to Mix Any Special Stain Using Only Five Commonly Available Colors

Start with this "palette" of commonly available stains to mix the colors listed below. These are starting points. Modify the proportions to get exact matches if you are trying to duplicate the color of another piece.

MAHOGANY
Almost always is a red. Brown mahogany is rarely available. See below.

LIGHT OAK
Tan or sand color.

BLACK
Used in very small quantities to deaden the brightness of any stain or mixture.

MAPLE
A yellowish orange.

WALNUT
Your basic brown. Sometimes *dark* oak can be substituted.

***ANTIQUE PINE**	4 parts Walnut 1 part Red Mahogany
BROWN MAHOGANY	5 parts Walnut 1 part Red Mahogany 1 part Oak
***ANTIQUE MAPLE**	2 parts Maple 1 part Oak 1 part Walnut
***HONEY MAPLE**	2 parts Maple 1 part Walnut 3 parts Oak
CHERRY (Brownish)	1 part Walnut 1 part Oak 1 Part Red Mahogany
***FRUITWOOD**	4 parts Oak 1 part Maple 1 part Walnut
DARK OAK	1 part Walnut 1 part Oak
SWEDISH WALNUT	4 parts Walnut 2 parts Oak Drop of Black
RED CHERRY OR MAHOGANY	1 Red Mahogany 1 Walnut

For blond and pickled finishes, see section on **FINISHES—OPAQUE.** Also on **FINISHES—DECEPTIVE.**

*Always start with full strength stain mixture, then thin down for lighter shades—testing on scrap wood first. The four marked * will have to be thinned quite a lot.

scrap of the same kind of wood that you want to stain. If your test patch doesn't look "warm" enough, add a little red mahogany. If the color is too dark, add some thinner.

Obviously, in this experimenting stage you will be mixing teaspoonfuls or less in a cup to get a general idea of the proportions you will need. If you put in too much red, you can throw your little batch away. It is only after you find your general proportion that you start mixing in larger quantities.

If you are familiar with mixing colors, this will come easily. For those who haven't the faintest idea of where to start, I have listed some general proportions. But these are only starting points. For instance, take the proportions given for fruitwood. You may think this is far too orange. In that case, leave out most or all of the maple.

If all this seems like a nuisance to you, I'm sorry, but that's the way it is. If you are going to be particular about the color and shade of your furniture, you are going to have to experiment. Even professional finishers have to do this. They may get the color they are after a little faster than you do, but they have to go through the same process. There is no easy way to match a color.

Of course, most jobs aren't too complicated. For instance, if you have a maple table, the only stains you have to buy are maple and walnut. It is then only a matter of finding the proper proportion for the particular shade of maple you want.

alcohol stains This term refers to an aniline dye, which comes in powder form and is dissolved in denatured alcohol. These powders vary in intensity. For the lighter colors such as light oak and maple, start with an ounce of powder to a quart of alcohol. The darker colors such as walnut and red mahogany are so strong that an ounce will make a gallon of stain in alcohol. However, dissolve them in only a quart to start with.

The advantage in using alcohol stains is that they dry a few minutes after application. This means that if the color of the wood isn't dark enough, you can apply an additional coat every five minutes until you get the degree of darkness you want. Also, if after two thin coats of walnut stain you think the piece should have a little more red in it, you can then apply a thin coat of red mahogany stain while the walnut is still wet.

I assume that the advantage in working from light to dark is obvious. But if the stain does get too dark, it is easily bleached with Clorox or any other liquid laundry bleach. After bleaching with Clorox the wood must be rinsed with water, and then allowed to dry for twenty-four hours in a warm place before staining again.

With alcohol stain, as soon as the wood looks dry, it is dry enough to apply a first coat of shellac. As I said above, this is usually within five minutes of having finished applying the stain. This coat of shellac should be a half-and-half mixture of shellac and denatured alcohol. If you are working in a warm, dry room, you can apply varnish over the shellac in two hours. However, this is a matter of judgment that should be based on some experience. The safe procedure for the amateur is to let any coat of shellac dry overnight, and any cost of varnish for at least twenty-four hours. Better safe than sorry.

See also listing for *aniline dyes*, which follows.

aniline dyes This is another subject on which the world is full of misinformation. People are always saying that aniline dyes will fade. Well, that was once true of some of them back around the time of the First World War. But it is not true any more. They are now made differently and from different things. In fact, the chemical trade now refers to them as synthetic dyes, but the name aniline has stuck for any stain or dye that comes in powdered form.

These dyes are now manufactured to dissolve in either alcohol or water. See separate listings for *alcohol stains* and *water stains*. They also used to be made to dissolve in oil or turpentine, but this has become quite rare because such stains bleed into varnish coats put over them. They are also slower drying than when the dye is dissolved in alcohol, which is almost universal practice these days.

A basic selection of aniline-dye colors is available through the larger paint stores, especially those doing a wholesale business. These are plenty for mixing stains according to the directions given at the beginning of this section. For those who want to go into the refinements of staining, a wide selection of colors is available from H. Behlen & Bro., Inc., 10 Christopher Street, New York 14, New York. They also have a complete selection of professional refinishing supplies. The store is open to the public daily, and they will supply you by mail if your order totals five dollars or more.

antique brown This is the color that pine and maple turn with old age. Obviously, it is not an exact color. It is basically walnut, tinted with red mahogany. Some people prefer to tint the walnut with orangish maple. Some just use a thin wash of pure walnut. It is a matter of taste or preference—except that we are essentially dealing with walnut, tinted mildly one way or another. There are several brands of this on the market, one of which is sold by The Furniture Doctor, East Poultney, Vermont. I know that sounds like an advertisement, but it does seem sort of fake to make believe I don't sell refinishing supplies by mail when a half a million people already know it.

blond finishes These are not really a result of staining, but I am listing them here in case some people don't realize this. They are usually the result of first bleaching the wood, and then wiping a flat, creamy-colored paint onto and then off the bare wood. A finish is then applied over this. See section on FINISHES: OPAQUE.

colors ground in oil Sold in any good paint store, these are tinting colors that can be used in any oil-base paint or varnish.

These are the kinds of paint that you thin with turpentine or mineral spirits. These "colors" are opaque pigments ground up in just enough oil to give them a pasty consistency. They are available in a wide spectrum, but the ones we are most interested in are:

burnt sienna (cherry or reddish-brown mahogany)
raw umber (walnut)
yellow ocher (light oak)
vermilion (orangish red)

With these four colors—plus black and white for blond and other trick finishes—we can match almost any finish found on furniture. These colors are the opaque equivalents of the four colors of clear aniline stains shown in the diagram at the beginning of this section. They are not exact matches for those four colors, but they are close enough to mix just about the same way.

These colors can be used to conceal defects or to camouflage wood to make it look like something it isn't. Here are some examples:

When the end grain of wood has stained too dark, you can smudge some of these colors on with your finger tip to lighten the area.

Using the same finger-smudging technique, they are useful for concealing cigarette burns and other surface injuries.

Rubbed onto and then off a sanded wood surface, they can be made to color the surface in an obscure, streaky way to make light woods such as pine and poplar look like cherry or walnut.

They are used to tint the flat white wall paint that you wipe onto and then off sanded wood to create a blond finish.

For use on large surfaces, you thin these pastes with mineral spirits or turpentine to the consistency of thin cream. In any event, they must be allowed to dry for twenty-four hours in a warm place, and the first coat of finish that goes over them must be shellac. If you try to varnish directly on top of them, they often dissolve into the varnish and make a streaky mess. The shellac seals them.

You can add japan driers to these colors to make them dry faster. Do not use more than one part drier to four parts of the paste as it comes from the tube or can. And for the experiment-minded, these colors can be added to varnish to create antique glazes or false graining when swirled around.

driftwood finish Like blond finishes, this is covered in the section on FINISHES: OPAQUE.

end grain When staining, say, a table, you will notice that stain is sucked into end grain and therefore darkens it far more than it does the rest of the surfaces. To prevent this, give the end grain a preliminary coat of shellac before staining the piece. This should be a solution of 50 per cent shellac and 50 per cent denatured alcohol. Paint this shellac on with a brush, quickly wiping off any that gets on other surfaces. After the shellac has dried for two hours you can proceed with your staining.

Now strangely enough, this applies no matter what kind of stain you are using—oil stain, Minwax, alcohol stain, water stain, any stain.

Some of these stains will penetrate through the shellac faster than others, and a lot depends on how porous the particular piece of wood is. But if the stain isn't penetrating the end grain well enough, rub the stain onto the end grain with a small tuft of 000 steel wool. This will gradually break down the shellac and let the stain in until you have just the degree of coloring you want.

fruitwood stain When people speak of fruitwoods, they mean the light ones such as apple and pear—not, for instance, cherry or dark plum. These light fruitwoods are usually stained with a thin wash of walnut stain. And some people like this walnut wash to be tinted slightly with maple or orange.

Thus any light wood such as pine or poplar can be given a fruitwood coloring.

honey tones In recent years this seems to have become a big word with the furniture manufacturers. It's honey maple, honey-tone pine, honey-tone cherry, etc. What does it mean? As far as I can see, all it means is that all the standard stains have been given a foggy whitish-yellow cast just to be able to sell something different.

Well, all right. If that is what you want, the way to get it is with yellow ocher and white. (For those who know color, that is the equivalent of Naples yellow, which can also be used.) At any rate, you buy a half-pint of flat white wall paint, the kind that thins with mineral spirits. To this add two tubes or about half a cup of yellow-ocher color ground in oil. Stir well, and then thin with mineral spirits to the consistency of thin paint. Brush this on the surface of the wood, and then wipe it off *hard* with a rag. Let this dry twenty-four hours, and then wipe any stain onto it. The degree of "honeyness" that you then have depends on the amount of pigment left on the wood. As with all trick staining techniques, you have to experiment first on some scrap pieces of wood or on the undersides of table leaves, etc.

maple staining The reason for giving maple a separate listing in this section is that it presents a special problem. Most maple is so hard that it won't absorb much stain. So when a stain doesn't seem to work on maple, don't blame the stain. The darker maples that you see in some lines of mass-produced furniture are the result of the wood being sprayed with an even coat of colored lacquer. The only way you can duplicate this effect is with *varnish stain,* for which see listing further on.

matching colors Most people don't realize what a job they are undertaking when they set out to finish something to exactly match a piece they already have. It's all right if the piece is a dark one—old-style mahogany or walnut, for instance. But the lighter tones are very hard for anyone who has not had experience in mixing colors. It takes patience, and a willingness to think of the time it takes as time spent on your education.

The "secret" of anyone who is successful in matching colors is his willingness to take a lot of time experimenting with small sample mixtures on scraps of wood similar to the kind of wood he is trying to stain.

When it comes to colors on modern furniture—and recently-made reproductions, too—the secret is that many of the honey tones and "off" shades are the result of the faintest tint of black or white (or both) having been added to the color blend.

What this amounts to is that the amateur should be satisfied to get something beautiful, and not make excessive demands on himself in the matter of getting exact color matches.

Minwax This is a widely distributed *sealer-stain* (see listing under FINISHES: CLEAR) that is primarily used for built-in cabinets and paneling. But it is also excellent for use on furniture. It is a very good product for beginners to use if they like one of the shades available. It is an easy product to use, and there is no point in my repeating the directions on the can.

The only drawback to Minwax is the limited range of colors, and the fact that they are not intense enough to use in mixing any of the stranger and darker colors.

Incidentally, these stains have a small amount of opaque pigment in them, but many finishers let this settle to the bottom of the can, and use the clear liquid on top. It is a good idea to try any given color both ways—first clear, and then after the contents have been stirred.

Minwax may be tinted with *colors ground in oil,* listed above.

oak staining Like other very hard woods, oak does not take stain well. The best way to get it dark—say, to match or simulate walnut—is to first soak the bare wood with ammonia. This will give a base of darkness over which you can stain when the wood is dry. The ammonia turns the wood a brown, walnut shade. You can then make this darker with more walnut stain, or shade it toward either the red or yellow tones (see staining chart at beginning of this section).

It is not possible to stain oak any of the lighter shades, such as fruitwood. The grain of oak is so obvious and characteristic that this is like trying to turn a sow's ear into a silk purse.

oil-base stains These are stains made by dissolving *aniline dyes* (see listing above) in mineral spirits or turpentine. They are not widely distributed, and become less so every year. They mix and soak into the wood the same way alcohol stains do. Their disadvantage is that they take longer to dry—at least overnight in a warm place—and have to be sealed with a prime coat of shellac before you apply a varnish. These are minor disadvantages, of course, but it is because of them that general usage has gradually switched to the alcohol stains, which are bought in powder form and mixed with denatured alcohol. See listing above for *alcohol stains.*

pickled finish This is what the trade calls a novelty finish. The large, open pores of oak or walnut are filled with white or another color which contrasts with the way the surface of the wood is stained. Obviously, there are about a billion possible variations of this because you can use any color—clear or opaque—for the surface of the wood, and any shade of paint in the pores. You can lacquer the piece a dull black and have white pores, or you can lacquer it white and have black pores. Between those two extremes lie all the possibilities of the spectrum.

Start out with a clean sanded surface. Brush any dust out of the open pores, and stain or paint the wood whatever color you want it to be. You can use any kind of stain. If you are painting the piece, use flat wall paint tinted to whatever color you want with colors ground in oil. Or, of course, you can use any color of paint as it comes out of the can. (Water-mixed paints can be used just as well, but finding them in the color you want is not so easy, and there is no simple way to tint them.)

After the stain or paint is dry—give the paint two days to dry thoroughly—give the piece a coat of shellac, thinned with an equal amount of denatured alcohol. About a cup of each will give you enough for a large table or chest of drawers. Use the clear shellac, not the orange. When dry, apply a second coat, and rub smooth with 000 steel wool.

When the shellac is dry, you will notice that the pores of the wood are still quite open. Filling them is never easy, anyway. The next step is to get contrasting color into those pores. Brush on a thick colored paste, and wipe it off the surface with rags, leaving the paste in the pores. As to the nature of this paste, many things can be used. The pigment that settles in the bottom of flat wall paint is the commonest thing, because it is easiest to tint with colors ground in oil, which you get at the same place you bought the paint. The thicker this goo is, the better. So if it is too thick to brush on, wipe it on with a cloth pad. Then wipe the surface clean with clean cloth pads.

For decorative little pieces that don't get a lot of use, it is not necessary to apply any more coats of finish. But for a table top, you will want to apply a final coat or two of clear varnish. Before doing this, be absolutely sure that the filler in the pores is dry. Test it by picking at one of the pores with a pin.

The advantage in not applying a final coat of varnish, if not necessary, is the desirable chalky look of the filler, which disappears when "wet down" with varnish.

pigmented stains One of the things that throws many beginners off the track is the distinction between pigmented stains and clear stains. Pigmented stains are very finely ground solids. They can be bought through paint stores in a dry, powdery form—they are then called *fresco colors* or just *dry colors*. They are more commonly available as colors ground in oil. These solids are also used as the opaque pigment in paint, whether flat or enamel, and also mix with varnish.

The trouble with pigment stains—as opposed to the clear aniline dyes—is that they conceal the grain of the wood. Therefore the only time they are used is when you are trying to do exactly that. See listing above for *colors ground in oil*.

pine staining Pine is a soft, porous wood that takes stain well. However, that very porousness sometimes gives trouble. See listing for *end grain*, above. See also entry for pine in section on THE WOODS.

poplar staining Poplar, in all its varieties, is a dream wood when it comes to staining. You may not be able to make a silk purse out of a sow's ear, but you can make maple, mahogany, walnut, rosewood, or anything else out of poplar. That wood has an absolutely even grain and absorbs stain in a slow but steady way that makes it easy to control the degree of darkness either over the whole area or in streaks if you are faking a figure in the wood. See listing for poplar in section on THE WOODS.

sealer stains Originally brought out for floors, these were quickly picked up by furniture restorers and finishers. Dura-Seal is one widely distributed brand. You can also get a good standard antique brown from Cohasset Colonials, Cohasset, Massachusetts, or from The Furniture Doctor, East Poultney, Vermont.

Sealers have the consistency of varnish, but penetrate into the surface of the wood, which hardens it, rather than resting on the surface the way varnish does. You brush them on, then after ten minutes wipe off any excess on the surface of the wood. When dry, just rub down with 000 steel wool and wax. For table tops, you can apply a top coat of dull varnish—before waxing, of course. A coat of sealer—it comes clear as well as in the basic wood colors—also makes an excellent first coat for a linseed-oil finish.

The basic thing that distinguishes a sealer-stain finish is that it is an easy, fast, one-coat finish that is very good-looking, and serviceable for everything except tops that get a lot of use or wear. It has no "built-up" look, and the grain of the wood is usually still visible. Whether or not you want this is a matter of taste. Sealers are now being used on both modern furniture and "country-style" antiques.

spirit stains This is merely an old-fashioned term for *alcohol stains*. See listing above.

tobacco stain Chewing tobacco has long been used to make an inexpensive antique-brown stain. To make it, chop up three or four plugs of chewing tobacco in a quart of water, and simmer over a very low heat. Or you can just let the tobacco soak in a warm place for a couple of days. If you want a warmer color, add some beet juice.

While tobacco stain is an excellent color, it has the disadvantage of being a water stain. This means that it will raise the grain on softer woods. To avoid this, wet the wood with clear water to raise the grain, let the wood dry, and sand down the roughness that develops with fine sandpaper wrapped around a sanding block. Do this a second time, and then use tobacco stain or any other water stain. After the stain is dry, any finish may be applied over it. But with a water stain, be sure the wood is dry by keeping it in a warm, dry place for two days.

varnish stain This is an old-time product which combines varnish and stain in one coat. It is, in fact, varnish with some aniline dye dissolved in it. Its disadvantage is that to get a good-looking job you must apply a perfectly even coating without any brush marks. And this is very hard to do even for a professional. It is easier to first stain the wood, and then apply a clear coat of varnish, which will not show up every little defect in the brushing.

The only way to overcome this difficulty is to spray varnish stain on. But if you have a spray gun, you might as well use lacquer colored with aniline dyes, because it dries without the constant danger of sagging that you have with varnish stain.

water stain Any stain dissolved in water, but especially aniline dyes dissolved in water. The same aniline powders that dissolve in alcohol will also dissolve in water although the colors will be slightly different. The disadvantage in this is that the water raises the grain of the wood. For handling this, see listing immediately above for *tobacco stain*. See also listing above for *aniline dyes*.

Section 8

FINISHES: CLEAR AND CLOUDY

The kind that reveal the true beauty of wood, but are easy to apply only if you will follow me, forsaking all others

Definitions.

A finish is a permanent coating put on wood to both protect the surface and to bring out the beauty of the wood. Waxes and polishes are not finishes. They are "dressings" for finishes—put on to protect finishes and, when finishes get worn, to improve their appearance.

You think I'm kidding, or trying to insult your intelligence? Not at all. You'd be amazed how many people are confused about the basic idea.

So let's go on from there, and don't raise your hand until the lecture's over.

To begin with, there are basically only two kinds of finishes. All the others are only variations of these two. And these two basic finishes are shellac and varnish.

Shellac is a rosin extracted by parasitic insects from the banyan trees in India. It dissolves in alcohol. It dries as the alcohol evaporates, but if you put more alcohol in it, it redissolves. Because alcohol is very volatile, shellac dries fast and is a quick, easy finish to use. It is a good-looking finish, polishes beautifully, and was the only clear finish used until around 1850. The obvious trouble with it is that alcohol, even considerably diluted, will wash it off. Less obvious, but just as bad a fault, is that if a wet glass is left on it, it will turn white. A coat of wax on shellac will delay this, but eventually—in a few hours—the water will get through the wax and presto—you have a perfect white ring on the shellac.

For clarity's sake, I will mention right now that lacquer is very akin to shellac, except that it is better. It is harder, tougher, takes longer to turn white under a wet glass. The reason home craftsmen don't use lacquer very much is that it is very hard to get a good coat unless you spray it on. So everybody skips over lacquer and goes right to varnish when they want a really good finish. Here's why:

Varnish, you see, was invented when someone had the fairly reasonable idea of boiling some linseed oil and shellac together to get them to mix. The shellac made the linseed oil dry hard—which linseed oil never does by itself. And the linseed oil made the mixture alcohol-proof, oilproof, resistant to the acids in vegetable juices—and it will not white-spot if you leave a wet glass or vase on it.

Varnish then, is the really good finish. And all sorts of refinements have been made since it was first invented to make it even better. Today's "plastic" varnishes are the best ever.

But just as we mentioned lacquer before leaving the subject of shellac, there is something that needs to be said about varnish: there is a kind of varnish that is simply no good for furniture. This is always clearly labeled SPAR varnish. It is hardly anything more than pure linseed oil, and when exposed to air, forms a surface film, but never dries all the way through. This makes it fine for outdoor work—especially for spars on boats—but impossible, of course, for furniture.

The reason I have to make a big point about this is that most clerks selling paint and varnish know practically nothing about the products, and care less. If you ask for their best varnish, nine out of ten of them will try to sell you spar varnish. The only thing you can do is to stamp your little foot, and insist on a varnish that clearly says "for furniture" on the label. If the store doesn't have any, go to another store. Or you can use a floor varnish. In other words, if the label says "for floors"—that's fine, too. In fact, just as good as the ones that say "for furniture." Obviously anything that is used on a floor has to dry hard, and that is the important thing in any furniture finish.

Here, then, are specific directions for applying shellac, varnish, and their variations.

dull glow You can also call this a "satin" finish, sheen, or hand-rubbed effect, or whatever words come to mind. However, whatever you call it, what we are talking about is a finish whose surface has been ground down with some fine abrasive.

Shellac, varnish, and lacquer all dry to a naturally glossy surface. Additives can be put into them to make them dry dull, but this is for fast, mass-production work, as the same effect can be obtained by abrasion.

This abrasion is done with either fine sandpaper or fine

steel wool, and the degree of dullness is controlled by the grade of sandpaper or steel wool you use.

The standard material for the small shop or home craftsman is grade 000 (called "three-ought") steel wool. You can get away with using 00 steel wool, which is a little rougher, but may make scratches. Going the other way, you get a progressively higher shine with 0000, 00000, and 000000 steel wool. So you can run up and down the scale from "just off shiny" to "very dull."

Sandpaper is never used in refinishing because of the danger of it cutting through the finish if there is any unevenness to a surface. Of course, if you have a perfectly flat surface, this

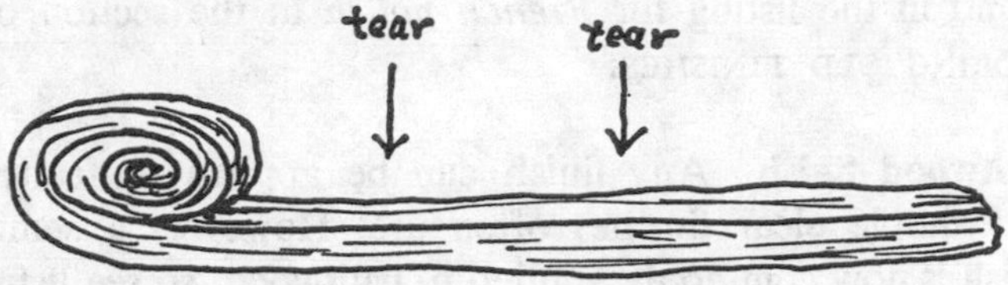

STEEL WOOL will go 10 times as far if you unroll the pad and use a little at a time.

danger is much less—especially if you wrap a piece of the paper around a perfectly flat block of wood about six inches long and three inches wide. The grades to use are 6/0 or 7/0.

When "polishing" a finish this way, you should always stroke with the grain of the wood, and when you are finished, wax the surface to "wet down" the dry, powdery surface.

You will read a great deal about using both steel wool and sandpaper with oil. The superstitious belief here is that this keeps the surface cool or something. Well, for machine polishing in a factory, this is true, but it is meaningless in handwork. In fact, it is much easier to see how you are coming along if you work dry.

Finally, when using sandpaper, use a very light pressure. With steel wool you can rub as hard as you like. Generally speaking, use the same pressure that you would use to give someone's back a good scrubbing.

French polish This is a shellac finish, polished with an oily pad of cloth to the highest gloss obtainable. In fact, it looks "glassy." To apply such a finish, start with two coats of shellac, both rubbed down with 000 steel wool. See listing for *shellac finish,* below.

Then apply more liquid shellac with an oily pad, rubbing briskly. Because this technique is mainly used in the restoration of old finishes, complete directions for the process will be found in the listing for *French polish* in the section on RESTORING OLD FINISHES.

fruitwood finish Any finish can be applied to fruitwoods, and simple clear finishes often are. However, a semiblond finish is now commonly applied to fruitwood, so see listing for *fruitwood finish* in the following section devoted to FINISHES: OPAQUE AND FANCY. See also listing for *fake fruitwood finish* in section on FINISHES: DECEPTIVE.

honey-tone finish See listing in following section on FINISHES: OPAQUE AND FANCY.

lacquer finish Lacquer is similar to shellac, but the solvent used is even more volatile than alcohol. This solvent is called "lacquer thinner," but its characteristic ingredient is acetone, which evaporates almost instantly. This finish was invented for use on production lines. You can spray lacquer on, and it is dry to the touch in ten seconds, dry enough to be "polished" with steel wool in a couple of minutes.

By spraying lacquer you can also finish a chest of drawers in five minutes. For those who wish to try this method, a spray gun, with air compressor and motor, costs about sixty dollars.

With this gun you can also spray shellac, varnish, and paint.

As to brushing on a coat of lacquer, most people don't bother with it, because it is harder to do than with either shellac or varnish, and not as good as varnish. (See introduction to this section.) However, the procedure is this:

Start with a pint can of brushing lacquer from a large paint store. If they only have spraying lacquer, all you have to do is add one teaspoon of castor oil (from the drugstore) to each pint of lacquer, and you will have exactly the same thing. This slows the drying.

Now thin the lacquer with an equal amount of lacquer thinner bought at the same place. Brush on a first coat, soaking it into the wood. When the wood is well-soaked, wipe off any excess with a soft cloth.

When the first coat is dry—in about an hour—rub briskly with 000 steel wool. Dust well. Now brush on the second coat with full body, and tip off with the brush. By "full body," I mean as thick as you can without getting runs or "curtains"—when the film sags on vertical surfaces before it dries.

As lacquer is quite full-bodied, this one coat is usually a thick enough finish, and trying to apply additional coats should be avoided.

Give this second coat overnight to dry, and then rub it down with 000 steel wool, and wax. See listing above for *dull glow*.

Additional coats of lacquer should be avoided since each new coat will redissolve the coat underneath, causing a "gooiness" in which you are very likely to leave brush marks. Very few people can work fast enough to escape this danger.

linseed-oil finish (See also entries on *raw linseed oil, boiled linseed oil, driers, mineral spirits, and colors ground in oil.*)

Linseed oil, like lye, is a highly controversial subject. As such, it is a great conversation starter, especially among people who cherish antiques or who like to put antique finishes on newer pieces and unfinished furniture. Thus, the people of the whole civilized world can be divided into categories by their varying attitudes toward the linseed-oil finish. (1) Those who neither know nor care—happy lot—what a linseed-oil finish is. (2) Those who know and adore it. (3) Those who know and abhor it. (4) Those who know and admire it, but reject it as too much work (the author's category). And finally, (5) those who have heard of or seen its beauty, but are unfamiliar with the techniques of its application and the problems involved.

It is to this last group that the following comments are chiefly addressed.

Although I accept the undeniable beauty of the linseed-oil finish, it is indisputable that I am prejudiced against it. So why try to deny my bias? Within the framework of it, I will tell the facts as they are commonly agreed upon, and with my prejudice publicly declared, you can better judge the truth for yourself than if I try to feign impartiality.

To begin with, when we talk about a linseed-oil finish, we do not mean the common, or "raw," variety that is used in house paint. This raw linseed oil is a pure organic product which in its natural state has the property of never drying—or at least not for several decades. A sealing skin forms on the surface, keeping the understrata of oils wet or at least sticky. This makes a fine flexible coating that stands up well out-of-doors, because it "gives" with the expansion and contraction caused by summer heat and winter cold. But naturally such a finish when applied in ordinary thickness cannot be rubbed down with steel wool or sandpaper because it immediately gums and tears away from the wood. Also, if you put a raw linseed-oil finish on a chair, no matter how long you dry it—even in the hot summer sun—when you sit on it, the finish will quickly take on the texture of the fabric of your pants, and hold it. If it doesn't hold the pants themselves.

With raw linseed oil out of the way, we now come to the real thing. Namely, *boiled linseed oil.* This is linseed oil that dries better. Not very well, but better. It will dry throughout the depth of the coating, if the coating is thin enough. In the old days this drying quality was built into the oil by literally boiling it. If you want to try this, you can still do it, but I warn you to do it out-of-doors, as the stuff smokes fiercely with an acrid odor that takes a week to air out of a house. (How I know this should be obvious without my relating the miserable details.)

In modern times, however, the same effect is obtained by the addition of *driers,* such as the common *japan drier* sold in paint and hardware stores, and the *siccative drier* sold in artist's-supply stores for use in oil painting. Which is best? Undoubtably the siccative. But from the practical point of view, it is not enough better to make any difference in this case. You can "load" the linseed oil with more of the siccative without the finish cracking in later years, but so little drier is used in linseed oil that this does not become a significant factor in wood finishing. As it can be in oil painting.

The usually recommended quantity of drier to add to linseed oil is a tablespoon to a pint of oil, but double that quantity can be used with safety. This holds for both the siccative and japan varieties.

Before the actual finishing is begun, the oil is diluted with from one-quarter to one-third turpentine or mineral spirits. Here I prefer the mineral spirits because of its superior drying quality, but certainly the old-timers stick to turpentine with excellent results.

Speaking of old-timers, you will also hear other charming formulas from them. The most common is one-third boiled linseed oil, one-third turpentine, and one-third vinegar. Sauterne and other wines are sometimes substituted for the vinegar. And both cider and wine vinegar have their partisans. In fact, one little old lady in New Hampshire tells me that anyone who uses anything but cow urine has come under the influence of foreigners.

So be it.

Now for the actual process of finishing the wood, which is where my back stiffens. To begin with, soak the oil into the wood for a couple of days, brushing it on freely to keep the surface wet as the wood sucks it in. When the wood has stopped absorbing the oil, wipe the surface as hard and carefully as you can. The piece should then be let dry for two weeks, in a warm dry room if the weather is cold enough for the heat to be on in the house. In the summer the process can be speeded up by taking the piece out into the sun every day for a week.

Now starts the "building up" of the finish, by rubbing the oil mixture into the wood once a week for six months. This is done with the palm of your hand or a soft pad of cloth, preferably flannel. After each application any excess oil must be wiped off with dry cloths or soft paper so that only the barest film of oil has been added to the surface.

Six months is, of course, a generality, but not an exaggeration. It is a matter of individual taste as to how much you want your finish built up. And there is also the school that holds that the job is never done. They continue to rub the table twice a year until their grandchildren take over the job. However, this is a matter of preference. Once the finish is established, it may be waxed, or polished with an oil-base polish, just like any other finish.

So the disadvantage of the linseed-oil finish is that it is a lot of work. There are three advantages. (1) There is no finer, deeper finish for a beautifully grained piece of wood—such as an old cherry table top. The way you seem to be able to see into the wood as if it were colored glass is unsurpassed by any other finish. (2) A linseed-oil finish is strongly resistant to alcohol, the acids in fruit and vegetable juices, and water from sweating vases. This has made it traditional for bar tops in New England. The accepted procedure is to sew a brick in flannel, and use this to rub the mixture onto the bar every night after closing, or as a hint that it's time to close. And (3) some people just love to rub or polish furniture, and this gives them the finest excuse ever invented.

Gummy surface. Besides the work, there is another difficulty with the linseed-oil finish that people commonly run into: After a few rubbings the surface becomes sticky or gummy. This is caused by trying to rush the world's slowest job, and building up layers of finish before they have had a chance to thoroughly dry. This brings us to the major rule, or warning, or pitfall to avoid, or whatever you want to call it.

Each application of boiled linseed oil must be wiped off thoroughly so that only the barest film of new oil on the surface is left.

Darkening of the wood. You will often hear people say that linseed oil darkens the wood. Which is a statement that is more or less true here and there. In the first place, some woods darken more than others when they are wet with any liquid—water, alcohol, lacquer thinner, paint thinner, varnish, shellac, or whatever. And they darken to the same degree whichever liquid is used. This is called the wetting effect, or how the wood looks when wetted. So if you want to see how a finish is going to darken a piece of wood, just wet it with water.

However, with linseed oil there is another factor. This is quite simply dirt. Because linseed oil is very sticky, it absorbs any dust that falls into it. And since by the nature of the beast a linseed-oil finish will be wet over a period of at least six months, a lot of dust is likely to fall on it and get absorbed. And when linseed oil is used over the years, this is magnified, and the darkening is considerable.

This cannot be said to be either good or bad. It depends on what you want. This darkening effect certainly gives wood a rich, aged look.

Stain in the oil. It is possible—and perfectly practical—to hasten the darkening of a linseed-oil finish or color it by adding small amounts of burnt umber or burnt sienna (or a mixture of them) to linseed oil. The burnt umber is almost black, a deep dead brown. The burnt sienna is a more reddish brown.

Stain in the wood. It should also be noted that a linseed-oil finish can be applied to a wood that has been previously stained to bring it to a desired color. For instance, maple is such a light wood in its natural state that you might well want to darken it with an antique-brown stain before applying the linseed-oil finish. This can be done with any stain in which the vehicle carrying the dye totally evaporates. These are stains based in water, alcohol, lacquer thinner or paint thinner, or turpentine. (These last two are usually called "penetrating oil stains.") The exceptions are any stains that contain a sealer or wax (sealer stains, varnish stains, Minwax) that will block the penetration of the oil into the pores of the wood.

Minwax Except for the limited number of colors that it comes in, Minwax (a trade name) is an excellent, easy finish for wood, especially paneling. As it does not have much body, it can best be described as a sealer stain. It soaks into the surface of the wood, sealing it so it will hold a wax or polish on the surface—and stains the wood at the same time, of course. This is obviously easy to do. Just brush the stuff on, let it soak in for fifteen minutes, and wipe any excess off with a dry cloth. Of course, this must be done to bare wood, sanded smooth.

You can apply a second coat of Minwax for a richer effect of the stain, but it never builds up body. To do this, apply shellac over the Minwax, and then varnish over the shellac. You cannot varnish directly over Minwax. A coat of shellac must come first, or the varnish will not dry properly.

As I said above, the Minwax colors are good wood colors, but rather toned down. If you like one, fine. However, they can be "doctored" by the addition of colors ground in oil, which like the Minwax comes from a paint store. See listing for *colors ground in oil* in section on STAINING.

oil finish The only oil used in finishing furniture is *linseed oil,* for which see listing above. The mineral or lubricating oils darken wood and bring out the grain, but never dry, and stay oily to the touch.

rubbing down This is the process of polishing the surface of a finish with a fine abrasive. The why and how-to of the process are discussed in the listing above for *dull glow*.

sanding Most finishers reserve all their sandpaper for smoothing the raw wood. Sanding finishes with very fine paper can be done under factory conditions or by a very skilled operator. See discussion in listing above for *dull glow*.

As to sanding wood, in the process of *re*finishing this is avoided if possible, first, because it is a lot of work. In the

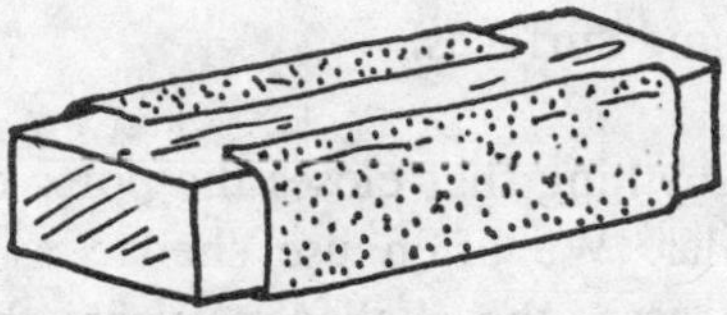

SANDING BLOCK— Saves paper,
Makes sanding faster and safer.

case of antiques, a second reason is that it destroys the old look or "patina" of the wood.

Nevertheless, there are times when we can't get out of sanding, and this is when the wood is badly pitted or scarred in one way or another. Then the best thing to have is a belt sander, but these cost sixty dollars. They are much better than the oscillating sanders, because the grit travels in a straight line. Thus, as you always sand with the grain, any small surface scratches are not apparent to the eye. The oscillating sanders make small circular scratches that you don't see until you apply the stain, and then you have to sand all over again.

Naturally, no one is going to buy a mechanical sander for just an occasional job. You can save too much money doing the job by hand. Start with rough paper to "cut down" the surface as far as you need to. Then smooth this with medium paper, and finally with fine paper. Then give a final rub with 000 steel wool.

It is important not to try to use ordinary, tan sandpaper. You get much more cutting strength as well as much longer life per sheet out of the reddish-orange or "garnet" paper, also called "cabinet" paper. Once you've tried it, in spite of its higher cost you will wonder why they still make the other kind.

Another important thing about sanding is that you will get far more mileage and better cutting out of your garnet paper if you wrap quarter-sheets around a small block of wood. The paper lasts much longer. Of course, this can't be done on turnings and round surfaces.

sealer finish Anything that closes the pores of the wood can be called a sealer. We often use shellac as a sealer under varnish. In this case, the shellac prevents the varnish from penetrating the wood, therefore keeps it floating on the surface to give us a finish with body.

But in recent years a product has come onto the market that is called "sealer" or "penetrating sealer" in its own right. This is a mixture of oils and resins—for drying—that is similar to varnish, except that because of the particular oils used, it will penetrate into the surface fibers of the wood far more than varnish will. Once in the surface fibers, it dries hard. This gives the wood a tough, wearable surface without any coating film on it.

This mixture comes clear and with stains already in it—when it is called "sealer stain"—and is widely sold for use on floors. But the same product also works beautifully on furniture. The sealers sold for use on furniture, in other words, are the same product as those sold for use on floors.

Because of its dullness, and the fact that it is cheap and easy to apply, this finish is being used more and more on furniture of modern design. But it is, of course, excellent for antique furniture.

After the sealer has sunk in for fifteen minutes, wipe off

with a dry cloth any that hasn't penetrated the wood. Next day rub it down with 000 steel wool, and wax it. See listing above for *dull glow*.

For better wearing qualities, you can varnish over a sealer. Just steel-wool it, varnish, rub down with steel wool again, and then wax. Shellac will go on top of sealer, of course, but is such a poor-wearing finish that there isn't any point to it.

sealer stain This is simply a *sealer finish*, for which see listing above, to which a stain has been added so that you can stain and seal the wood at the same time. They are very satisfactory, and the easiest of all finishes to apply. They come in all the standard wood colors, and are usually sold for floors but work fine on furniture. Apply the same way as described in listing for *sealer finish*. When you first apply sealer stain to some porous woods, the result may look very blotchy, but don't worry about this as the color will even out as the sealer dries. As with clear sealers, you can also shellac or varnish over sealer stains, and a sealer stain with varnish over it is an excellent two-application finish for table tops. None better.

shellac finish Shellac is not only the beginner's finish, it is basic to all finishing. This is because:

(1) Shellac is a perfectly good finish for everything except table tops or other work surfaces. So the common procedure is to finish the piece in shellac, then put a coat of varnish over the top for added protection. (See introduction to this section.)

(2) Shellac is used to seal any stain that has been applied to the wood, which is necessary before applying varnish.

(3) Shellac is an excellent undercoat for varnish. A first coat of shellac seals the surface of wood so that varnish will not penetrate into it. That way you can get a good "build," or thickness of finish, with only one coat of varnish.

And here is the time to lay an important ghost: I know that

it is widely believed that you shouldn't varnish over shellac. This idea probably got started because the varnish manufacturers were naturally loath to promote the sale of shellac. So their labels usually said in one way or another that shellac is not a suitable undercoat, and they recommend several coats of varnish. Fair enough. But professionals still use shellac for an undercoat because it applies easily, rubs smooth better than anything else with 000 steel wool, and a varnish finish is just as good over shellac as over a first coat of varnish.

Now for the specific directions for applying this easiest of all finishes:

(1) We will start by assuming that the wood has been either sanded smooth or, if you have removed an old finish, that you have wiped the surface absolutely clean of any removers with lacquer thinner. You can use mineral spirits for the wiping, but lacquer thinner is always the best cleaner-offer, just as it is the best brush cleaner.

We will also assume that you have applied any stain that pleases you. See section on STAINING.

(2) To do a chest of drawers or a drop-leaf table, for instance, you will need about a cup of shellac and a cup of denatured alcohol. (It makes no difference whether the shellac is called "three-pound cut" or "four-pound cut." This is an obscurity that some "experts" like to dwell on, but it really makes no difference. Forget I even mentioned it.)

Pour these two solutions into a soup bowl, and stir with a clean brush.

(3) Apply the shellac to a section at a time—that is to say, the leaf or center of a table, the side of a chest, etc. Cover the surface you are working on as quickly as possible. Smooth it out with a few quick strokes, and then *let it alone*. Don't try to get the brushing perfect, as this doesn't matter, and the shellac will start drying under your brush.

If you are brand-new at this sort of thing, don't brush anything onto vertical surfaces. If you want to do the side of a chest of drawers, turn it so the side is up and level.

(I know I said shellac was easy, and it is easy. I'm just trying to think of every possible thing you could do wrong—or that will help the real novice.)

(4) In a warm room, shellac is often completely dry in an hour—and you should be working in a warm dry room anyway. If you work in damp air, shellac—being anhydrous—will absorb moisture from the air, and turn white. In case you *have* to work in dampness, thin the shellac with lacquer thinner instead of alcohol. Then it won't turn white. It may take twenty-four hours to dry in the damp air, but it won't turn white. Don't ask me why. I don't have the slightest idea, but it works.

(5) After the shellac is dry, rub it down with 000-grade steel wool. See listing for *dull glow,* above. Apply a second coat the same way as the first, and when dry, rub down with steel wool. Some people apply a third coat, but you won't notice much difference.

(6) After final steel-wooling, wax, and there you are.

If you want to apply a coat of varnish to the top of your piece, see listing for *varnish finish,* below.

spirit varnish An old-timers' name for shellac, based on the fact that shellac dissolves in alcohol, which was called—as it sometimes still is—"spirits."

spraying Any finish can be sprayed, and it is always considerably faster than brushing. But don't waste your time or money with the small self-contained spray guns. They simply don't have the power to spray any but the thinnest liquids. Every finisher I know has tried them and given up. You simply have to invest in about sixty dollars' worth of equipment. One of the best-known and most widely sold spraying outfits is called the Speedy-Sprayer, and both Montgomery Ward and Sears Roebuck have very good basic outfits.

The only trouble with spraying is that it's something like riding a bicycle. You have to learn how by practice. And it is just as impossible to tell someone how to use a spray gun without having one in hand as it is to tell someone how to ride a bike. The only way to learn how to use one is to get one and try it out for a couple of evenings. It's not really hard, but—like riding a bike—you have to get the "feel" of it.

As to specific directions for filling, thinning, mixing, and so forth, these naturally come with each gun.

steel wool The basic material for "polishing" finishes as a last step before waxing. See listing above for *dull glow*.

tack rag This is another subject dwelt upon at length in popular craft magazines. However, I've yet to see a professional finisher that bothered with one.

The idea is that you wet a rag—preferably cheesecloth—with varnish, then squeeze it out. You keep this in a tightly closed jar so that the varnish won't dry out, but stays sticky. This rag is then used—after you take it out of the jar, of course—to wipe a surface free of dust before applying any coat of finish.

Well, yes, it works. But so does dusting the piece well with a dry cloth, or just dampening a cloth with mineral spirits or turpentine.

varnish finish In spite of all the old wives' tales about how hard varnishing is, it can be very easy. The only trouble is that first you have to forget every single thing you have ever heard or read on the subject. I won't go so far as to say that it's all lies, lies, lies. But there certainly has been more misinformation published on this subject than on any other I know of.

For instance, one of the first things you hear about varnish is that you must never shake the can, because this will make bubbles in it. And the second is that you have to "flow" the varnish on carefully. Well, I believed this sort of thing, too, until one day I stopped in at Cranston Howe's boatyard over on Lake Bomosene. There was a lad there about eighty-two years old who had been varnishing the transoms of boats for the last sixty years, turning out a job as smooth as silk every time. And do you know what he was doing? He was pushing his brush into an old pail that was crusted an inch thick with dried varnish. Then he didn't wipe the sides of his brush against the edge of the can (another bugaboo), but slapped his dripping brush against the mahogany and brushed away with short cross-strokes so hard that he actually worked up a lather. When he had evenly spread the varnish over the surface, he stroked it lightly once with the grain of the wood, and climbed down from the low scaffold on which he had been standing.

Naturally, I asked him some questions, and got him to talk about the performance I had just witnessed. "The secret is," he said, "that you always thin varnish with a couple of dollops of thinner." (This turned out to be about one part mineral spirits to seven or eight parts of varnish.) "Then," he went on, "you have to really scrub it in, because this stiffens the varnish so it won't sag. And the bubbles disappear because you thin the varnish."

So I went home and experimented, and by gosh if the old fellow wasn't right. Now—about five hundred experiments later—my working procedure boils down to the following steps, and if you follow at least half of them, I don't see how an eight-year-old could botch the job. And if you're eight years old, you should be out playing marbles, anyway.

(1) Prepare the surface of the wood. It should obviously be clean and dry. Not quite so obvious is that the temperature of the room—and of the piece you are working on—should be about seventy degrees Fahrenheit.

(2) Whether you have stained the surface or not, start out by applying a sealer coat of shellac. Always buy shellac in small quantities so it will be fresh. Thin it with an equal amount of denatured alcohol. For the average piece of furniture, mix about a cup of each in a soup bowl. Brush this on

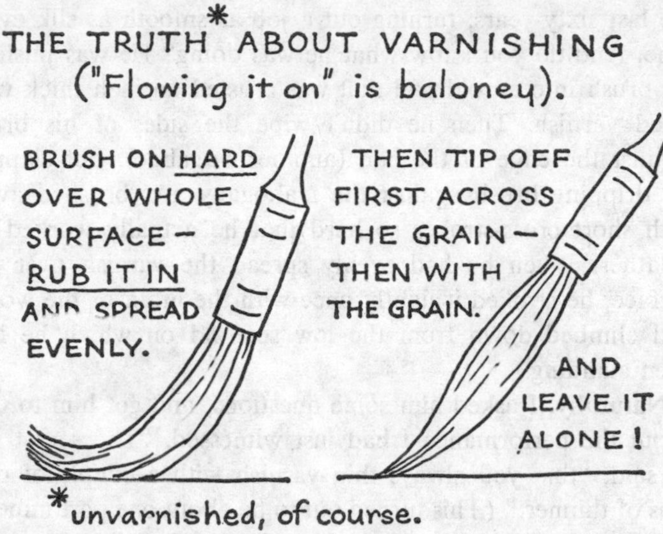

with an inexpensive, clean or new, two-inch brush. (See instructions above for *shellac finish.*)

THE TRUTH* ABOUT VARNISHING
("Flowing it on" is baloney).
BRUSH ON HARD OVER WHOLE SURFACE— RUB IT IN AND SPREAD EVENLY.
THEN TIP OFF FIRST ACROSS THE GRAIN— THEN WITH THE GRAIN.
AND LEAVE IT ALONE!
*unvarnished, of course.

(3) After the shellac is dry—overnight—rub down with 000-grade steel wool for a silky-smooth surface. Dust this well, and you are ready to apply the varnish.

(4) What varnish you use is not very important so long as it isn't spar varnish. (See introduction to this section.) If the label says the varnish is for furniture, that's fine. If it is for floors, that is just as good. Don't worry about these varnishes being "glossy," because you can make them dull or soft or "satin," or whatever you want to call it. That's the last step, below.

(5) Quantity needed and thinning: buy varnish in the smallest quantities you can, because it spoils once the can has been opened. A half pint (one cup) is enough for two coats on the average piece of furniture after you have thinned it by adding about three tablespoons of mineral spirits.

Very few people want more than one coat of varnish on

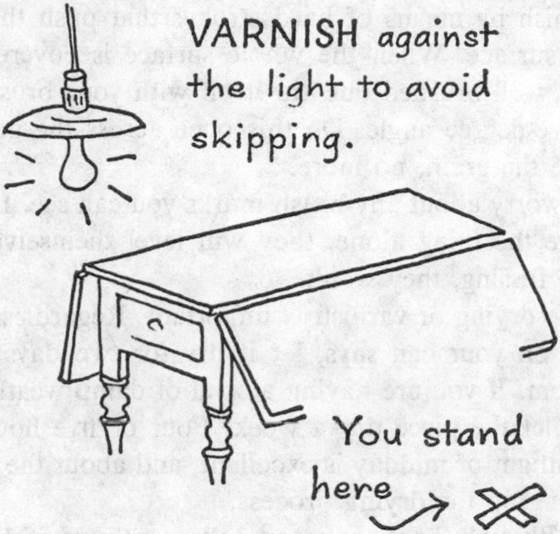
VARNISH against
the light to avoid
skipping.
You stand
here

furniture—because there is no advantage to more than one. If something is alcohol-proof, it's alcohol-proof, and two coats aren't any more alcohol-proof than one is. When you want a thick or "built-up" finish, simply apply two or three coats of shellac before the top one of varnish.

(6) Brushing the varnish on is done with any clean two-inch brush. The expensive ones don't work any better than the cheap ones, so save your money. The important thing is that the brush be clean, which means that immediately after the last time you used it, you rinsed it out in mineral spirits, then lacquer thinner, and finally washed it with Lestoil and water. It is usually less trouble to buy a cheap new brush for each varnishing job, and after one such use, you demote it to painting.

(7) Always work in a good bright light to avoid skipping small areas, which is easier to do with varnish than any other finish.

(8) Work on one section of a piece at a time: a single drawer front, the leaf of a table, the side of a chest, etc.

First, get the whole surface you are working on wet down with varnish by means of hard strokes that push the varnish onto the surface. When the whole surface is covered with a thin coat, well brushed out, tip it off with your brush held at a forty-five-degree angle. Do this once across the grain, then once with the grain, no more.

Don't worry about any brush marks you can see. If you will now leave the thing alone, they will level themselves out. If you keep fussing, they won't.

(9) The drying of varnish is important. Regardless of what the label on your can says, let it dry for two days in a dry warm room. If you are having a spell of damp weather in the summer, let the piece dry a week. Four or five hours in the direct sunlight of midday is excellent, and about the only way of speeding up the drying process.

(10) Although there are some dull or satin varnishes on the market, they only speed up the job of dulling the finish. The safest way to do this is with steel wool. See listing at the beginning of this section for *dull glow*.

That's all. It's easy.

varnish stain A number of paint companies also package a furniture varnish to which has been added a clear dye. These come in the standard colors of oak, maple, mahogany, and so forth. And they work fine when used right, but horribly when you demand too much of them.

You simply cannot expect to put a mahogany-tinted varnish on raw pine and have it look like mahogany. It would take five coats, and the brush strokes would show. You would have to stain the pine with straight stain first. Then if you put a mahogany-tinted varnish on, you will get a very good effect. Or you can use mahogany-tinted varnish on real mahogany—if the mahogany is a dark enough kind to begin with.

What this adds up to is that the amateur will do much better staining the wood to the color he wants it first, then covering the stain with clear coats of finish.

wax finish There really isn't any such thing as a wax finish, but the term is used, and means that you have simply rubbed wax onto raw wood. This works best on the hard woods such as maple, and they must be sanded to a really silky smoothness first. This is done most often to turned bedposts.

The trouble with using wax on soft woods such as pine—and on used surfaces—is that you can't build wax up to any thickness without it starting to look smudgy. And the thin coats that you do get on don't stand up long.

What most people mean when they refer to a wax finish is a sealer finish that has been rubbed down with steel wool and waxed. The sealer—which penetrates into the surface of the wood and hardens it—provides a foundation for the wax. See listing for *sealer finish,* above.

Section 9

FINISHES: OPAQUE AND FANCY

(See also Section 11)

Such as "antique white" and
other popular ways of making silk purses
out of sows' ears

It's a funny thing about trick and decorative finishes, but the fancier they look, the easier they are to do. Getting a flawless clear film of shellac or varnish on a piece of wood takes considerable care. But the finishes in this section are ones that are based on irregularity and unevenness of texture, which makes it impossible to get a bad-looking job—assuming that you are using the right materials in the right order.

These finishes—and they are the important ones in this section—are

antique white
 (also pale green, gray, blue, etc.)
blond finishes
driftwood finish
honey tones
milk-paint effect
pickled finishes

I have included another fifteen odds and ends (or cats and dogs, as they say on Wall Street) in an effort to be encyclopedic on the subject, but the ones above are the ones that count, and they are really quite delightful to work with because every time you do one you get something a little different from the last time. And that is the basis of the charm that these finishes have—their individuality.

This brings us to the trouble with opaque and fancy finishes: it is almost impossible to duplicate them unless your knowledge of colors and glazes and what's likely to happen when you use them is at least pretty close to the professional level.

You can do a set of pieces that match, all right, if you work on all of them at the same time. This means undercoating them all at the same time, glazing them all at the same time, with exactly the same mixture, and so on.

What you can't do is decide that you like some piece that you have seen, and that you are going to duplicate it. You can get roughly the same thing, but you can't get a match.

Finally, while opaque and fancy finishes are usually thought of as high-style or sophisticated, they have a wonderful bonus value, as they say in the ads. They are just the thing for that period in our lives when the house is full of small children. I won't try to make a list of all the ways tots and toddlers can think of to deface furniture. But the signs of their activity show up least on the finishes in this section.

This is particularly true of any finish where signs of wear are part of the character of the finish—the glazed-paint effect of antique white and the milk-paint finishes. It is also almost as true in the case of the mottled-effect finishes such as pickled finishes and fake graining. And while blond finishes will show the marks of hammers and screw drivers (Bless their little hearts!) they show them a lot less than the traditional dark finishes will.

antique white There are many variations of this style of decoration, and in fact, some of the loveliest pieces result when pale greens or blues are substituted for the white. This style originated with the French, of course, and is usually applied to the carved Louis type of chair. But it can be done to any furniture—especially chests of drawers, beds, small tables, and old pianos that have been bought for a few dollars from a secondhand furniture store. In fact, there are many small shops that get their main income from this practice.

The basic process is this:

(1) You don't have to clean the old finish of the piece you are going to work on, which is a great advantage of this finish right there. Wipe it well with a cloth and mineral spirits, used freely, of course, to remove any wax. Also with soap and water if it is needed.

If you are working on raw wood, give the piece a base coat of shellac. See *shellac finish*, above.

(2) Now that the surface has been prepared, the next step is to gild or gold-leaf the high spots on the carving—that's right, *before* painting.

For gilding, mix pale-gold, yellow-gold, or red-gold bronze powders (from an art-supply store) with bronzing liquid or varnish. About equal quantities by volume, and about half a cup is all you'll need for the average chair. Brush this on all raised carving (also on edges of table tops), and let dry thoroughly.

Using gold leaf instead of bronze powder is usually considered pretty fancy, and is rarely done even by posh interior decorators. But if you insist on being very special, directions for gold-leafing are given in the section on DECORATION.

(3) The paint usually used is flat white, and usually a water-mix paint. Oil-base paint (interior wall flat white) can be used just as well. And, of course, either of these can be tinted to your taste. However, you will find that the pale blues and greens are the best. They go best with the gold, and the brownish glazes used over the paint.

The paint is applied in one coat, just thick enough to cover, with a brush. Cover the whole surface, including the gilded carving. Then when you are finished painting, fold a soft cloth or a piece of burlap into a pad about as big as the palm of your hand, and with this pad, wipe the paint off the top of the carving so that the gold peeks through.

Next come the possible variations. Wiping with a smooth cloth will give a soft effect. Burlap will give a scratchy textured look. Which you use is a matter of taste. It is also a matter of taste as to how much paint you wipe off. On your first try at doing this, avoid wiping too much off.

(4) Now let the paint—with the gold peeking through—dry thoroughly. When it is dry, give the whole piece a coat of clear shellac. For a chair, it will take a half cup of shellac mixed with an equal amount of denatured alcohol.

When the shellac is dry, give it a light scuffing with 000 steel wool, preparatory to applying the glaze. Here is another variation: some people use rough steel wool (grade #1) with the very purpose of scratching through the shellac. These scratch marks will turn into dark lines when the glaze fills them. This idea is not recommended on your first try at this sort of thing. You are likely to scratch too much of the shellac off the paint.

(5) The final step is the application of the glaze. To make this, start with a half cup of varnish, and add to it a teaspoonful of raw umber from a tube of colors ground in oil (from a paint store). If you want a warmer, more reddish-brown tone, add a very small amount of burnt sienna—a little of it goes a long way.

This glaze is now brushed over the whole piece. The half cup will be enough for a chair. When the whole piece is covered, wipe the glaze off the high spots and out of the centers of any panels, sides, tops, or other smooth areas. This leaves the glaze in the crevices of the carving and fading out from the edges of the flat areas toward their centers.

If the varnish begins to get too sticky to wipe off easily, wet your wipe-off cloth with mineral spirits, and then squeeze it out as hard as you can. This will then pick up the varnish.

Don't worry about technique with this glaze, because if you don't like what you did, for the first fifteen minutes you can wipe the whole thing off with a cloth which is good and wet with mineral spirits. You need about a cup of it to clean the glaze off the average chair. Then try again, until you get the shading effect you like.

(6) When the glaze is dry, scuff lightly with 000-grade steel wool, and wax. Finis.

There is, of course, an alternate method for getting the gilding on the high points of the carving which should be obvious to everyone, and that is to wipe it on with a cloth pad *after* the piece has been painted and shellacked.

For my money, this works just as well, and I defy anyone to tell the difference in how the finished job looks from more than six inches away. The technique for doing this is to wipe the gild on with a pad of soft cloth about two inches square. You will get the gold on exactly the same raised areas as are exposed when you wipe the paint off. And there is a definite advantage in this for the beginner. If you get too much gold on the carving, you can wipe it off with a cloth wet with mineral spirits, and try again until you get the exact effect you want.

black finish See listing for *black* in section on DECORATION.

blond finish Contrary to popular belief (to coin a phrase) blond finishes are not the result of bleaching, but of rubbing pale-yellow or tannish paint onto finely sanded wood before applying the finish.

(When the wood is obviously bleached and no pale opaque pigment is on it, you don't say it has a blond finish, but call it "bleached wood, finished naturally.")

The technique for getting such a finish is easy, and as discussed in the introduction, it is a finish that shows wear and tear a lot less than the traditional stained wood, finished clear.

To begin with you have to start with raw wood, fine-sanded to satiny smoothness.

For the pigment, use ordinary interior flat, oil-base paint, which thins with either turpentine or mineral spirits. For a dining-room table, say, you will only need about a cup of paint and a cup of mineral spirits (or turp) to thin it with. It is best to start with white paint and tint it with colors ground in oil, also from the paint store. The colors you use are raw umber, raw sienna, and yellow. The best of the yellows is "chrome yellow, light," but any chrome yellow will do.

If you start with a pale-yellow paint, all you will have to do is add the raw umber to it, doing this at the rate of a quarter of a teaspoon at a time until you have the shade you want, or one that matches some other blond piece.

This thin mixture of paint and mineral spirits is then brushed on the wood, and immediately wiped off with a dry cloth. The "blonder" you want the finish, the less hard you wipe.

Let this pigment dry for six hours, and then apply a sealer coat of shellac. After the shellac is dry, you can apply more shellac, lacquer, or varnish. But the first coat must be shellac, as anything else tends to pull the pigment off the surface of the wood.

Directions for applying shellac, lacquer, and varnish are found in the section on FINISHES: CLEAR. Varnish is best.

bronzing The fine bronze powders in many shades of gold, copper, silver—and all the colors of the rainbow, for that matter—that are sold in art-supply shops, can be mixed with any clear finish—shellac, lacquer, or varnish. The bronzing liquid sold for the purpose is simply varnish with a little extra japan drier mixed in. The advantage isn't noticeable.

Mix these powders with an equal bulk measure of the liquid. Then you invariably have to use the appropriate thinner to thin the paste to brushing consistency.

driftwood finish This is done exactly the same way as the *blond finish* listed above—except that you use gray paint instead of tannish-yellow. Start with either a flat gray as it comes out of the can, or tint flat white with lampblack. If this is too bright a gray for you, add a little raw umber, which will give you a dirty brownish-gray. Driftwood finishes are commonly done both ways.

A natural driftwood effect—actually, weathered wood—can be made by sanding wood smooth and leaving it out in the sun and rain for ten or fifteen years. But a quicker way is to soak the surface with a mixture of one can of lye to a quart of water. Do this once a day for three days running. Then you only have to leave the piece out in the weather for one year. But a driftwood surface such as this—or any natural driftwood or weathered-wood surface—cannot be finished in any way. Anything you put on it will mat down the fine ends of wood fiber that give the surface its luster.

enamel finish Enamel is a gloss varnish to which finely ground pigment has been added. This is a generalization that any paint chemist would howl about, because special resins are added and each company has its own formula. But from a practical point of view, this is what we are dealing with.

Therefore, the directions for enameling are the same as those for varnishing. Also see listing for *enameling* in section on DECORATION.

fruitwood finish This is one of those loose terms that means many things to many men, so it is hard to know whether to put it under clear finishes, opaque finishes, or decorative finishes. Most commonly, it is halfway opaque, and halfway clear. But you might also be talking about a clear finish on fruitwood, and when you start making the finish semiopaque, you can gradually move over into false graining. (For *false graining,* see listing in section on DECORATION.)

Naturally, fruitwood can be finished either clear, or clear after having been lightly stained with a walnut or brown-mahogany wash to bring out the grain. The other extreme is false graining, which can be done on any wood, or even on metal. But between the two lies a middle ground which is the one most frequently plowed. This we will call the semiopaque fruitwood finish, and it can be applied to either the duller-looking real fruitwoods or to any pale wood. Maple, birch, poplar, gum, and even pine are used.

Fruitwood is basically a pale, whitish tan with shadings of burnt umber—which is a reddish-brown. Be very careful when mixing any burnt-umber coloring into anything, because it is very, very strong and intense. A very little goes a long, long way.

First, the wood must be sanded smooth.

Now, the first job is to put the characteristic fruitwood figure into the wood. This is a thin, wavy curve, but it is ridiculous to try to describe it with words, and if you are a serious person, the only thing to do is to look at a piece of fruitwood while you are working. Anything short of that is sloppy. Or a picture will do.

These lines are made, or faked into the wood, in the following way. Mix a quarter of a cup of furniture varnish with an equal amount of mineral spirits. Now run down to the paint store, and buy a small tube of burnt-sienna colors ground in oil. When you get back, squeeze out the equivalent of about a rounded teaspoonful of the color into your thinned varnish. Stir well.

In your right hand take a tail feather from a chicken, duck, partridge, or similar-sized fowl. Hold the quill end of this between your thumb and forefinger. Dip the feather end about an inch into the varnish-stain mixture. Now simply draw the figure lines on the raw wood. If you have something to copy, it is easy. The trick is all in the feather. It wobbles in just the right way. And the stain is thin enough so that it spreads a little around the line to give the effect of a wood figure.

Let the figure lines dry twenty-four hours.

Now prepare a thin, wash paint by mixing a cup of ordinary flat white paint with a third of a cup of mineral spirits. Tint this with raw-sienna colors ground in oil to get your tan. It will take approximately one rounded tablespoonful of the paste as it squeezes from the tube. Mix well. Brush on freely over the whole piece, and then wipe off. Let dry six hours. Apply a coat of clear varnish or shellac.

For a paler and more opaque effect, a second coat of the tan wash can be applied before varnishing. For an antique effect, add one rounded tablespoonful of burnt umber per cup to the varnish you apply as a top coat.

When you use this technique, the grain of the wood still shows through the tan wash coat, and your figure lines are obscured by it. So this can be called the "fruitwood-effect" finish. The strange thing is that it is also used on real fruitwood that already has a strong, attractive figure marking. In this case, of course, omit drawing in the figure lines with your feather.

honey-tone finish Here is a very popular finish that is being used on all kinds of wood—walnut, cherry, maple, pine. It is especially popular in the better grades of factory-made furniture. It gives the effect of softening the natural grain and figure of the wood without noticeably changing the color, though in some cases the color tends to have a yellowish-tan cast.

The way this effect is obtained is similar to that for getting a *fruitwood finish,* described above in this section. But there are differences, so I will describe it from the beginning:

First, the wood must be sanded bare and very smooth.

Then the wood is stained with a clear stain to the color you want it to be. The easiest stain to use is an alcohol stain. These are aniline-dye powders that dissolve in denatured alcohol. See section on staining.

Over the stain apply a sealer coat of shellac. This is "white" or clear shellac (as opposed to orange shellac) that has been thinned two-to-one with denatured alcohol. For the average job, start with a half cup of shellac, and stir in a cup of the alcohol.

Brush this sealer freely on the surface—no matter what kind of stain you have used. And any kind can be used, but alcohol-solvent aniline dyes are the easiest. Let the sealer-coat shellac soak in for a few minutes. Three minutes. If wood is porous, keep applying coats until it stops soaking in. Then, wipe the excess off with a cloth wet with denatured alcohol and then squeezed out hard.

When this is dry—in an hour—you will see that the grain of the wood is still visible and unfilled. But you and I know that the shellac has penetrated into the surface fibers, where it will resist the penetration of any liquid that doesn't have alcohol in it. Now if we were in a factory, we would simply spray on a coat of lacquer with some finely ground pigment in it. But the easiest way for the home-craftsman type of fellow to get such a semiopaque film on the surface is to mix some colors ground in oil into some varnish, and brush that on. The following directions can be modified according to individual taste, but here is a basic mixture for honey-tone maple or pine.

(1) Surface of wood has been stained and sealed as described above. The stain should be a little darker than the color you want for your finished product—say, approximately 25 per cent darker. But don't worry about how to determine such a percentage. Just make it a little darker, and everything will be all right.

(2) To a cup of varnish, add a half cup of mineral spirits. Add to this a rounded tablespoonful of the yellowish umber called "raw umber" and a level teaspoonful of the blackish-brown umber called "burnt umber." Both can be bought by the tube in almost any paint store. Finally add a level teaspoonful of ordinary flat white wall paint. That was:

1 rounded *tablespoonful* of raw umber
1 level *teaspoonful* of burnt umber
1 level *teaspoonful* of flat white paint

The mixture you now have is called a semiopaque glaze, and it will not penetrate into the sealed surface of the wood, but rest on top of it. Now brush on a thin even coat. First cover the whole surface. Then squeeze the brush dry, and go over the surface again to pick up the excess glaze. If you want to pick up even more of the glaze, go over the surface with a soft, clean, dry cloth. Let the glaze dry twenty-four hours, and then cover it over with a protective coat of varnish.

An alternate method of doing the same thing is to use only a half or third as much coloring pigment in your glaze. In that case, brush on a thin coat, and don't wipe any off.

Before applying the final coat of varnish, see listing for *varnish finish* in section on FINISHES: CLEAR.

japan finish (Also see listings in section on DECORATION.) If finely ground opaque colors are added to shellac you get the equivalent of enamel, except that the liquid dries faster, is much more brittle, and can be brought to a very high gloss by *French polishing,* for which see listing in section on FINISHES: CLEAR.

The pigment you add to shellac (though it can also be added to varnish) comes in a wide range of colors as a prepared paste in cans and tubes. It is not widely used, as the finish is not very serviceable. However, for those interested, the colors are available through arts-and-crafts supply houses and stores.

lacquer (colored) Pigmented lacquer is available only through supply houses catering to manufacturers. It must be sprayed, and with pretty good equipment at that. So even small professional shops prefer to use enamel paints instead, and brush them on—though enamels can be sprayed as well as any other finish.

milk-paint finish Although they are tough and wear well, milk-paint finishes are rarely used except on antiques, for two reasons. They are a little trouble to mix, and, like most flat paints, they spot easily even when oiled—which is something we will come to in a minute.

Their main use, I am afraid, is in perpetrating frauds.

Let us say that you buy a fine old pine washstand at an auction. You get it home, and start scraping off the green shutter paint that some idiot has put on it, and you find that the top has been burned with an electric iron, or battery acid, or gosh knows what. Anyway, the top is ruined. Maybe it has dry-rot holes in it that some humorist has filled with plaster of Paris. I've seen it.

Well, the only answer to this problem is to sand all the old green paint smooth, give the piece a coat of beautifully antique-looking milk paint, and either learn to live with your mistake, or try to sell the unhappy thing to someone you don't like. I wouldn't want to come right out and say that I've ever done this, or that I've ever heard of an antique dealer doing it. I'm too idealistic to have a knowledge of such low and scurrilous practices. But in case anyone ever asks you, this is the way it's done:

The advent of easy-mix powdered milk has made it fairly simple. To begin with, mix the powder with water until it has the same brushing consistency as any flat paint. And there you are. That's milk paint. The only trouble is that now it has to be colored. Originally, this was done with blood. In the olden days, paint-making time came right after slaughtering time. But any handy colored clays and berry juices were also used—the same materials that the Indians used to decorate their bodies. And as time went on, dry colors were imported to this country from England, and these were the paints used on Windsor chairs, simple pine furniture, and interior paneling. Pine that is finished clear is a very modern idea. Our ancestors preferred to have a little color, and they used bright ones, too.

They also used to mix any old thing they had around the house in their paint, especially any oils, even shellac. But this doesn't concern us, because except for the blood, none of these additives really helped the paint, and most of them weakened it. Sometimes, they used to paint their houses first with the milk paint, then apply a couple of coats of linseed oil or cotton oil over it to give it a gloss. Shiny houses sound pretty strange to us, but in the old days it was a mark of distinction to have one. For Early American status seekers!

As to coloring the milk paint, you can use blood or berries if you want, but it is a lot easier to go to a big paint store and get a package of "dry color," which is used by house painters for tinting purposes, and is exactly the same kind of coloring that the colonists imported from England. These colors are inexpensive, but fairly pure and bright for our purposes. So along with whatever color you are after, it is also necessary to buy packages of brown and black, which you mix in sparingly to deaden your basic color.

The trick of mixing is to experiment with small batches. If you want a dead yellow, start with half a cup of the white paint, and add the yellow color by the teaspoonful until you have about what you want. Then add a pinch of black and a pinch of brown. If you get something awful by adding too much of something, throw the half cup of paint away, and try again until you find the proportions you want. Only then mix up any larger batches.

One of the basic tricks of any good paint job is to sand the surface smooth first, so don't try to skip this. Then brush on the paint the same as you would any other. (See instructions given under *enameling* and *varnishing*.) Milk paint will dry fairly fast—in an hour—but you should let it cure for two or three days before "distressing" it. In this case, distressing can mean several things. Rubbing it down with steel wool will give a nice effect. Rubbing a good black mud over the whole surface and then washing it off is good. Leave a little dirt in the crevices of turnings, etc. Mix equal amounts of soft paste wax (mineral spirits will soften hard wax) with pumice powder (from the paint store). Throw in a little dark-brown furniture oil. Wipe this on, and then off. In other words, get the thing dirty, and then clean it up—but not all the way. See other distressing techniques in section on FINISHES: DECEPTIVE. Linseed oil is a good surface treatment for milk paint, too. But not until the distressing has been done. Leave it until last.

Old English finish This is also variously called a Gothic, Old World, or antique finish. Reference is especially made to the very dark oak pieces that look as if they had been standing around some castle for five or six hundred years. At least a simple majority of such pieces are fake, and they are still being made both here and in Europe.

Technically speaking, these aren't really finishes as much as they are staining jobs. First you mix two or three ounces of walnut aniline dye in a pint of denatured alcohol. All the stain won't dissolve in this small amount of alcohol, and some will settle to the bottom. But this way you know you have the stain as strong as you can get it, and as you use up the alcohol, simply pour some more in. Then, with a brush, soak this stain into the wood until it won't take any more.

Now you can put a one-ounce package of black aniline stain, which is very strong, into a pint of alcohol, and use this for shading. Brush this into crevices, cracks, corners of side panels, etc. Then wipe off the surrounding areas and high spots.

If oak or mahogany are the basic woods, make no attempt to fill the pores, as this was never done.

At this point, there will be so much stain sitting on the surface, not completely absorbed into the wood, that you have to be careful about brushing on the sealer. This can be a *sealer stain* (see section: FINISHES: CLEAR AND CLOUDY) or a *varnish stain* (also listed further on). Or it can even be a thin coat of boiled linseed oil. The varnish stain is probably best, because it is a glaze and adds further darkness and obscurity to the wood. In no event should you use either shellac or lacquer, as these will pick up the stain from the surface of the wood, and you will have a mess on your hands.

When the sealer coat is dry, steel-wool it with 000-grade steel wool. Finally you can apply a pretty good imitation of the dust of ages by mixing up equal parts of pumice (from a large paint store) and paste wax—about a half cup of each. Unless the wax is very moist, you will also have to add about a tablespoonful of mineral spirits to the mixture. Now wax the whole piece in the usual way, and when the wax is thoroughly dry, you will notice that some of the pumice has remained in the crevices and corners. For a darker dust, you can add some dark-brown "dry color"—about a rounded teaspoonful. Dry color is obtainable at large paint stores.

pickled finish This covers any finish in which the open pores of a wood are filled with a pigment that contrasts in color with the rest of the wood. Therefore, the finish can only be applied to wood with large open pores: chestnut, oak, walnut, and mahogany. Of course, even poreless wood such as pine can be scratched with a wire brush to simulate pores, but this would come more under the heading of a novelty finish rather than a pickled one, even though the finish is applied in the same way.

Sometimes the wood is painted a solid color such as black or green, and then the pores are filled with white or gray pigment. But the wood can also be stained either lightly or heavily, and the pigment then put in the pores. In this case, the pigment put in the pores is either white, gray, or a lighter shade of the same color used to stain the wood. And the base color of the wood can range from pale blond to dark walnut. I once saw a stunning piece in which oak had been stained a dark greenish-brown, and white had been put in the pores. In other words, in using this finish you are limited only by your imagination and courage.

The first step is to sand the surface of the wood smooth, and remove any filler or dirt from the pores. Liquid paint remover will usually soften any filler in the pores of wood, but if this doesn't work, you have to scrape or sand down the surface a sixty-fourth of an inch to reveal the next layer of pores.

Now, to give us something that we can talk concretely

about, let's say that we have a bleached walnut table that we want to stain a pale brown and fill the pores with white. What we do here applies to all stained and pickled woods. (After we have run through this, we will take up the painted and pickled surface, but read this anyway to get the general idea.)

First, stain the wood with either alcohol or oil stain. See section on STAINING.

Second, after the stain is dry, seal it with one coat of shellac—two parts of shellac mixed with one part of denatured alcohol, about a cup of shellac to a half cup of alcohol. This is pretty stiff for a sealer coat, but we want it that way. In a warm room this should be thoroughly dry in four hours, but leaving something overnight never hurts. Then you are ready to lightly rub the shellac down with 000-grade steel wool. Finally, brush and blow out all dust in the pores. A dry paint brush is best for this.

The easiest pigment to put into the pores is a flat water-mix wall paint such as Kem-Tone. But oil-base flat wall paint will do just as well. In any event, you want the thickest paint you can find. Now simply brush the paint on the surface undiluted, and scrub and push it into the pores. When the whole surface is covered, wipe off the excess with a soft, dry cloth. Let this pigment dry in the pores for twenty-four hours in a warm place. Then if you wish, you can do the same thing over again to get more pigment in the pores. But when using this method, one never tries to get the pores completely full so that they are flush with the surface. That can only be done by brushing the pigment on raw, unstained wood, letting it dry without wiping off, and then sanding the whole surface down to raw wood again. And that is a difficult operation which takes professional equipment and know-how.

To get back to our table, the wood is now stained and sealed with shellac, and the pores are filled. All that is needed is a protective coat of furniture varnish. But even this can be omitted if the piece will not get much use or wear.

Now for the case of an opaque or painted finish that is

pickled. The only difference here is that instead of staining and shellacking the wood, a coat of enamel or colored lacquer is brushed onto the wood. For this, definitely read the directions for *enameling* to be found in section on DECORATION.

After the enamel is thoroughly dry—and that means letting "four-hour" enamel dry two days in a warm, dry place—steel-wool it smooth just as you did the shellac, and proceed to rub in your pigment in the same way. Varnish may be applied as a protective top coat as you decide.

wrinkle finish Usually found only on metal—for example, on typewriters—this finish is a lacquer, and must be sprayed on. No special process of application, other than spraying, is involved. You simply have to buy the right kind of lacquer in the first place. It is available only from professional supply houses such as H. Behlen & Bro., Inc., 10 Christopher Street, New York City.

Section 10

FINISHES: DECEPTIVE

In which we frequently bump into the simply impossible

There is a certain group of people in this world who are never satisfied—and sometimes I think all of them write to me. These are the people who want their mahogany tables to look like fruitwood, their oak tables to look like cherry, their cherry tables to look like oak, their oak chairs to match their maple tables—and on and on, ad infinitum.

Out of the depths of their happy faith in Ye Olde Furniture Doctor, they write me letters that ask for detailed directions for doing what is often impossible, and sometimes embarrassing.

The big trouble is that there is no sharp line between what you can do and can't do in this kind of fakery. You can make a stab at anything, and your success depends to a great extent on how good a job you will be satisfied with.

Let's put this in specific terms. Let us say that you want to make an oak chair match a reddish cherry table. From my point of view, this is lunacy. Because you can't possibly disguise the large pores of oak, and you can't possibly simulate the characteristic sweeping figure of cherry on oak, which is a brittle, nonabsorbent wood (a feat that can be very nicely performed with poplar, for instance).

But I know a lady who is quite satisfied that she has turned an oak chair into cherry. What she has done is to rub dark-red paint on it, and then put a coat of varnish stain over that. And if you don't get any closer than fifty feet, I will have to admit that it does look like cherry.

And she is happy as a lark about it. So who am I to disillusion her. And if this is the kind of a job you will be satisfied with, of course you can do anything. But when I speak of a fake or deceptive finish, I am talking about the kind of thing that will fool all but the practiced or professional eye. And there are quite a few of these. Some are based on similarity of grain between two differently colored woods. Others are based on the fact that certain porous, fine-grained woods (such as poplar, gum, apple, and to some extent even maple and pine) will "take" stain in such a way that you can imitate the figure of other woods.

For instance:

Walnut and mahogany have in many cases such similar grains and textures that color is the only important difference between the two of them. To make one look almost exactly like the other is simply a matter of bleaching and restaining. Sometimes you don't even have to bleach.

Chestnut and oak are also so similar in grain (an interchangeable word for pores) and in color that they offer little problem.

But I guess I've labored the point far enough. In the following pages, then, I will discuss the deceptions that can be carried off with reasonably good success. If you do not find directions for making the deception you want to make, that is because it is in the class of rubbing red paint (at least she did it in a streaky way) on an old oak chair and calling it cherry. Nobody needs directions for doing that. And if he does, it shouldn't be given him.

Let there be no argument on that. I know what is right and wrong, and I know what can be done and can't be done. I'm like that old fellow Paul McCormick told me about once. It seems that this old duffer and his wife lived way up in the hills on one of those mountainside farms outside Rutland, Vermont, that you have to see to believe.

This was back in the days when the railroad first came through, and the old lad had never seen a steam engine. So one fine summer day, a couple of his younger friends (some "boys" about seventy-five years old) decided to take the old couple down the mountain to see the train come in—which was a sort of national sport in those days.

When they pulled up to the station in their buggy, the train was already in, and the giant iron engine stood there quietly puffing small wisps of steam while its water tanks were being filled.

The old fellow climbed down from the buggy, walked up to the engine, slowly walked around and looked at it from the other side, and while he was standing there with his head cocked back considering the whole affair, one of his friends asked him, "Well, Everett, what do you think of her?"

Old Everett pursed his lips, looked down at the ground in front of him, and shaking his head slowly said, "They'll never start it."

Well, that was good enough, and made the day for the whole crowd that was hanging around the station, but just about then the engineer blew his whistle, and grunting and groaning the train slowly started. Then in a few seconds it was tearing down the straight track at about eighty miles an hour.

As the end of the last car faded to a speck and finally disappeared around a curve, somebody asked, "Well, Everett, what do you think now?"

The old boy shook his head as he looked at the spot where the train had disappeared. Finally he turned and looked straight at his questioner and said, "They'll never stop it."

antique brown This is a listing found in a number of places in this book not because I'm confused, but because so many other people are. They will say to me, can you put "an antique-brown finish" on cherry or oak or whatever. Well, the answer, of course, is yes. You can put an antique-brown finish on anything because anything can be stained a little browner than it usually is, and then you put a shellac or varnish finish over that, rub it with 000 steel wool to a dull glow, wax it, and there you are. See listing for *antique brown* in section on STAINING, and the listings for the various finishes in the section on FINISHES: CLEAR AND CLOUDY.

faking cherry You can get a reasonably good simulation of cherry from the following woods: poplar, gum, basswood, any pale fruitwood, and pine. These are all pale woods that suck in stain. You can also get a "sort-of" cherry effect on the harder pale woods such as maple and birch.

As it happens, I have described this process in the introduction to the section on AGING TECHNIQUES AND FAKE ANTIQUES. The techniques are also discussed fully in the listing in the section for *false graining*.

faking fruitwood Here the only woods you can use are poplar, gum, and basswood. And pieces of these three woods are often found in furniture that is mainly of fruitwood. The process is described in detail under the listing for *fruitwood finish* in the section on FINISHES: OPAQUE AND FANCY.

faking mahogany Because of its darkness it is easier to fake mahogany—whether brownish or reddish—than it is to fake maple or pine, or the fruitwoods. Also you can "make" more woods into mahogany. In addition to the pale woods—poplar, pine, basswood, maple, and birch—we can add walnut and oak. Or at least we can add them when they are cut so as not to have large pronounced pores, which frequently occurs. Cherry can also be made to look like mahogany, and the two are often confused.

The staining process is described under the listing for *false graining* in the section on AGING TECHNIQUES AND FAKE ANTIQUES. Also see the discussion on faking cherry in the introduction to that section, because the processes are very similar. The only difference is in the colors of the stain used.

faking maple The only time this can be done is when the wood you have is a very pale one—birch, pine, poplar, etc. And about all the faking amounts to is staining that wood with a maple stain—see section on STAINING. This works on chairs and other spindle furniture, but does not come off very well on board pieces because you cannot fake the figure of maple the way you can fake the darker figures of cherry and mahogany. Just look at a piece of maple, and you will see why. There is a depth to the figures that simply cannot be imitated in a pale stain job.

faking pine This is pretty silly, because why not just go out and buy something made out of pine—it is always cheaper than a comparative piece made out of one of the more valued cabinet woods.

In the case of pale woods, you can obviously just stain them a sort of brownish-oak (which is what pine is) or antique brown. The darker woods cannot be made to look like pine without actually painting them with a tan paint. This is not as silly as it sounds, because you sometimes run into the case of a commode or something which is all pine except for a single piece which is of a darker wood—often a piece of dark-streaked tulip poplar. And, seriously, the only thing to do is to wipe or brush a coat of tinted flat white paint onto the offending wood.

Stain and finish the rest of the piece before you do this so that you will have the color you are trying to match right before you. Raw sienna and burnt umber are the two most useful colors—and just the slightest suggestion of burnt umber—for arriving at a shade the color of pine. After the paint is dry, apply a clear coat of shellac or varnish over it. For mixing such a tinted flat white paint, see listing for *colors ground in oil* in the section on STAINING.

faking rosewood This is a tricky job, and must be done on a pale, poreless wood. Commonly: pine, basswood, poplar—and birch or maple only when they have very little figure in them.

This comes so close to decoration that it is described under *false graining* in the section on DECORATION.

faking walnut Because of the similarity between walnut and mahogany, there is no point in repeating what has been said above in the listing for *mahogany*. All the same things apply.

honey tones See listing for *honey-tone finish* in section on FINISHES: OPAQUE AND FANCY.

Section 11

THE DECORATOR'S GUIDE

Concerning the secrets and tricks of the quietest craft

Decorated furniture comes in two kinds. First is the decoration of the Colonial period, which was mostly imitation woodgraining on ordinary pine furniture. The wood that was imitated the most was mahogany, the most colorfully figured wood, and the most popular wood in fine English furniture of the period.

This false graining was applied to paneling and floors as well as to furniture, and as a side line, some pretty great imitations of marble were also made. This was mostly on floors and walls, but is seen on some furniture, too.

All this work ranged in quality from as good as trompe l'oeil to just plain crude. But by now there is so little of it left around that even the worst of it is good enough for a museum —maybe not the Metropolitan, but certainly for places like Old Sturbridge Village. So if you ever run across any, don't say, "Oh, isn't that awful," and tear into it with paint remover and a scraper. If the fake graining is in good condition, you can sell the piece for enough to buy four or five others that you do like.

Even if the false graining has been painted over, if it is of good quality, there are some people who feel it is worth the painstaking job of removing the paint without disturbing the false graining underneath. Of course, this is not always possible, but it does happen, because sometimes a layer or two of thick shellac was put over the false graining before the paint was applied. So by working in small areas—about two inches by two inches—you can soften the paint with paint remover, and wipe it off before it penetrates through the shellac. You can then clean up the shellac by wiping it gently with a cloth moistened with denatured alcohol—the solvent for shellac, no matter how old it is.

The second kind of decoration was ornamental—all the flowers and fruit, ears of corn, and shafts of wheat that began appearing on furniture about 1815. This kind of decoration started on Sheraton chairs that were being made here in the United States, and the decoration was originally imitative of the decoration that was done on French furniture of the period. It was part of the casting around for anything different that characterized English cabinetmaking at the end of the 1700s. (See section on FURNITURE PERIODS.)

But this decoration soon became purely American as the idea was picked up by cabinet and chair makers far from the big cities where English influence still prevailed. The Sheraton-type fancy chairs were covered with Grecian urns and little strings of forget-me-nots. Being basically agricultural, Americans preferred bunches of grapes and bowls of fruit, with some eagles, corn, wheat, etc. By 1830 this sort of thing was being mass-produced and sold in great quantity all over the country. It was one of the first "fads," and culminated, as everyone knows, in Lambert Hitchcock's factory, which opened in 1820 and closed in 1843. And fancy chairs, as they were most often called, were made for only a few years after that.

In recent years, as they become rarer, these chairs have come to be highly valued. If their decoration is in very good condition they can sell for as high as two hundred dollars. Even those with no decoration left on them at all will go at auctions for up to fifty dollars.

So decoration on chairs of this kind is well worth preserving—even if it looks half worn off. And, of course, there is a great deal of redecorating done with stencils and bronze powders in duplication of the original method.

Finally, both painted designs and stenciling with bronze powders was widely done at the same time on tin boxes, trays, and miscellaneous household articles. These, then, are the techniques of decoration that we will deal with in the following listings, from the point of view of either reproducing them or restoring them. Of course, we will also cover a few related techniques such as gold-leafing, striping, painting on glass, and so forth.

The materials used in this kind of work fall under the classification of artist's supplies, and can be found in most "Arts & Crafts" stores. That is the listing used in the Yellow Pages of the telephone book. If you want to buy them by mail, see the YELLOW PAGES section at the back of this book. A particularly good source for designs and precut stencils is The Peg Hall Studios, Brookville, Massachusetts. Catalogues will be sent at no charge.

> Note: *A number of listings related to decoration, especially about preparation of surfaces, will be found in section on* HOW TO STAIN *and* FINISHES: OPAQUE.

antiquing The basic *antique-white finish with gold peeking through* is covered in the section on FINISHES: OPAQUE, and methods of making things look older are discussed in the section on FINISHES: DECEPTIVE. In terms of decorated furniture, the important technique is *glazing*, for which see listing in section on AGING TECHNIQUES AND FAKE ANTIQUES, as well as below.

asphaltum This is a kind of black paint found mostly on tinware from 1800 on, but it was used before that, and also on some furniture and carriages. It was made by dissolving asphalt, as it's found in the earth, in turpentine. Then it was boiled with shellac and resin to give it drying qualities. In a single coat it is fairly transparent, and has a very brownish cast.

The use of asphalt started as a way of preventing tinware from rusting. A single coat was baked on in an oven. From there it was a logical step to apply more coats with lampblack mixed in, and then decorate the boxes, trays, and so on.

It was a hard material to work with, and a very poor drier. As shellac became more available in the early 1800s, shellac with lampblack in it was used instead. Incidentally, early phonograph records were made of shellac with lampblack in it. In fact, this went on until the unbreakable records came along. By crushing these old records and dissolving them in denatured alcohol, a good black shellac can be made, and still is by many an old-timer. The dissolving takes at least a week in a good warm place—in the warming oven over your iron kitchen range, or near a radiator if you go in for new-fangled heating methods.

black Much decorated furniture has a black base coat. To begin with, see listing immediately above. In mass-produced furniture—such as reproductions of Hitchcock chairs and Boston rockers—the material used is black lacquer. This is fine if you have a spray gun, because that is the only practical way to apply lacquer, due to the speed with which it dries. And it is not commonly available. It's a professional material. However, if you should happen to come across some, you can convert it into brushing lacquer by thinning with about an equal amount of lacquer thinner and adding one teaspoonful of castor oil to each pint of the thinned mixture. Castor oil comes from the drugstore, of course, and when stirred in well has the property of making the lacquer slow-drying. The same thing works with clear spraying lacquer.

But the material used by home craftsmen—and most of them are craftswomen—is flat black paint bought in any paint store. This is the same kind of paint that you use on interior walls—except that it is black. It thins with mineral spirits or turpentine.

The best way to apply it is in two thin coats, as any paint smooths out better in a thin coat. Then it can be shellacked or varnished.

If you are going to decorate the piece, the best procedure is:

(1) Two thin coats of flat black.

(2) Lightly rub the second coat, when dry, with 000 steel wool to further smooth the surface.

(3) One coat of thin shellac (one part shellac to one part of denatured alcohol).

(4) Lightly rub the shellac down with 000-grade steel wool.

(5) Now do your decoration on the shellac.

(6) When decoration is thoroughly dry, give the whole piece a protective coat of dull varnish. (Make it thin by adding one part of mineral spirits or turpentine to each three parts of varnish.)

(7) When dry, lightly steel-wool the varnish, and apply wax or polish.

Here you may say that this seems like a lot of steps before you get to the decorating—why not just paint the chair with black enamel in the first place as a substitute for the first four steps? And the answer is that it is easier to get a good-looking smooth surface my way than it is with your enamel. Also, my way will give you professional-looking results whether you are working on a Hitchcock chair or ebonizing a modern table. Enamel won't—unless it is sprayed on under ideal conditions.

casein paint This is a derivative name for water-mix interior wall paints, and means that they are simply a modern version of the old-fashioned milk paints. They are very tough, and can be shellacked or varnished over—though they darken when so "wet down." In the natural state they have a completely dull finish.

Their main use is as a substitute for milk paint as they can be colored and tinted with the dry colors sold in paint stores. See listing below for *milk paint*.

découpage Just as *collage* means a picture made of pasted-up pieces of paper, *découpage* refers to an object—often furniture—that has been decorated with paper pasted on it. Naturally, this doesn't mean any old paper, but interesting printed matter. Old valentines are often used, with pictures in the middle of a panel, and the lacy paper pasted around the edges as a border. Early documents, prints, and letters are also used. These are often combined with painted decorations or trompe l'oeil painting. (See below.) In other words, anything goes.

The way you go about this is:

(1) First, the surface is prepared for decoration. For this see listing below for *painting*.

(2) Apply the paper with "white" glue such as Elmer's. Thin the glue with about a tablespoonful of water—a little more if you prefer—to a cup of glue. Brush the glue evenly on the back of the paper, and then press down on the surface. Press paper down hard, and smooth it outward from the center.

(3) Wipe off any excess glue that squeezes out, and let the paper dry twenty-four hours in a warm place. Then apply a thin coat of shellac over the whole surface of the piece you are decorating. You can use a spray-can of shellac if you want, and don't mind the extra expense. When brushing the shellac on, it should be thinned to a mixture of one part shellac to one part denatured alcohol.

(4) The shellac, when dry, should be lightly rubbed down with 000 steel wool; then apply a coat of dull varnish, two coats if this is the top of a desk or table that will get much use. Steel-wool both coats, of course, and wax or polish the final one. (See listing for *varnish* in section on FINISHES: CLEAR.)

enameling Getting a good enameling job with a brush is one of the hardest jobs known to man. The good enamel work that you see on manufactured furniture is done either by dipping or spraying.

Physically, enamel is varnish with opaque color finely ground and mixed into it. This makes it pretty intractable to brushing unless (1) the surface you are enameling has been perfectly sanded and sealed with a coat of shellac, (2) your brush is absolutely clean, (3) the enamel has been thinned with mineral spirits to just the right consistency—which depends on the temperature of the room you are working in. Finally, enamel is very slow-drying, and does not smooth off well with steel wool, or even sandpaper, both of which tend to stick in the surface.

For these reasons even professional workers prefer to work with flat paints and put shellac and/or varnish over them to get a durable surface. Such a finish also has a depth to it that makes it look more like grownups' furniture. No matter how good a job of enameling you do, it still always tends to look as if it belonged in a nursery or kitchen.

false graining For a discussion of what it is, see introduction to this section. It's not hard to do from a technical point of view, and we'll get to that in a minute. The important thing is that you shouldn't jump in cold. Preferably, you should have someone else's job of false graining in front of you while you work. Or you should have a good-sized sample of the kind of wood you are trying to imitate. And this is just as true if you are trying to do something modern as it is if you are trying to imitate antique mahogany.

First, paint the whole surface with a color that matches the light tones in the figure of the wood grain you are trying to copy. Do this with a flat paint, and seal it with a coat of shellac.

Then mix a darker color to streak and swirl over the shellacked surface. Use oil-base flat paints, which will not pick up the shellac.

The best way to get this darker color is to use the same paint that you used for a base color, and add raw umber to it. Also try black oil color to darken your base paint. You can keep trying different mixtures, and just wipe them off the shellac with a dry cloth until you get one you like.

To get the streaky effect of wood figure, you can use a stubbly brush, small pieces of rough cloth, a natural sponge, the frayed end of a rope, anything like that. Sometimes it works very well if you put the first streaks on with such a rough applicator, then smooth them out a little with a dry, fine-haired two-inch paint brush.

After the streaking is dry, varnish the surface with a glaze to further soften the effect. In this case, you can make a good glaze by starting with a cup of varnish. Thin with a tablespoonful of mineral thinner. Add one tablespoonful of raw umber and one of burnt sienna. (These colors can be bought in small tubes in a paint store, and are called colors ground in oil.)

Apply one coat of this glaze, and top off with a coat of clear varnish.

floating color This is the same thing as a glaze, described immediately above, and further in listing for *glaze*, below.

freehand painting See *tray painting*, below.

gilding Gilding is simply a coat of shellac or varnish (or even wax) into which some very finely ground bronze powder has been mixed. These bronze powders can be bought in art-supply stores, and come in five or six different shades of gold, and a whole rainbow of other colors. The most used of the gold colors is called "pale gold."

The special bronzing liquids that are sold to mix with these powders are simply varnishes with a little extra japan drier in them. Regular shellac or varnish work just as well.

After mixing the powder in, the shellac has to be thinned to brushing consistency with denatured alcohol, the varnish with mineral spirits or turpentine.

glass cutting Cutting glass is really very simple if you have any kind of manual competence at all. But you have to know how, and these are the simple rules of the game:

(1) Place the glass on an absolutely flat surface. Don't cleat. Use the top of a dining-room table, padded with four layers of newspapers. Don't use more paper than that. It's only to protect the table top, anyway.

(2) Get someone to help you hold a straight-edge, so it won't slip. Any straight piece of wood will do.

(3) Use a new glass cutter, or one that you know hasn't been used much or allowed to rust.

(4) Make one firm cut with the glass cutter along the edge of your straight-edge. Do not chew back and forth with the cutter. How deep your cutter went is not important. That there be just *one* cut is.

(5) Now tap along the cut with the "ball" end of the cutter just as the glass lies. Then pick the glass up and tap from the other side. You are actually getting the score mark your cutter made to develop into a straight crack in the glass. Tap for half a minute on each side.

(6) Finally, place the glass down on the table with your cut-mark exactly over the edge. It must be a square edge and not a rounded one, of course. Now break the glass by holding down the part on the table, and pushing down on the part that sticks over the edge.

If you follow these rules exactly, it will work every time.

glass painting Reverse painting on glass is an old art, and can be a fine one. But the work done since Colonial times in this country isn't hard for anyone to reproduce. In fact, most people find it harder to cut glass—see listing above.

In case someone doesn't understand what we're talking about, the subject under discussion is the small decorative panels found under clock faces in shelf clocks and over mirrors. These pictures are always rather primitive, and have a lot of charm. Happily, it's a trick that always comes off no matter how inexperienced the artist.

The way you proceed is to first cut the glass to size. Then make a simple drawing of a church, a tree, some grass, and a sky with a cloud in it. Place the glass on top of the drawing, and first paint in any thin lines with ordinary enamel from the paint store. These are the lines that outline the buildings and tree trunk, etc., and are made in black. If you have any thin lines in lighter colors, put them in next. Sash in a window, for instance.

These are your drawing lines, and now you let them dry. After that, fill in some larger areas of color that don't meet, and let them dry before putting in adjoining masses. This gives you good clear lines between masses that don't have drawing lines separating them. For instance, you don't want a black line around a cloud. So paint the cloud in first. After the cloud is dry, fill in the sky, brushing right over the cloud.

Obviously, this is not the most sophisticated kind of painting on glass, but if you keep to this simple method, when you finally turn the glass over and look at the picture, you will have something that looks exactly like the originals.

glaze Any transparent coating with some color in it. The commonest way to make a glaze for use on furniture is to mix raw umber or burnt sienna—or a mixture of both—into a cup of varnish. The colors used are called *colors ground in oil.* (See listing in section on staining.) These are bought in any paint store, and about a tablespoonful of color (it's a paste) to a cup of varnish will produce an average glaze. Put in more or less of the color, according to taste.

Raw umber is a dead, cold brown about the color of silt in a river bed or on a clam flat. This is the basic color for an antiquing glaze. It is warmed—moved toward a reddish brown —by the addition of burnt sienna.

A glaze can be applied with a cloth pad, or brushed on and wiped off with a cloth pad. Wiping more off the centers of panels than in the crevices and corners gives the appearance of age to a piece of furniture. You also wipe the glaze off of any high spots on carving or wherever natural wear would occur.

gold leafing This is one of those things that people try to make a big mystery of. Nothing could be easier to do. You wet the surface with varnish and let it set for a half hour to an hour —that is let it get "tacky," or "set" but not really dry. As it takes at least four hours for any varnish to dry, this is easy.

Over this varnish, lay a piece of gold leaf, let it settle, and pat it down gently with a cloth pad.

Special varnishes are sold for this purpose, but any furniture varnish will do. (Never spar varnish, because it doesn't dry well enough.) That is, any varnish will do *if* you thin it with an equal amount of mineral spirits, and brush on a thin coat.

If the gold leaf breaks as it goes on, and it usually does, just put another small piece over the area where the ground is exposed, press down, and blow away the excess that isn't sticking to the varnish.

Gold leaf used to come in stacks, and you picked up the top piece by laying a piece of wax paper on it, then when you picked up the piece of wax paper, the top layer of leaf would come with it. Now it comes with pieces of conveyer paper between the leaves, and also in roll form.

On mirrors the foundation for gold leaf is usually polished plaster, to get the smoothest possible surface. This is burnished twenty-four hours after application. Any rough spots polish out as the gold works into itself. For burnishing, use a soft flannel cloth.

On "antique-white" furniture—usually French and with considerable carving—you often see carving on which gold leaf has been laid, but allowed to crack as it was laid on the carving. Through these cracks shows a bright vermilion (red-orange) or Chinese red. To achieve this effect, the carving was first painted red—any kind of paint will do—and then when the paint was dry, a thin coat of varnish was laid on it, and when tacky, the gold leaf applied in the usual way.

Gold leaf does not have to be protected, but, especially in any piece that gets wear, it usually is. Varnish, lacquer, or shellac can be used. A spray can of one of them is the best because you get the most perfect film that way.

graining See listing for *false graining,* above.

Hitchcock chairs Decoration on these consists of stenciling with *bronze powders, striping,* and freehand designs done with the same techniques used in *tray painting.* See listings for those subjects elsewhere in this section. For preparing the base black paint, see listing for *black,* at the beginning of this section.

japan colors These are a fairly professional material, and are the equivalent of colors ground in oil with japan drier as a solvent or carrier for the dry colors instead of linseed oil. They are used for the same purposes as *colors ground in oil,* for which see section on STAINING.

japan drier A boiled solution of resins and shellac that, when added to paint, varnish, or linseed oil, improves their speed of drying and increases the hardness of the dried film. It can be used in its pure form, but the dried film has little body and tends to be brittle.

Japan drier is used in oil-base finishes only. There is never any trouble about the drying of shellac and lacquer, or of water-base paints either.

japanning This term covers a wide field. Originally, from about Chippendale's time, it meant any painted decoration of Oriental subjects. Then it came to mean a mirror-polished, opaque-colored finish on furniture—the equivalent of a French polish over a painted surface, usually black.

In this country at the beginning of the 1800s it came to mean a baked-on asphalt finish applied to tinware to prevent rusting. (See listing above for *asphaltum.*) This tinware was often decorated, and this decoration was then called japanning, though the original Oriental motifs had disappeared.

Hitchcock chairs and all the other fancy chairs of the early 1800s were usually sold as being japanned, though they were only painted black.

marbleizing You do it with a feather. And you can do it quite fast over large areas once you get the knack of it. (See reference to origins of the technique in listing above for *false graining.*)

For illustration, let us say that you want to marbleize the top of a chest of drawers. Sometimes whole pieces are marbleized, as well as floors, paneling, and even entrance halls to houses—especially those of the Greek Revival period in America.

But let us say you are doing the top of a Victorian chest of drawers.

First the wood must be sanded smooth and sealed with two coats of shellac. Both are rubbed down with 000-grade steel wool to make them good and smooth.

Now you paint the surface with white or gray enamel. Use a clean or new paint brush, thinning the enamel with a tablespoonful of mineral spirits to a cup of enamel. Quickly get the whole surface covered, then brush lightly, first across, then lengthwise, just as if you were applying varnish.

For the characteristic streaking in marble, you now use a large feather, say eight to twelve inches long. Holding the feather by the quill end, dip the feathery end into brown, gray, or pinkish-tan enamel that has been thinned with two tablespoonfuls of mineral spirits to a cup.

Using the edge of the feather, make a thin, but wobbly line

across the surface of the wet paint. At irregular intervals, flick the feather out to one side and, without lifting it from the surface, continue with the line.

You'll be perfectly amazed at how good you are at this, because the skill is all built into the feather. The only real difficulty is making yourself stop before you have put in too many streaks. To get a good idea of how much of this streaking is needed, look at a real piece of marble. In fact, start out by copying some piece, or make a drawing of the pattern in some marble and take it home with you.

When the paint is dry, you don't have to put a protective coat of varnish over it, but if you do—getting the clearest varnish you can—it will increase the illusion. When this coat of varnish is dry, polish it with 000 steel wool, and bring it to a high shine with wax.

milk paint In the early days people made paint with whatever materials they had at hand. What they had on hand most often was milk, and at slaughtering time, blood. Colored clays and berry juice were also used for coloring. For making and duplicating milk paint, see listing in section on FINISHES: OPAQUE.

painting (This listing is devoted to painting in general. For decorative painting, see listings below for *tray painting*.)

Some people can paint anything and make it come out looking wonderful. Others invariably make a mess. The difference, of course, is that the good painters are careful workmen who take pains in preparing for the actual application of the paint. The others plunge into the job, expecting the paint to work some kind of magic for them.

So let's look at the few simple things a good painter does:

(1) First, the surface has to be smooth. If this means removing a coat of chipped paint, that's what you have to do. If there are only a few dents in the surface, they can be filled with Plastic Wood, and then the whole surface sanded smooth.

The dust should be brushed off, wiped off, and then wiped off again with a damp rag.

In the case of raw wood, all the same things apply. You fill, sand smooth, and dust carefully.

(2) Whether you are painting over old paint or starting with raw wood, apply a base coat of shellac before painting.

When you do this over a previous coat of paint, you are assuring equal absorption of the paint in all parts of the surface. Shellac is a sealer, through which paint will not penetrate. Neither will varnish penetrate through it.

Also, any patches you have made in the surface will now have the same nonabsorption as the rest of the surface.

The same thing applies to new or raw wood, even if the surface is perfect and you have had to make no surface patches. Besides sealing the surface evenly the shellac also raises and hardens the minute wood fibers on the surface so they can be abraded with fine steel wool (000 grade) before you apply paint. For doing this, the shellac should be mixed with an equal amount of denatured alcohol, and when the wood is particularly fuzzy, two coats should be applied and both rubbed down with steel wool.

Naturally, the dust caused by steel-wooling the shellac should also be carefully dusted and wiped off.

(3) In applying the paint, we come to the oldest chestnut of advice in the whole how-to-do-it field. Namely, use a clean brush. The only thing I can add to this is that the only way I know for an amateur craftsman to have a clean brush is to buy a new one. In fact, many professionals follow this plan. They buy the cheapest kind of two-inch brushes, and throw them away after each job.

This is because people who paint a lot soon come to see that the expensive brushes aren't any better than the cheap ones, and you have to spend such a lot of time cleaning the good ones to get your money's worth out of them. This brings us to our next point. . . .

(4) It isn't how much you paid for the brush that counts, but how you use it.

The trick in applying a smooth coat of paint is to thin it "just enough." There is no rule for this, because some paints are thicker than others. Also, paints flow better in a warm room and on a warm surface than they do if the room or surface is cool. However, as a rule of thumb, you can't go wrong if you thin every pint of paint with two tablespoonfuls of the appropriate thinner.

When putting the paint on, brush it in hard over the whole surface you are working on, then tip it off, holding the brush almost vertically. Don't try to smooth it out perfectly as you go along. The work is separated into two operations. First, get the whole surface wet. Then, smooth it out. By the surface you are working on, I don't mean the whole piece of furniture, but the seat, or side or leg or top. Finish one such section, then go to the next. (To paint chairs, turn them upside down, and do the inside of the legs first.)

I won't insult your intelligence by going into all that business about putting newspapers on the floor, not letting people throw sawdust around while you're working, and all that.

I won't even tell you not to sit on a painted chair before it is dry. But I will make a final revelation: The secret of many perfect paint jobs is that they really aren't paint.

Some of them are opaque colored lacquer that has been sprayed on, rubbed down with 000 steel wool, and then waxed. You can do this to lacquer because it is more brittle than paint. Steel wool tends to discolor the paint and stick in it as it heats up from the rubbing. There are some enamels that are exceptions to this because they are mainly plastics. But you have to experiment with each new brand to be sure. The ones to try, of course, are the modern, new brands, especially the ones whose labels proclaim them to be "plastic base" or "alkyd."

The other kind of painted finish that isn't really paint is the kind you often see on redecorated Hitchcock or fancy chairs. Here the wood has been colored with a flat paint, over which several coats of shellac have been applied. They may even have a top coat of varnish. The reason for doing this is that each coat of shellac can be smoothed with steel wool before applying the next, and this results in a very smooth surface.

These shellac coats can be applied over any color of paint, but for some reason known only to myself, I have described the process in the listing above for *black*. I mean the reason was known to me at the time, but no longer.

peasant decoration The paints used for this are enamels applied on an enamel base coat. As to painting the designs, that is a whole book in itself. And furthermore, it has already been written. It is the ***How-To-Do-It Book*** by Peter Hunt. It is available through book stores, and is in most good public libraries. I worked one winter for Mr. Hunt, scraping furniture. At the time, he was doing an enormous business. He used to buy late-Victorian furniture from the Salvation Army by the truckload. He would knock off the excess carving and gewgaws, then paint and decorate it. He shipped it out by the trailer-truck load to leading department stores across the country. When he was done with it, a three- or four-dollar chest of drawers finally retailed for one hundred and sixty dollars. But the difference wasn't just paint. It was imagination and talent, all of which he has shared—as best one can—in this book. (See listing below for *tray painting*.)

stenciling with bronze powders I think more fuss has been made over this pretty art or craft than any other in the history of the world. The trouble is that the people who know how to do it make such a big mystery out of it. I suppose this is because if you know the trick, you can look like a fabulously skilled artist even if you don't have any more talent than a matzoth ball.

The whole basis of the trick is that you do it while the

varnish with which you have covered the chair or tray is still tacky—that is, almost dry, but still sticky to your finger tip. Your finger doesn't leave an impression in the varnish, but it sticks, makes a sound when you pull it away, and leaves a beautiful fingerprint on the surface of the varnish.

The advantage of this is that your stencil also sticks snugly to the surface so that you can wipe bronze powders into the exposed areas of the stencil, and still have crisp edges. By wiping the powder into the exposed area from the edges, it is also quite easy to get a beautiful shaded effect.

There is no limit, of course, to the ways this technique can be combined with striping and decorative brush-painting, though the combination work is much more frequent on trays than on furniture. The pieces of furniture most often stenciled with bronze powders were fancy chairs, Hitchcock chairs, and Boston rockers, but it was even done on pianos at one point.

To give us something specific to talk about, let us say that you have bought an old Hitchcock chair at an auction. Because the designs were completely worn off, you have stripped it down to the bare wood, and now want to make it match another Hitchcock that you own that is in perfect condition—or at least, the decoration is all clearly visible.

The process then breaks down into the following steps:

Trace the design on the good chair onto any good tracing paper. Cut the paper into strips about six inches wide, and fasten the edges to the surface you want to trace with Scotch tape or masking tape. Now trace the design with black ink and the finest pen point you can find. The best point is called a crow-quill and, like the rest of the materials involved, will be found in artist's-supply stores. For buying these supplies by mail, see YELLOW PAGES section at the back of this book.

Stencils are made out of architects linen. You place pieces of this semitransparent material over different sections of your tracing so that you will end with a set of stencils rather than one unwieldy large one. You also make a separate stencil for each different color of bronze powder. If you have a red apple, a green leaf, and a yellow pear, make a separate stencil for each shape.

Use the same quill point and black ink to trace the forms onto the architects linen. You can't use the linen to make your original tracing because the linen isn't transparent enough—not nearly as transparent as real tracing paper.

Cutting the stencil is done with a single-edged razor blade, X-acto knife, or cuticle scissors. And most people use all three. Incidentally, don't get involved in this unless you have plenty of time. So far it has taken two hours to make the tracing on the tracing paper, and another two hours to trace this onto the linen stencils. Cutting the stencils is good for four or five hours. Of course, the stencils can be used over and over again once you have them. That is, they can be used over and over providing you wash them with Carbona or a similar cleaning fluid after each use. Never use water to wash them, as it dissolves the starch and ruins them in a flash.

Prepare the surface to be stenciled by painting it with flat oil-base paint, the kind thinned with mineral spirits or turpentine and sold in paint stores for walls. Yellows, grays, and greens are sometimes used, but the basic color is black. After the paint is dry it is shellacked—the process is described in the listing above for *black*. Follow the same procedure whatever base color is used.

At the same time, paint a piece of smooth cardboard black and then shellac it. Or buy black poster board, and give it two coats of shellac. This will give you a similar surface to experiment on as you go along with your work. Try out each stencil on the cardboard before using it on the chair.

Apply the varnish you are going to stencil the powders into with a regular two-inch brush. Make it a smooth, clean thin coat. For best results add a teaspoonful of mineral spirits to a half cup of varnish. Do not think that you need a lot of varnish. A thin coat brushed out well is best.

Depending on the temperature and amount of moisture in the air, it will take the varnish from half an hour to two hours to get tacky. An hour is the average time, and don't worry about hurrying, because it will stay tacky enough for another hour, at least.

Place the first stencil on the varnish, starting from the middle of the design to help you in placing the following stencils evenly. Press the edges of the opening down with your finger tip with the same pressure and smoothing motion that you would use to apply Scotch tape to something. As a matter of fact, you have just about the same adhesive situation, except that after stenciling, you will peel the stencils off before the varnish dries. There's no hurry about this. You've got a couple of hours at least, but on the other hand, don't forget.

The powders are applied with a "finger tip" of velvet. You make this by sewing a small piece of velvet into a one-and-a-half-inch sleeve that fits on the end of your finger. Some people prefer flannel or chamois. Others just roll the velvet or other material into a small ball, which they hold with their thumb and first two fingers.

To see how this works, varnish a piece of the shellacked black cardboard at the same time that you do the section of the chair that you are going to work on, and try your stencil out on this before actually applying it to the chair.

Tap some of the bronze powder out on a piece of scrap paper. A quarter of a level teaspoon is about the amount to begin with, though you can always pour any extra back in the bottle after you have finished.

Smudge the edge of the pile with the velvet finger tip and then, working from the edge inward, smudge the powder into the hole in the stencil.

Let us say you are doing a pear that is standing straight up. By looking at the piece you are copying, you will see that the powder was first smudged around the whole outline of the pear, starting full-strength at the edge, but smudging in only about a quarter of an inch. Then from one side, the powder was smudged in with smooth curved strokes to the middle, where it fades out. This gives an illusion of roundness, and is really the simplest thing in the world to do. It ought to be, after all the time it has taken us to get ready to do it!

Sometimes a larger shape such as a pear will have a highlight of a lighter-colored powder. This is done freehand, just smudging a little of the paler color into the highlight area with a circular motion of your finger.

When you have stenciled in as many designs as you can without overlapping stencils and thereby smudging your work —stop.

After the varnish is dry—just leave it overnight—rinse off any excess bronze powder with mildly warm water and a soft brush. If you have finished the work, blot the surface dry, let it air dry for another hour, and apply the final protective coat of varnish.

If you haven't been able to do all your forms, apply thin coats of varnish to the areas still to be done, and proceed as described above.

A final trick should be described here. Sometimes a colored glaze is put over different forms. For instance, you often see leaves that are bluish silver. This effect is obtained by mixing colors ground in oil or artists' oil paints into varnish to make the varnish blue, but still transparent. This glaze—or "floating color," as it is sometimes called—is then carefully painted in a thin coat over the form that has been stenciled in with silver-colored bronze powder.

stenciling with paint On decorated furniture, you will often see shapes that have perfectly crisp edges, and just don't look as if they were hand-painted. Well, they aren't. They were stenciled on, and the job doesn't look messy like most stencil work because it was done the same way that stenciling with bronze powders is done. In other words, the stencil is pressed down on a tacky coat of varnish just as described in the listing above.

People who absolutely refuse to learn to use a striping brush because the tension of the whole thing makes nervous

For a better STRIPING BRUSH than you
can buy, steal 6 to
10 long hairs from
an old paint brush
and tie them with
wire or thread to a wooden match.
(Use rubber cement or glue to
hold hairs in place while you tie).

wrecks of them, even cut stencils for stripes. This works all right if you work in lengths of eight inches or so; much longer and the stencil becomes too hard to handle. However, see *striping*, below.

striping As mentioned above, striping is difficult for people with a high level of anxiety. They are so worried about their hand wobbling that it wobbles.

Well, like everything else, it's all in knowing the tricks of the trade. The first trick is that a professional decorator wouldn't even try to draw a stripe unless he had a special striping brush. The second is that you always use a yardstick as a guide to run your fingers down. And the third is that if you are striping in enamel or even flat oil-base paint, you do it on a finish that has been covered with a sealer coat of shellac so that if you make a mistake, you can wipe the paint off the shellac and start over again.

Striping brushes are hard to find, but easy to make, and I've never been able to figure out how you use the kind you buy anyway. To make one that will really work, steal about ten hairs from an ordinary paint brush, and tie them to the

To draw line, rest hand on surface and pull brush along to you like this.

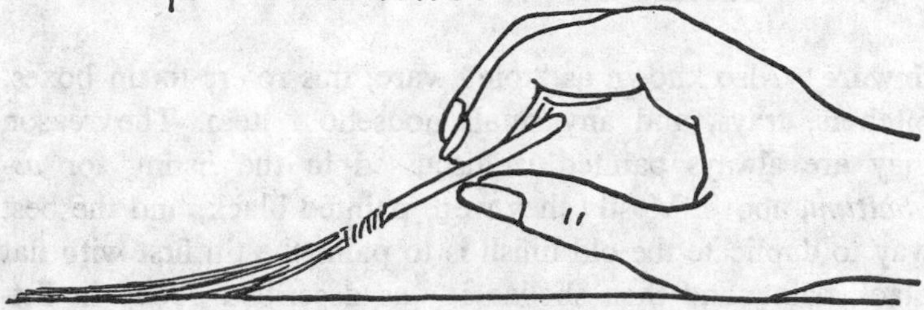

end of a wooden match or toothpick. The hairs should be between two and three inches long, and the more hairs, the wider the stripe will be. Eight or ten hairs will give an average, thin stripe. You can have as few as four hairs, or up to twenty-five for a wide stripe.

And here are a few other things:

Before you begin, wipe the surface with mineral spirits and let it dry. This will remove any waxy or other matter that tends to repel the paint.

It is preferable to make the stripe with enamel, thinned with a tablespoonful of mineral spirits to a half cup (quarter-pint can).

Now dip the brush in the paint to the top of the hairs, drawing out against the edge of the can to remove excess paint. Use up half the paint on the brush with a practice stroke on any handy surface, and use the second half to make your actual stripe.

To guide your hand, run your third and fourth fingers along the edge of the surface you are striping. This makes curved stripes inside of curved edges just as easy as straight stripes. If you are too far from an edge, lay down a yardstick, and have a friend hold the ends while you use it for a finger guide.

Curved lines in the middle of large surfaces are usually done with quarter-inch-thick patterns that are laid on the surface and used as finger guides.

Simple, isn't it?

Or do I just think so?

tinware Also known as "tole" ware, this refers to tin boxes, pitchers, trays, and any small household item. The reason they are always painted is discussed in the listing for *asphaltum*, above. Mostly they were painted black, and the best way to duplicate the old finish is to paint the tin first with flat black paint, and then shellac it—as described above in listing for *black*.

Of course, tinware was painted in many other colors—pale blues, greens, gray, and white. Here the technique of antiquing the surface with a glaze is very effective. For doing this, see listing for *glazes*, above.

These items were also commonly striped, or decorated by freehand painting. *Striping* is listed above, and directions for all hand painting have been put in the listing below for *tray painting*.

tray painting Freehand painting is done on all sorts of tinware and furniture, but the art or craft runs riot on tea trays, so it is in them that all possible kinds and techniques of decoration are found. Early American trays were often stenciled with bronze powders, just as the fancy chairs, and the best source for these classic designs is The Peg Hall Studios, Brookville, Massachusetts. Send for catalogue of wide selection of designs, materials to decorate, and even painting courses by mail.

Let me kid you not, though, by saying right away that there are no short cuts or tricks about freehand decoration. You are either talented this way or you are not—and by the time you are old enough to read this book, you will know it. If you don't have it in your hands, all the instruction in the world won't help you. If you do have it, you don't really need instruction. All you need is to know the tools and the techniques that are used. Then copy a couple of pieces that someone else (good) has done, and you are off on your own. Just don't chew gum. You'll never be a good painter unless you give up such habits.

Here then, are the materials you need:

(1) A small set of artists' oil colors. If they are not already in the set, you will want to add tubes of Indian yellow, yellow ocher, raw umber, burnt umber, raw sienna, burnt sienna. And as any painter will tell you, you always need an extra tube of white.

(2) Turpentine, drier, and lacquer thinner for cleaning brushes. (It is the only thing that really cleans them—because of the acetone in it.)

(3) Brushes. First a set of camel's-hair brushes ranging from #0 to #4. And here, if anywhere, lies the trick in decorative stroke painting: you will also need a set of square-end camel's-hair brushes. No, you can't cut the ends off the pointed ones. It just doesn't work. They are put together in a different way. Numbers 2, 4, and 6 are a good selection of these.

If this sounds as if I am being exact for a change, I am. This isn't something you do just to keep your house looking nice. You've got to be really interested. And if you remember the old saw about a good workman never complaining about his tools, you might notice the next time you see a good workman that he always has exactly the tools he needs, and the best ones he can find. He never has any reason to complain about them, that's why he doesn't!

Now we come to the technique, or use of the brush. Here we notice a remarkable thing. Regardless of whether the decoration is Early American, Peter Hunt peasant, or Pennsylvania Dutch, all the designs break down into an amazingly few basic strokes. Five, the way I count them.

The probable reason for such simplification is that all the artisans that were doing this work—regardless of where they were—were getting paid by the piece, and naturally tried to turn out as many "works" a day as they could. You will notice in a few minutes that once you have become familiar with the basic strokes, the painting can go very fast.

To begin with, use a large piece of glass as a pallet, as you want to work with the colors in a fairly liquid state—about the consistency of light cream. An 11″ by 14″ piece of glass is good. Squeeze out about a half inch of paint to start with, and thin it with turpentine. This will dry flat, of course. If you want it to dry glossy, use linseed oil. Whichever thinner you use, add a tablespoonful of japan drier to each half-cup of the thinner (i.e., either turpentine or linseed oil). The reds especially won't dry well unless you do this.

Now you are ready to begin, and here are the five strokes that you will notice all the accompanying illustrations are composed of:

(1) The straight line, and crosshatch of straight lines.

These are painted with one of the smaller, square-end brushes. Otherwise the ends become too pointed. Never try to draw a line—or any other shape—without having your third and fourth fingers sliding on the surface you are painting. It gives you both steadiness, and control of pressure.

(2) The squiggly or alternately thick and thin wavy line.

Here again, having your fingers rest on the surface is all-important, because all you have to do is rock your hand to make the wider parts of the stroke. Use either a square-end or pointed brush for slightly different effects.

(3) Most typical of all the strokes is what I call the "push-pull" stroke, because that's how it is done.

This stroke must be done with one of your square-end brushes, and you start with the blob, then pull and lift the brush away from it at the same time. Once you have the hang of it, you can make them one a second: plop, draw—plop, draw. . . .

It is possible, of course, to make this "mark" with a pointed brush, but you are in constant danger of one of the shorter hairs of the brush flicking out to one side and ruining everything. This doesn't happen with a square-end brush, because all the hairs in it are the same length, and so they stick together better.

(4) Then there is this variation of the "push-pull" stroke, which is obvious.

(5) And finally there is the dot. And even this is best made with a square-edge brush. The purpose of your pointed brushes is mainly to touch up your basic strokes wherever the paint skips, and for fine details.

And that is all anyone really needs to know from the technical point of view. From the artistic side, it is very hard to make up these designs unless you have had artistic training. It is always best to start with something that has already been composed, and to copy it with your own modifications.

After the design is painted, the next step is thorough drying. At least a couple of days in a warm dry room, or out in the baking sun.

Then most people apply a varnish glaze of burnt umber (see listing above for *glazes*) and finally a coat of clear varnish on trays or other pieces that may get washed. The overcoat of varnish is not usually applied to furniture, except decorated table tops.

trompe l'oeil Anybody who says he can tell you how to do do this is a liar. Unless you're in the habit of selling cover portraits to *Time* magazine, forget it. If you are in that habit, you already know far more about the subject than I do.

water paint Water-base paint can be substituted for oil paints in any furniture-finishing or decoration. You can even do decorative painting with show-card colors from any stationery store so long as you cover them with a protective coat of shellac and then one of varnish over that.

In fact, many decorators use water-mix wall paint in doing "antique-white" chairs. This base coat is then given a coat of shellac before glazing, and this gives the white a very mellow, old-ivory look. Of course you cannot apply a glaze directly to a water-mix paint or a milk paint, because they are too absorbent if not sealed with shellac.

Windsor chairs When originally made, Windsor chairs were invariably painted. However, times change, and tastes with them. Nowadays, they are scraped down to the raw wood, and shellacked. At least, that's what's been done for the last fifty years. However, they have become so rare by now that it would be a great mistake to do this to one you ran across these days. The really knowledgeable collectors prefer them with the original finish. See listing for *Windsor chairs* in section on FURNITURE PERIODS.

If you do want to paint a Windsor, milk paint would be the preferred finish. See listing for *milk paint* in section on FINISHES: OPAQUE.

Section 12

AGING TECHNIQUES AND FAKE ANTIQUES

A shameful guide to some nefarious practices that I am sure no reader of this book would ever stoop to using

When I opened my first refinishing shop, I used to do a lot of work for a lady antique dealer. This is not profitable work, because antique dealers can't afford to pay much for repairs and refinishing. And even when they can afford to, they're not likely to. But it is a good way to get experience. It's the hard way, because it keeps you hungry, but that makes it a good way because you have a powerful incentive to learn fast.

The fastest I ever learned was with this lady dealer, who for reasons of libel shall be nameless. One day she called me on the telephone to come over and look at a cherry table she had just bought from one of her pickers way up north somewhere. So we looked at it. And after my usual protests that the price she offered to pay me for refinishing it was highway robbery, I hauled it off in my truck, and started to work on it that night. She paid cash on delivery, and the coalbin was down to about a bushelful.

As the top was all pitted and scarred, I decided to take about an eighth of an inch off the surface with my pride and joy, a three-inch belt sander that I was buying for a dollar and a half a week from Sears Roebuck. With the innocence of those who sand where angels fear to tread, I tore into one of the leaves with a medium-coarse grit, and had gone about two feet before I saw that I was leaving a band of almost pure-white poplar behind my sander. I didn't know immediately that it was poplar, but I did know that it wasn't cherry. So I called up my antique lady, and told her the tragic news. Her response was depressing.

"George," she said, "I gave you a cherry table, and I want a cherry table back."

I said, "But—but—it wasn't cherry."

"George," she said, "I couldn't possibly have made a mistake, and since you don't know your business I'll tell you what to do. Get some brown-mahogany paste wood filler. You can get it at any boatyard, or at any of the paint and hardware stores that supply boatyards. I'm sure Dick Lippincott will give you some. Thin it down, and wipe it on the poplar in streaks. Or wipe it on evenly and wipe it off in streaks. You'll have to experiment. It's just the right color, and the streaks will help some more. Then, when that is dried and sealed with shellac, use a walnut varnish stain, or even better, darken some clear varnish with raw umber. Then finish off with a coat of clear varnish. You'll have to experiment, I know, but by next Monday I want my *cherry* table."

Yes, ma'am. And by Monday she got her cherry table. It took some experimenting, all right, but, by gosh, she knew her business.

Since then I have learned that this was only the simplest kind of faking. The extremes that some people will go to to be dishonest would make them rich men overnight if they devoted their energy to some legitimate enterprise. For instance, I once met an old duffer who was making two-hundred-year-old chairs. The craftsmanship he put into them would have made them just as valuable as reproductions. But that somehow went against his grain. It sort of took the fun out of it for him. Not only did he use all the usual "distressing" methods on his chairs after they were finished, but he even faked the inside of the wood so that if you cut into it with a knife, it looked aged inside. After turning the posts and legs on a lathe, he would bury them in a mucky swamp out in the

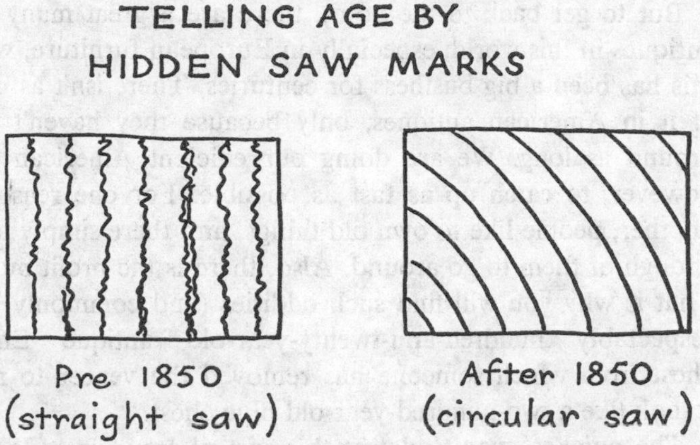

woods for a couple of years. Wood won't deteriorate when it is under water like that, and the dry open fibers of the wood sucked a darkening color right into the wood.

Of course, this man was an eccentric. In fact, an eccentric among eccentrics. Most furniture forgers use old wood. And where do they get two-hundred-year-old wood? The answer is simple. From two-hundred-year-old houses. And not just abandoned ones or ones that are being torn down. There is a regular, going market for attic floor boards. The price ranges from fifty cents to over a dollar a square foot, depending on the width of the boards, the kind of wood, and the age of the house.

In fact, down in Connecticut there is a sort of supermarket for old house parts. You can buy beams, doors, clapboard, paneling, hardware—everything. In fact, in the back-country sections of Rhode Island and northern New England there is many a two-hundred-year-old house you can buy for a few hundred dollars. You just have to haul it away. This is usually done piece by piece, but sometimes they are cut in half, braced, and moved by truck to a new location nearer civilization.

But to get back to the point, there are a great many fake antiques in this world, especially in European furniture, where this has been a big business for centuries. There isn't as much of it in American antiques, only because they haven't been around as long. We are doing our efficient American best, however, to catch up as fast as possible. For one reason or another, people like to own old things, and there simply aren't enough of them to go around. Also, there is the profit motive. That is why you will find such oddities (and commonly) as a respectably hundred-and-twenty-year-old antique Empire chest from which someone has removed the veneer to make it look like a two-hundred-year-old pine chest.

The quickest way to detect this sort of fraud is to look at the way the sides of the drawers are mortised into the fronts. In a really old chest, there will be only three or four tenons, and these irregular because they were hand cut. (The mortise is

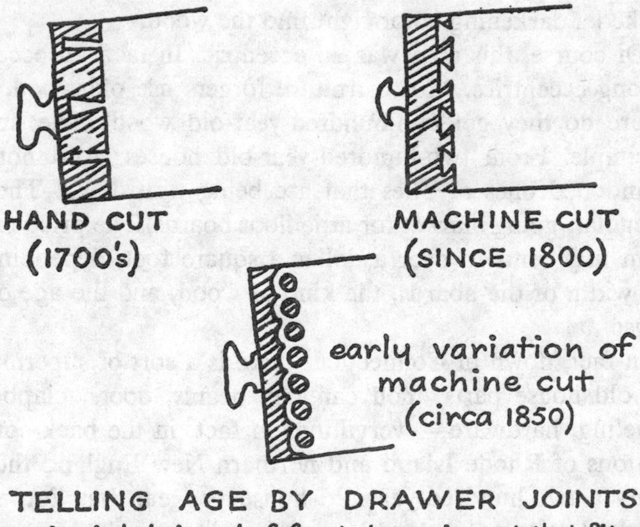

TELLING AGE BY DRAWER JOINTS
(Mortise is hole in end of front, tenon is part that fits in.)

the hole in the end of the drawer, the tenon the triangular projection from the end of the side that fits into the mortise. Hence, a mortise-and-tenon joint.)

By the time Empire furniture came along, machinery had been invented to make these joints, so that the tenons are not only regular in size, but smaller and more frequent—say ten or more of them to the average-size drawer.

All the ways of faking age in furniture probably haven't been invented yet, but the basic methods are listed in the following pages. After these, you are on your own.

bird shot This is really a legend. It's fun if you have a shotgun, of course, and it will get you a lot of attention in your neighborhood—but it is far from the best way to imitate worm holes. The shot doesn't go in far enough. Of course, if you hold the muzzle close enough you can blow a hole through the side of a chest of drawers and say that it happened in some battle of the Revolution. Or even in the French and Indian Wars. And if you have no shame at all, you can get shotgun shells that contain a single large ball. After shooting this through the side of a chest, you can leave this rattling around in one of the drawers. Let's face it, most people will believe almost anything.

burning Combined with staining, going over a piece with a blowtorch is also a good trick, because it will darken the wood the most in corners, where the most real darkness would actually occur. This is far better than spraying dark stain in corners and crevices, because the spray goes on too evenly and makes the piece look like a cheap reproduction. The flame darkens the wood irregularly, darkening the softer parts of the wood more than the hard streaks of figure, just as occurs in true aged wood.

chamfering Wear is a basic sign of age, and the most obvious way to indicate this is to round off all sharp edges. If you are starting from scratch—on an antique you have just made out of new lumber—the basic tool you need is called a wood rasp, and these are carried by the larger hardware stores that specialize in hand tools. But not by the ordinary store.

These rasps cut a lot faster than anything else, and in the right way. It's hard to describe what I mean by that, but they sort of tear the wood away, and do it more where there is least resistance, which gives a better imitation of wear than you get with a cutting tool such as a plane.

When duplicating wear this way, take a look at a piece on which the wear is real, and you will see that the wear is not even—around the edge of a table top, for instance. One edge or corner is invariably worn more than another just by accident of use. There will also be pit marks, which you can duplicate with the sharp edge of the rasp, and some deeper wear spots for which no one can ever figure out a reason. Throw one of these in, or an unexplained hole drilled right through a top, something eccentric, and since people can't conceive of your doing this sort of thing on purpose, you will be way ahead of the game.

After doing the basic job with a rasp, you will want to smooth off the wear with progressively finer sandpaper. But a touch of the erratic is the real key.

chemical burning The basic things to use for this are lye or ammonia. First use the lye as described in the section on REMOVING, but if you want the piece darker or more chewed up, just keep applying the lye. After you have neutralized the lye in the wood with vinegar, and let the piece dry, go over it with rough (grade 0 or rougher to suit your taste) steel wool to abrade the loosened surface fibers. Do not use sandpaper, because it can cut through the irregular dark surface of the wood and reveal the lighter shade underneath.

Ammonia will turn many woods dark without chewing up the surface the way lye will. Especially oak and cherry. See listing for ammonia in section on REMOVING.

distressing In a limited usage this term refers to a stylized spattering of black paint. The idea is to indicate worm holes, but in a way that isn't expected to fool anybody. In the case of painted finishes, they are actually chipped to make them look as if they had been used a few years. I suppose the original idea behind this was that it was vulgar to own anything new.

In a wider sense, distressing means any sign of usage that would suggest a piece was old. In faking antiques, you can break a leg off and glue it on again. You can mash up the foot of a leg with a hammer, and then restore it. Dents in a piece—either before or after it has been finished—are always good. A ball-peen hammer is good for this as the marks left by a regular hammer are too recognizable. Odd-shaped pieces of metal that will cause puzzling marks are best.

Distressing particularly applies to messing up a finish, as opposed to the wood underneath the finish. (See listings for *chamfering*, *burning*, and *chemical burning*.)

false graining False graining has been practiced since Colonial times, when it was rather crudely done with paint on a lot of "country-pine" furniture. In Victorian times, it became a fine art, especially in faking rosewood. (See listing for rosewood in section on WOODS.) Then it gradually became more stylized, so that it could better be classed as decoration. For specific directions, see listing for *false graining* in section on DECORATION.

But in the field of counterfeiting antiques, our specific interest is in making pine or poplar look like maple (or birch, which is similar) or cherry (or mahogany, which is similar). Now this takes a little experimenting and practice, so the best thing to do is get some pine boards from a lumber yard. When you have finished experimenting, you can make a bookcase or shelves with them.

Anyway, the technique is this: First get a sample of the thing you want to forge. Nobody can make up figuring, and you can't remember what it looked like while you run home from somebody's antique shop. You have to borrow the piece and have it right next to you.

Second, find or mix a stain to match the lighter areas of the wood you want to duplicate. Then mix another stain to match the darkest areas of the figure. This will always be the same color, only much stronger. If, in the case of cherry or mahogany, you can't get the stain dark enough, add a little black. If you can't get it dark enough in the case of maple or birch, add walnut.

In all cases, use aniline dyes dissolved in water or alcohol—alcohol is best because you don't run the danger of raising the grain of the wood. See chapter on STAINING.

The lighter base color is first applied in an even coat. Then, while it is still wet or moist, the streaks of figure are put in with the darker stain. This can be done with a stubby, ragged brush or a small scrap of cloth held in the finger tips, or with a toothbrush or fingernail brush. It all depends on what best imitates the particular figure you are after.

The secret of bringing off the stunt lies in the wetness of the surface as you apply the darker stain. The wetter it is, the more the dark stain will bleed into the lighter areas, and this creates the illusion of true wood figure. Controlling this degree of wetness—quite wet for a spreading figure, only moist for a definite line—is easier with water stain because it doesn't dissolve as fast as alcohol. But this can be solved by rewetting the surface with clear alcohol as needed, and working on as small an area at a time as is possible. For instance, with a drop-leaf table, first do the top, then one leaf at a time.

Now comes the problem of sealing this stain without disturbing it. If you have a light touch with a soft brush, you can flow on a sealer coat of shellac by cutting it with two parts of denatured alcohol to one of shellac. But it is much safer to use a spray can of shellac or of clear lacquer to apply the first coat over the stain. After that you can use a brush if you promise not to scrub with it.

The final step in this process is a coat of dirty varnish which will obscure your false figuring, and add to the illusion. This is done by coloring a cup of varnish with a couple of teaspoonfuls of raw umber ground in oil, which you can get at any good paint store. This is a basic proportion, but for a fake of light wood you may want to use only one teaspoonful. Or you may use as many as six to a cup of varnish if you want a dark effect. This is called a glaze, for which see the following listing.

With the addition of the color ground in oil you will probably want to thin the varnish a little to get a smooth coat free of brush marks. See listing for *varnish* in section on FINISHES: CLEAR.

glazes Basically, a glaze is any colored but transparent or semitransparent film, and the simplest way to mix one is with colors ground in oil and varnish. A basic proportion and amount for an average piece of furniture is three tablespoons of color, three tablespoons of varnish, and two tablespoons of mineral spirits or turpentine. An added teaspoonful of japan drier will speed drying.

The color used is usually raw umber, but some people prefer a warmer tone, and substitute a tablespoon of burnt sienna for one of umber.

The commonest use for such a glaze is in what is called the antique-white finish. In this case, it is brushed onto a piece (usually one with a lot of carving) and then wiped with a rag off the high spots and center of panels and tops. The idea is to simulate the grime of ages.

In faking age, this is also done on pieces that have been stained and shellacked. Then a final varnish coat is applied.

An interesting variation of this idea is to apply a fake dust of ages by mixing equal amounts of pumice and a soft wax. Then after the final finish coat has been rubbed down with steel wool, wax the surface with this mixture. When the wax has thoroughly dried, a light dust will be seen in the corners and crevices. This is done more often to European and Oriental antiques than to American ones.

milk paint More Early American antiques were originally painted than most people realize. Also, paneling in early houses. Windsor chairs, primitive desks, trestle tables, and tavern furniture in general were almost always painted with milk and whatever local coloring was available from clay deposits. And, of course, the commonest coloring matter was blood, which had the advantage of adding to the toughness of the dried film.

Because such a finish conceals the nature of the wood underneath, milk paint is very valuable to the antique forger. Of course, the reproduction should be pretty well battered before applying the paint, and then distressed again afterward. See *chamfering, snow chains, chemical burning,* and *worn rungs.*

For mixing and applying the paint, see the listing for *milk paint* in the section on FINISHES: OPAQUE. After the paint is dry, another application of *snow chains* is good. You can then brush on a coat of linseed oil and wipe it off well. Wipe on a raw umber *glaze* (see above listing) and finally use the pumice-and-wax trick described at the end of the *glaze* listing.

This is definitely the easiest job of faking to get away with.

shading Over the years recessed areas on a piece of furniture will darken more than exposed areas. Faking this has been going on for so many centuries that it is now even done in a stylized way with spray guns. But that is in mass-production furniture. For good faking in this respect, see the listing above for *glazes.*

snow chains For use on either raw wood or a finished piece, nothing will give a piece of furniture a worn and used look as well as a rubdown with a set of chains.

Use the chains after the piece has been chamfered and then sanded smooth.

To use the chains—the ideal situation—you first get them good and dirty in a mud puddle, and then literally beat the piece of furniture with them. Of course, you must understand that we are talking about old, rusty chains, because they have a rough, pitted surface that will hold the mud and grind it into the surface of the wood. Shiny, new chains are worthless.

Five or six swings at the piece are usually enough for the dents, and it is very important at this point not to be observed by the neighbors, who are likely to call the police on the premise that you have gone crazy. Then, you will find that pulling the chains back and forth over the edges produces excellent results, and you can keep this up until no further improvement is noticeable.

Ordinarily the use of chains should come after the piece has been stained and has received a sealer coat of shellac—or after it has been darkened by *chemical burning,* (see above). After the application of the chains, wash or wipe the piece clean with wet rags, steel-wool any places that have got too rough, make your worm holes or smashed feet, touch up with stain wherever necessary, and apply a top coat of dull varnish.

spattering This is another stylized form of aging. It was originally meant to simulate worm holes, but is now done in such a way that no one is fooled—or expected to be. Like shading (above), it is thought of as a decorative thing to do, and they often go together. Use any thin black paint or shellac colored with black aniline dye. Then apply this by shaking a raggedy brush at the surface. It is done after the sealer coat, and before the final coat of finish.

A good way to get control of the spatter pattern—so you get it where you want it—is to knock the brush against a stick held in your other hand. For making authentic *worm holes,* see listing below.

veneer removal Probably a quarter of the supposedly Colonial pine chests for sale in antique shops today began their lives as veneered Victorian pieces. All "ogee" pine frames—and I repeat, *all*—were originally veneered Empire. And so were 90 per cent of the small squarish ones that look so Colonial.

To get the veneer off, simply soak the piece in water. Picture frames can be put in a tub. With a chest, the only answer is to have a lake or pond nearby. Take the drawers out and throw the whole thing in. In fairly warm weather, in a week the veneer will practically fall off. (With hot water in a tub it takes only an hour or so to loosen the veneer on a frame.)

You will undoubtedly notice that this treatment also causes the glue in all the joints of the piece to loosen. The easiest thing to do about this is to let the piece drain superficially dry for a couple of hours. Then stand it on its legs, push it into a fairly square shape, and tie it with clothesline while the old glue in the joints dries—which will take two or three days in a warm, dry room. You can also stand the piece out in the sun. It will take a week or more to dry if just left in a barn.

When the piece is dry, it is time to make any major revisions that are needed in its shape. Moldings and carvings come off first. Sometimes the whole top-drawer section of a chest is cut off, and then the top replaced.

Finally, steel-wool (grade 00) the roughness caused by the water-soaking the wood has had, stain and finish it. Here is another case where a glaze can make all the difference in a fake. See listing for *glaze,* above.

weathering This aging technique is used only by the true artists in the game to whom time means nothing. These are the lovely old codgers to whom creating a masterpiece means more than making a fast buck.

However, for those who wish to indulge in the practice, let me say that you don't just buy something and then stand it out in your back yard. First, the surface must be prepared.

If it is an old piece, any finish must be removed. Then signs of additional wear must be made by *chamfering* and *snow chains,* (see above). If the piece is to be darkened by *burning* or *chemical burning* (see above), that must be done first, too.

Then you must remember to put the piece in an open spot where it will get the sun as well as rain and snow. The top of a windy hill is best if you can find one.

A year is the best length of time for the treatment. One summer and one winter. And in the middle of each you should turn the piece, especially a chest, so that both sides get equal exposure to the sun. Also—and this is very important—if you live in a climate where it snows, you must brush the snow off after each fall, or any top surfaces will become too badly warped. That a crack or two develop in a top piece is, of course, desirable.

After weathering, restain the piece and finish it. A sealer finish and then just wax is very good on a piece that has been treated this way. See listing for *sealer finish* in section on FINISHES: CLEAR.

worm holes The best way to make these is with an ice pick or a nail that has been sharpened to a long, tapering, needle-like point. The reason is that worms are not all the same size, and the holes they make aren't either.

Of course, you can use four or five sizes of finishing nails and brads—the smaller sizes. But the tapering, pointed nail or ice pick is easier.

Remember that worm holes do not appear regularly over a whole piece of furniture, but are usually concentrated in one or two legs or in one section of a table top—over one of the legs, of course, because they have to come up through a leg to get to a top. They are not often found in hanging leaves. Holes made this way can be made either before or after staining.

There is a refinement here. The true artist will make his holes with a small drill after the finish is completed and then blow some pumice into the holes—or he can even use dust from some rotten wood he has saved for this purpose. If you think I am making this up, believe me, it's true. I've worked in places where a fellow who didn't know his worm holes was considered an amateur. Mostly this sort of thing is left to the real craftsmen with European training who create the highest priced imported antiques. Only last summer I talked to an elderly craftsman who had been asked to authenticate a $25,000 Chinese screen. He was in a real dilemma, because he had made it himself some twenty-five years before, and was still friendly with the man he had been working for when he made it.

worn rungs This is one of the most obvious places where wear must be indicated in a good forgery. A wood rasp is the best tool to use. See listing for *chamfering,* above.

Here, as in all signs of wear, the key to success is in copying what happened to some authentic piece. You can't just make it up. Rungs—whether a front chair rung or a stretcher between table legs—don't wear evenly. There is always something a little eccentric about true wear and usage signs.

Section 13

FURNITURE PERIODS—EXPOSED AT LAST!

Or, "Please, Mr. Chippendale, couldn't you slice the baloney just a little bit thinner?"

Americans are funny people. In the last two hundred years, we have had the intelligence to organize the richest industrial society in the world. And we have had the talent to produce more than our share of the world's writers and artists. But for some reason we still cling to our inferiority complex about European furniture of the 1700s—most of which is pretentious, some of which is vulgar, and all of which is effete.

Let's look at the record.

When our forefathers first came to this country and couldn't get English furniture, they used their crude tools to create one of the first really new styles of furniture since the Greeks—most others having been evolved styles. This was furniture designed in relationship to its basic function and to make the most of the material used. As such, it was clean-lined, getting its beauty from its essential shape rather than from decoration, and was three hundred years ahead of the furniture then being made in Europe. We call this style Colonial, and because we have some sense, it has become increasingly popular in the last forty years.

But as soon as the colonists began to get settled, cabinetmakers opened factories in all our major cities to imitate anything that was being made in England. When these commercial-minded imitators ran out of English designs (Chippendale, Sheraton, and Hepplewhite) they turned to the French for Federal and Empire. Both the French and English designs were already hand-me-downs, but we'll go into that story a little further on. Meanwhile, masterpieces of Colonial design were being put in the cellar or broken up for firewood!

The final indignity was the Victorian era, when mass-production techniques were wedded to the grotesque taste of the German ruling family of England. (Victoria was 75 per cent German, and her husband 100 per cent.) This ornate and garish stuff was copied over here with the usual American zest.

Then in the Roaring Twenties we found Spanish furniture. By the Thirties, it was cubistic French Modern, and it wasn't until after the Second World War that Americans were even trying to design their own furniture for their own needs.

Of course, in spite of this the majority of the furniture being produced by Grand Rapids is still in the incongruous and anachronistic style of the English cabinetmakers of the 1700s. And our wealthier classes are still buying imported English and French antiques by the boatload. These, of course, are being forged on a production-line basis—as they have been for the last hundred years. This is made obvious by the fact that we've already imported enough to more than twice fill the country houses of both England and France, and there is no slowdown in the supply flowing across the Atlantic.

If this sounds as if I am against antique furniture—and therefore biting the hand that feeds me—that's not quite the point I'm trying to make. I like these things as antiques—as interesting relics—but I can't accept the idea that the art of designing furniture came to a dead stop back when people wore cocked hats. Wouldn't people who fill their houses with Federal furniture think I was crazy if I came to dinner dressed as John Paul Jones or somebody? Of course they would. And with all the world of antiquity to choose from, I refuse to believe that Americans really like English furniture of the

1700s that much. They just still haven't got over their inferiority complex about European culture.

Just how ridiculous this is, comes into even sharper focus when we examine where the Chippendale gang got their ideas in the first place. More of that in our "Bird's-eye View," which follows. Meanwhile, let me say that the main purpose of this section is to give you a series of keys that will make it fairly easy for you to tell one style of furniture from another. Each style has one or more oddities that none of the others have, and once you have noticed these peculiarities, it is hard to forget them. Then you may not be an expert, but at least you won't have to worry about people thinking you're *nouveau riche*.

THE BIRD'S-EYE VIEW

To begin with, there are really only four styles of period furniture that are worth perpetuation to any degree at all. These are the only four fundamental styles to emerge in the last five hundred years:

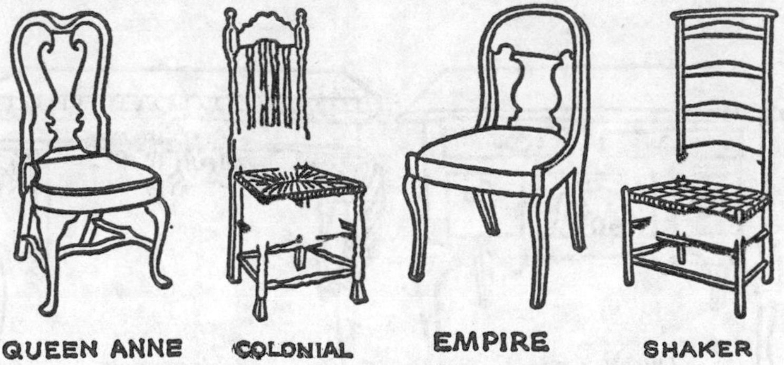

By calling these styles fundamental, I mean this: when you compare them to the other styles illustrated in this section, you cannot help but notice that what distinguishes them is the nature of their essential lines rather than tricks of design or applied ornamentation. By tricks of design, I mean such things as giving fancy shapes to the backs of chairs (the Hepplewhite shield-back, for instance) that have nothing to do with the purpose of the piece of furniture. In fundamental designs, chair-backs are designed to support your back.

It is this nonessentialness—mostly based on Greek and Roman motifs—that makes the work of Chippendale, Hepplewhite, Sheraton, etc., basically trivial.

For the best contrast, look at the lines of Colonial furniture—and in lessening degree to Queen Anne, Shaker, and Empire. This is also true in the rather special case of French Provincial when it is truly a country-made, simplified version of Louis XV.

These fundamental styles were created by new or isolated societies—or cultures, if you prefer that word. A perfect illustration of what I am talking about is made when we compare Queen Anne, one of the fundamental styles created by a "jelling" society, with the style that follows it—the vastly overrated Chippendale.

Queen Anne

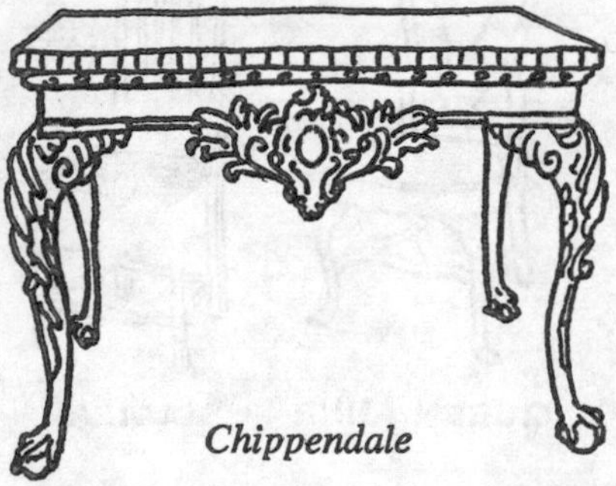

Chippendale

I think it is embarrassingly clear from the illustration that all Chippendale did was "gussy" things up. He was the designer only of some decorations laid on the Queen Anne style. And these weren't even his own, which becomes apparent when we look at the drawing of the three basic kinds of capitals used on Greek columns. These were the years when Europe was first discovering "the glory that was Greece," and when Chippendale saw his first Corinthian column, it obviously went to his head. After that, he probably had more success on the basis of one small, stolen idea than anybody else in history.

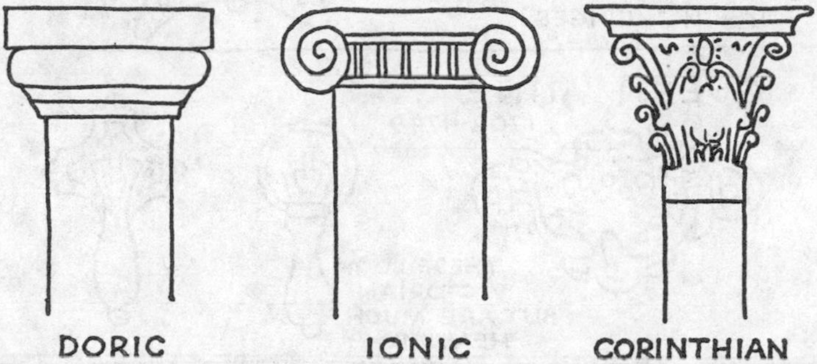

Of course, this plunges us right into the middle of the myth about the 1700s being the "Golden Age of Furniture Design." This palpably untrue concept was foisted on the American people by the antique dealers and interior decorators of the last hundred years. It wasn't a conspiracy—or even a particularly brilliant idea. It was simply that the lumber rooms of the eighteenth century were what they had to sell, and they naturally talked up their merchandise.

The way this came about was that the early 1700s saw the first growth of the cities in Great Britain as England thrived on trade with its colonies. This also produced a new merchant class that represented a new and monied market for the cabinetmakers of the day. These fellows soon stopped being traditional craftsmen, and organized shops employing as many as a hundred men. One made legs all day, one made arms, and

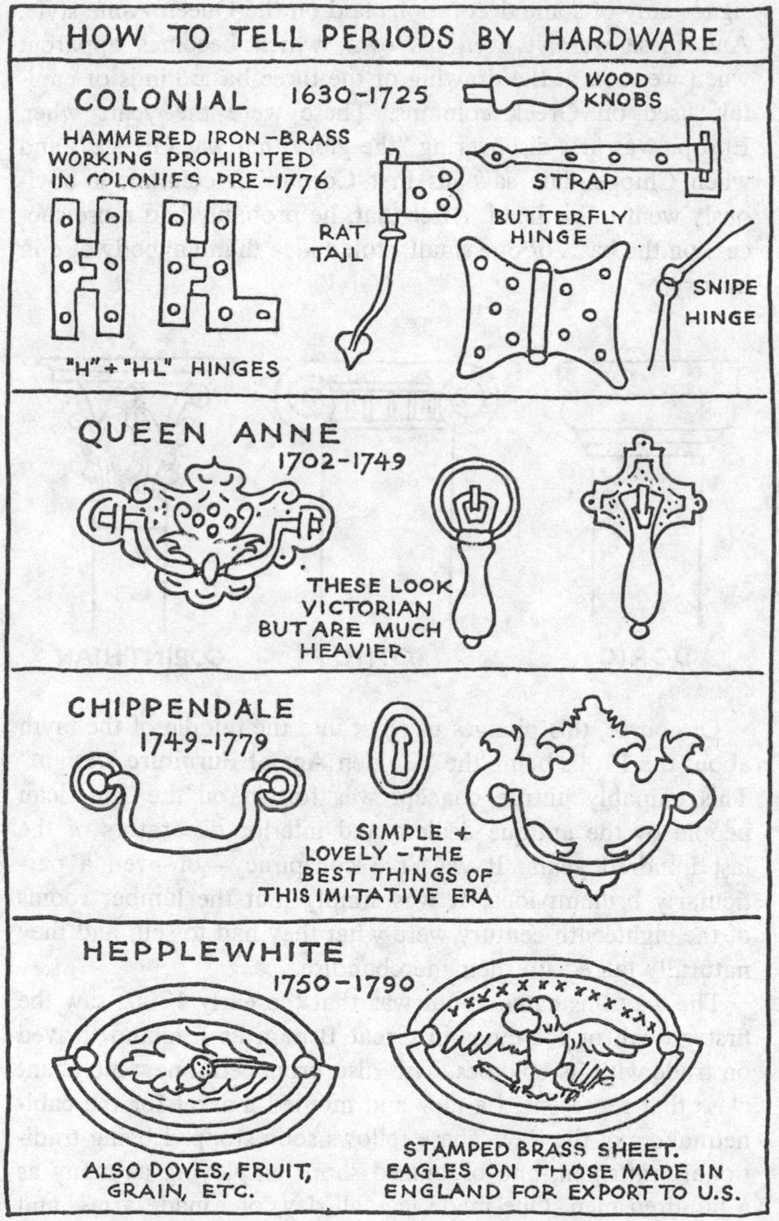
HOW TO TELL PERIODS BY HARDWARE
COLONIAL 1630-1725
WOOD KNOBS
HAMMERED IRON-BRASS WORKING PROHIBITED IN COLONIES PRE-1776
STRAP
RAT TAIL
BUTTERFLY HINGE
SNIPE HINGE
"H" + "HL" HINGES
QUEEN ANNE 1702-1749
THESE LOOK VICTORIAN BUT ARE MUCH HEAVIER
CHIPPENDALE 1749-1779
SIMPLE + LOVELY - THE BEST THINGS OF THIS IMITATIVE ERA
HEPPLEWHITE 1750-1790
ALSO DOVES, FRUIT, GRAIN, ETC.
STAMPED BRASS SHEET. EAGLES ON THOSE MADE IN ENGLAND FOR EXPORT TO U.S.

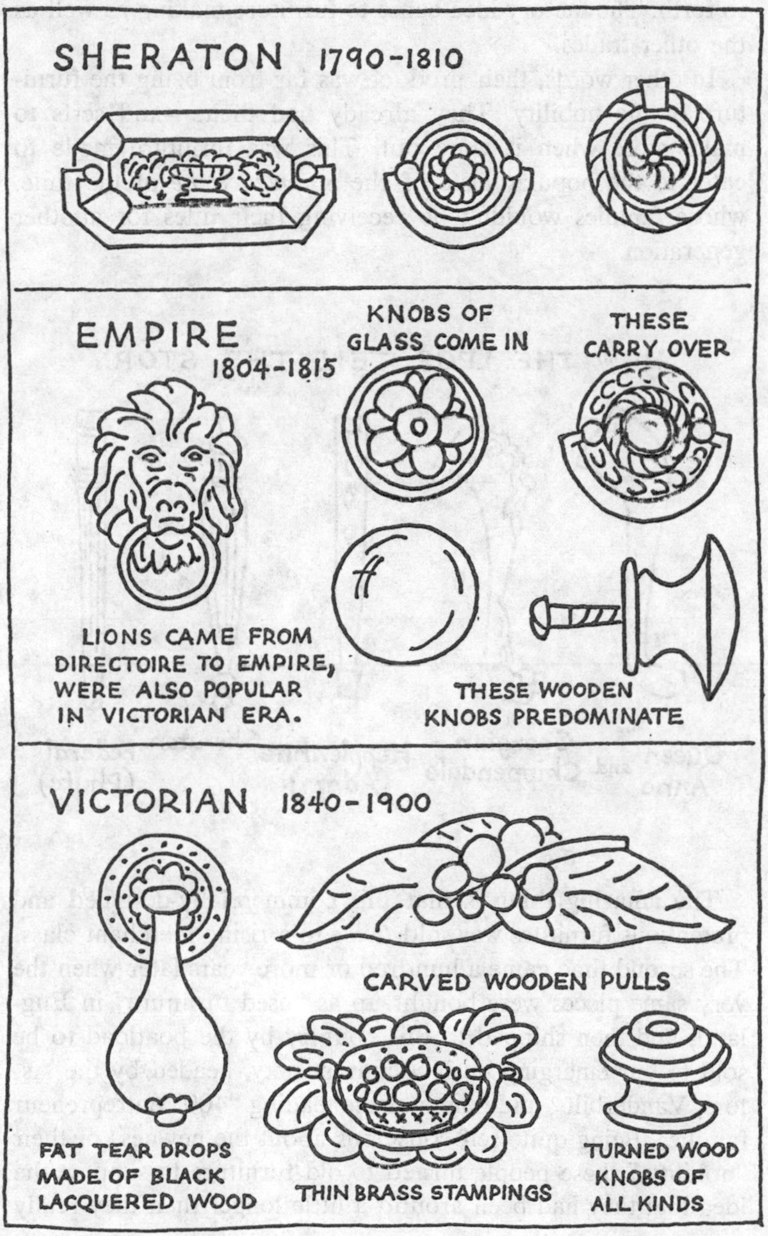
SHERATON 1790-1810
EMPIRE
1804-1815
KNOBS OF GLASS COME IN
THESE CARRY OVER
LIONS CAME FROM DIRECTOIRE TO EMPIRE, WERE ALSO POPULAR IN VICTORIAN ERA.
THESE WOODEN KNOBS PREDOMINATE
VICTORIAN 1840-1900
CARVED WOODEN PULLS
FAT TEAR DROPS MADE OF BLACK LACQUERED WOOD
THIN BRASS STAMPINGS
TURNED WOOD KNOBS OF ALL KINDS

so forth. The factory idea came to furniture-making as well as the other trades.

In other words, their product was far from being the furniture of the nobility. They already had theirs—and serfs to make more when it wore out. This was furniture made to cater to the popular taste of the *nouveau riche* of the time, whose families wouldn't be receiving their titles for another generation.

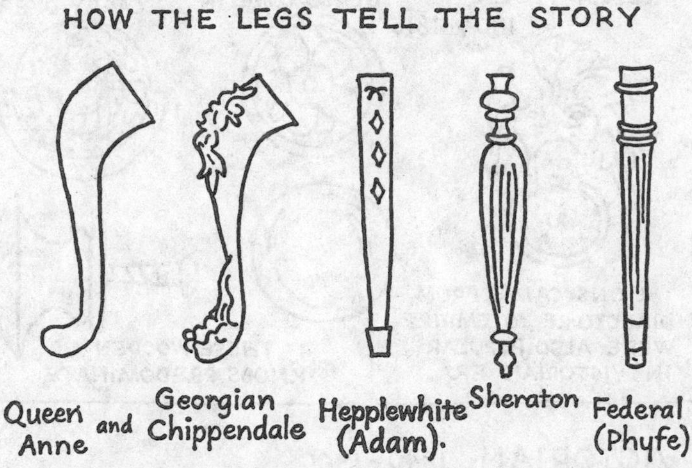

The amazing thing is that this commercially-designed and pretentious furniture was sold *twice* to a rising merchant class. The second time came a hundred or more years later when the very same pieces were bought up as "used furniture" in England, and then shipped to this country by the boatload to be sold to our emerging businessman society, headed by the Astors, Vanderbilts, and others of the leading "400" entrepreneur families. Being quite self-conscious about the newness of their "nobility," these people turned to old furniture to support the idea that they had been around a little longer than they really had. Later on, Hearst would be rich enough to buy Greek temples, but at the time, the used furniture of the 1700s was all that was available.

Thus, period furniture becomes a lot easier to understand if we take a bird's-eye view of its development in relationship to what was going on. In the "Family Tree of Furniture Styles," (see endpapers) the fundamental styles have been put in bold type. Each, you will see, begins with the start of a new society. In each case, the reasons for these new beginnings were different but new beginnings they were.

Back in the 1400s everything was pretty much of a hodgepodge of Renaissance influence on Gothic and medieval forms, with cross-influences by the intermarriage of nobility among the countries. But this influence was slow in filtering down to the masses, who were yet to become wealthy enough to stimulate any real production.

No one is quite sure how the Queen Anne style came out of this in England. What happened when the colonists went to America to start their new culture is obvious. The Shakers, of course, were a strange pocket in history. And the blood bath of the French Revolution accounts for Empire.

When it comes to a lack of originality, the use of Greek forms and motifs by the English cabinetmakers is outstanding, but this was also going on in France. There, of course, nothing much really happened except the application of Greek and Roman ideas to basic Renaissance forms—until the Revolution.

Incidentally, to see how consistent was the use of Greek ideas by the English cabinetmakers, compare Chippendale's stealing the Corinthian column with what Duncan Phyfe, at the end of the century, was still doing as a member of the English school, but working on this side of the Atlantic. A few pages further on there is a drawing of a classic Phyfe chair. Compare it to the drawing of the top of the Ionic column a few pages back.

ENGLISH

Now let us look at the various styles one at a time, as well as in their historical groups. The first two are the early English styles that precede Queen Anne. These represent a confusion of influences on the "tight little island," whose population, we tend to forget, was built up by one invasion after another. There were the German tribes, the Norsemen, the Romans, the Norman invasion, and many minor influences due to the coming and going of nobility from other countries.

Thus, we start our glossary at the beginning of the seventeenth century. All dates in this period are pretty arbitrary.

JACOBEAN

Jacobean 1603–1689: Curved lines—the Flemish scroll—appeared under James I, the period getting its name from the Latin for James. Also, there was a technical advance, in that the carvings and ornaments were made separately and glued or pinned on. You might say that this is where mass production was born.

William and Mary 1689–1702: Although a Dutchman, William of Orange brought a sophisticated French influence

WILLIAM AND MARY

to English furniture. The transition is still gentle, but now we have the start of veneers, inlays, and exotic decorations—lacquered cabinets with pictures of pagodas and Japanese figures running across little bridges. The carving becomes more graceful, less bulbous and heavy.

Queen Anne 1702–1749: How Queen Anne furniture evolved from the preceding is hard to see, but there it is. Suddenly furniture became gracefully sculptured pieces of wood—as opposed to the previous decorated posts and panels. With no decoration at all, the leg of a pure Queen Anne chair is a

QUEEN ANNE

thing of unique beauty, as pleasing in its lines as anything man has ever designed. And it was brand-new in the history of design, too. On top of that it is a practical improvement over the straight leg, giving extra bracing at the top where it is needed, and extra wood at the bottom where most wear occurs. Incidentally, the introduction of mahogany to England at this time had a lot to do with the birth of this leg design, because mahogany combines carvability with the strength that makes the design possible. Also, the fact that the wood has so much beauty in itself probably had something to do with the dropping of ornamentation.

The same gentle curves of the typical leg are then carried through the rest of the parts—still without frivolity, and at first little or no carving. Of course, there were those who couldn't resist this temptation. To this tendency the name Early Georgian was given.

GEORGIAN

Early Georgian 1720–1749: As you can see from the dates, this period coincides with the second half of the Queen Anne period. It is a transitional style which was really cashed-in on by the cabinetmaker who gave his name to the beginning of the overrated era of English cabinetmaking that depended on Greek and Roman designs. . . .

Chippendale 1749–1779: In Chippendale we have the old story of a man and a time meeting. For no matter how else we depreciate Chippendale, no one can deny that he was a master carver. Mahogany had just arrived full-force in England, and the demand for a more ornate furniture was also there with the emergence of England's new merchant class. (See introduction to this section.)

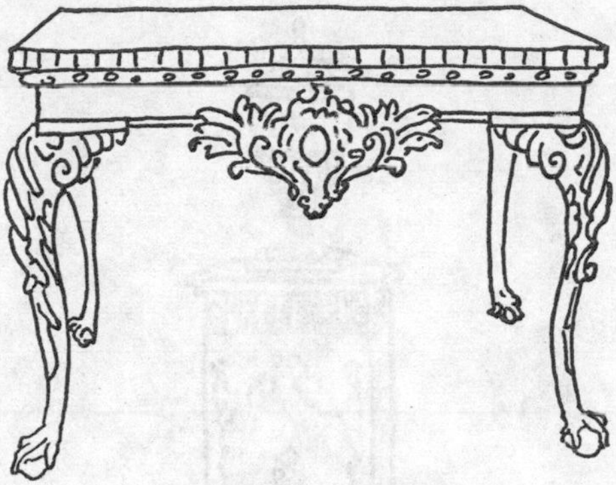

CHIPPENDALE

The best way to describe Chippendale furniture is to say that it is rococo Queen Anne. Here come the claw-and-ball foot, ribbon carving, and intricate pierced carving. In the legs of a typical Queen Anne chair this simply gives an Oriental effect. In the backs, it causes real structural weakness. Original Queen Anne chairs are still sturdy today. Chippendale chairs are fragile pieces that you either have to keep in glass cases or continually repair.

This lack of strength does not occur in the tables and chests, but the most untrained eye can quickly see that they are merely overdecorated Queen Anne.

Adam 1758–1792: It is with Robert Adam that the influence of Greek and Roman designs comes undiluted to English furniture. Chippendale would use anything—including Chinese ideas. But Adam unashamedly wanted his furniture to look like a Greek temple. And it does. The most typical detail in this furniture is the fluted-column leg, sometimes with a block foot that looks like the base of a Greek column, too. Also typical are draped garlands on the fronts of drawers.

ADAM

Adam used light woods—especially satinwood—and sometimes the furniture was even painted white. After all, marble is white, isn't it? All in all, it was a perfect style of furniture for furnishing a Greek temple.

Incidentally, a lot of this can be understood if we know that Adam was originally an architect, and it was as the King's architect that he turned to designing furniture—a common function for an architect in those days.

Hepplewhite 1750–1790: While his designs all retain a basically Grecian look, Hepplewhite had to have something new, so he came up with two basic innovations. First was his straight tapered leg, sometimes with a spade foot, at other times tipped in brass. We still have a few garlands and inlays, but less than with Adam—though there is no question but that Hepplewhite was working from Adam.

The other typical Hepplewhite development was his shield-back chair, which is structurally one of the worst things ever designed by man. They were made purely for looks, never for leaning against.

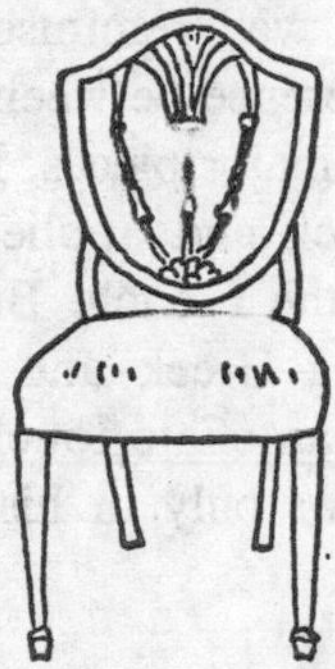

HEPPLEWHITE

The best things Hepplewhite did—and after all, he was casting around for new items to add to his line all the time—were his armchairs and so-called Martha Washington chairs. Again we have the case of simplicity and practical design turning out to be better-looking than all the ornamentation and trick carving in the world.

Sheraton 1790–1810: With Sheraton we have a mild, safe blending of the immediately preceding styles that makes this designer a close contender with Chippendale for the position of the most overrated cabinetmaker in history. He also turned to the French styles of the day to add a little fillip.

SHERATON

Basically he stuck to the straight legs of Hepplewhite, but made them round, in a way reminiscent of the Adam leg. Aside from this, the difference between Sheraton and Hepplewhite is academic in the major pieces. It was in his chairs that he introduced a lyre back and applied some of the slightly more ornate carving of the French. But since all the French were doing was applying Greek and Roman ideas to their own Renaissance—with an effete touch—the French element isn't outstanding. It shows only in his later, more decorated pieces.

Phyfe 1800–1815: Although Duncan Phyfe worked in America, it is ridiculous to classify him as anything but an English cabinetmaker. Phyfe's work was a continuation of

PHYFE

Sheraton's, and his factory in New York City employed up to a hundred men at a time. What he added to Sheraton's work was curved chair legs with a line similar to that in the Greek Ionic column. Also, eagles and other Federal motifs are seen in Phyfe.

It is, of course, somewhat doubtful whether Phyfe can be thought of as having a style, as his work responded yearly to any popular change in taste. Of his distinctive pieces, you can say that they have a curved Greek look as opposed to Adam's straight-line look. And he was getting this from the beginnings of the French Empire style that was just emerging.

So all in all, those who say there is no such thing as Phyfe style do have a good point.

Federal 1790–1825: This is the loosest classification in the world, and is used to cover the American interpretations of the styles popular in England during this period—in other words, Hepplewhite and Sheraton, along with the work of Duncan Phyfe. Except for the use of patriotic American symbols, there just isn't any such style.

The reason we have to class this as an English style—even though we've just said that it wasn't really a style—is that the work was being done by cabinetmakers who still thought of themselves in a cultural sense as Englishmen. And culturally speaking, they were. In fact, by leaving them in the English column, we clear up a good deal of confusion that has been caused by calling them American.

Victorian 1840–1900: Although it is easy for anyone who grew up in this country to recognize a Victorian piece, it is very difficult to pinpoint a Victorian style. The basic idea of the Victorian furniture designer was that anything goes. And just about everything did. Some Victorian looks like Empire, some like Gothic, all of it is madly ornamented with anything that could be machine-carved. Eastlake furniture was a variation that ran contrary to the carving trend, and looked like an exercise in mechanical drawing.

VICTORIAN

The most typical Victorian furniture would be the rococo work of John Belter, starting around 1850. His work carried the rococo idea the furthest, with bunches of grapes, leaves, and flowers running wild. Realistically machine-carved bunches of grapes and fruit—with leaves—are the most typical Victorian motif.

In other words, Victorian furniture was more a state of mind than a style, and as such it ran rampant in the United States, where an expanding population had more need for new furniture than did the English. Therefore you might say this "style" belongs in the American column. Certainly more Victorian furniture was made in the United States than in England. But in terms of its sources, Victorian certainly has to be classed as European, and more English than anything else.

FRENCH

French furniture from the Renaissance up through the 1700s is of interest to us mainly because of its influence on the English line. It showed considerably less development than went on in England. However, the influence of the Court and nobility were dominant, as opposed to the influence of England's rising merchant class. The effeteness and decay of France's ruling class are reflected in the furniture of the Louises. When Marie Antoinette said let them eat cake, she may have been referring to the furniture of the nobility—it certainly looked like it. The exceptions, of course, were the country-built Provincial and, after the Revolution, Empire.

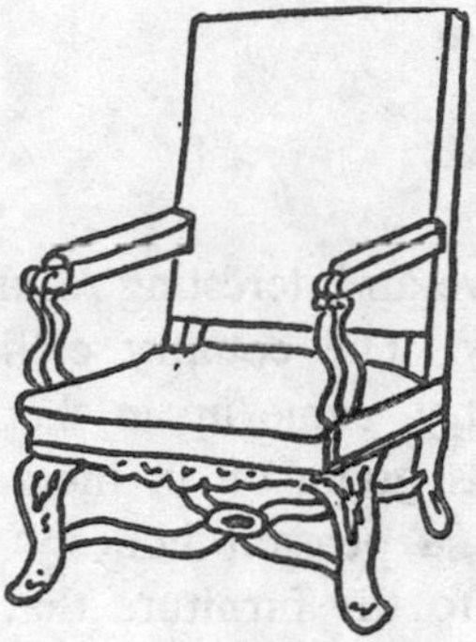

LOUIS XIV
1643–1715

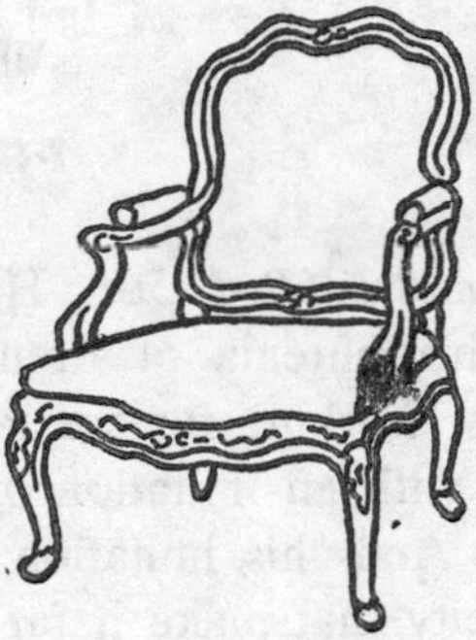

LOUIS XV
1715–1774

LOUIS XVI
1774–1793

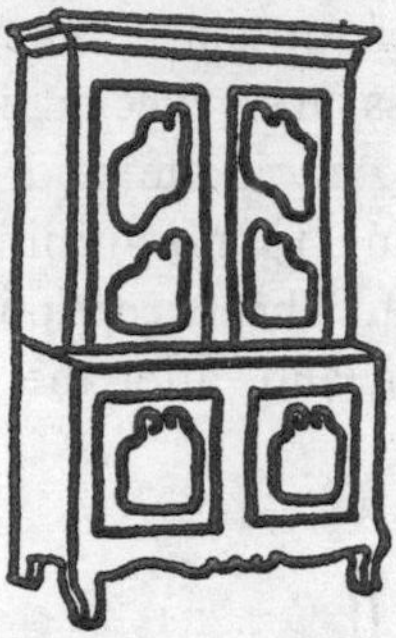

PROVINCIAL

Provincial 1750–1850: Here we have an interesting result of the schizophrenia of French society. The country cabinetmakers, working for the landed gentry, came up in the late 1700s with an imitation of what was going on in the royal Court. And this imitation possessed a peasant honesty and simplicity that make it far superior to the furniture that inspired it. It has the good, simple lines of practical design and restrained curving panels without any of the garish ornamentation popular in the Court. It compares quite closely to American Colonial, the other great country-made furniture. The difference is in a certain warmth or softness caused by more use of soft, curved lines in moldings.

DIRECTOIRE

Directoire 1795–1804: Although a continuation of the work that went on under the Louises, Directoire is a picturesque expression of Napoleon's glory, and especially of his trip to Egypt. The fabulous chair illustrated has Egyptian goddesses supporting its arms, but as a hangover of neoclassicism, there is a Greek urn on the back.

Empire 1804–1815: Up to now, in both English and French furniture, we have seen the use of Greek and Roman motifs to modify each following style, an essentially trivial thing to do. Why, then, you may ask, isn't Empire—with its straight

EMPIRE

use of Greek lines—the height of trivia. And my answer would be, because it was done so wholeheartedly by an energetic new society that wanted to cut itself off completely from the past and start anew.

Certainly, Empire was consciously taken from the Greeks, but it doesn't come out looking like a Greek temple the way the furniture of the Adam period did. There is no niggardly adaptation of a swag here and some fluting in the leg there, which was the way Hepplewhite and Sheraton worked. Empire is immediately recognizable in any piece of furniture, and is completely different from anything that went before it. When the Victorians used Empire for side chairs, you still can't miss the lines underlying the bunches of grapes.

Whether you like Empire or not, is not the question. It is a fundamental design idea, unlike anything else. It is a new start, made by a new society created in revolution and inspired to greatness under Napoleon. It was a time, you will remember, when the French people believed they could make Europe their empire—and almost did.

AMERICAN

Colonial 1630–1725: It is only in recent years, as Americans become increasingly sophisticated about art, that Colonial furniture has been really appreciated.

Only in the last twenty years have Americans become artistically sophisticated enough to appreciate Colonial furniture. At long last, our inferiority complex about the English furniture of the 1700s has begun to fade to the point where we can see that it is not only mostly rickety, but overornamented and showy. Placed next to the dignity and character of Colonial designs, it looks weak indeed.

This is because Colonial furniture had what artists call "functional design." This is the idea that if something is made from a purely practical point of view, it will be beautiful. Two things are involved: the use which is intended for the thing, and the material it is made of. The material becomes the deciding factor. If you are going to make a chair out of iron,

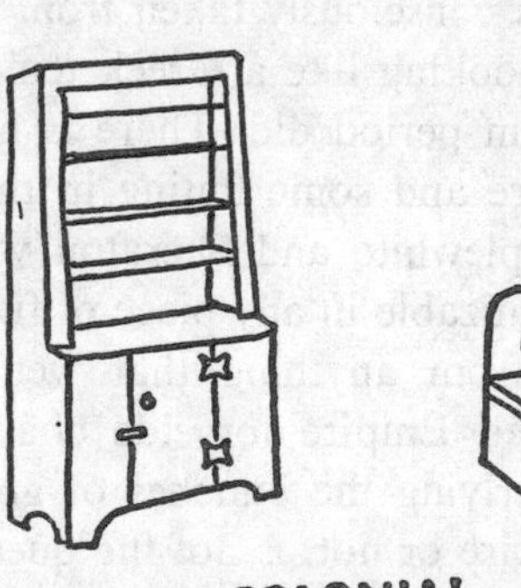

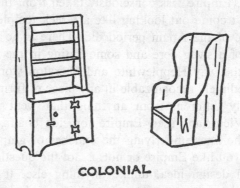

COLONIAL

try to do it to get the most strength with the least material, and you'll get something beautiful.

And that is what happened with Colonial furniture. The people who designed it, by trial and error over several generations, were trying to get the most out of a very particular material—pine wood. Then, as better tools became available, harder woods such as cherry and maple became part of the problem. And you might say that American Colonial is a series of answers to the problem. The tavern table, the sawbuck table, the hutch cabinet, the settle chair, the Windsor chair—all were built to do a job, and to do it well. And the beauty is there in their simple, economical lines—not in tricks of carving or ornamentation. The woods and workmanship are not as good as in Queen Anne furniture, but the same fundamentalness of line is there.

Windsor chairs 1725–1825: Windsor chairs are an important subdivision of Colonial furniture. They are a real triumph of functional design, because in spite of their lightness of weight they are among the strongest pieces of furniture ever built. Many that are already two hundred years old are in

AMERICAN WINDSOR

such perfect condition that they could be kept in daily use for another two hundred years.

The seats were poplar or pine, the spokes and curved backs of springy ash and hickory, the legs of rock-hard maple. They were not glued, but fitted together—with wooden wedges being used to spread the ends of spokes where they came through the arms or curved back sections. Sometimes the ends of the spindles that fit into the seat were carved to a small ball. This was then popped into a cavity in the edge of the seat whose mouth was smaller than the ball. This was naturally called a ball-socket joint. The result is that even when one of these chairs has completely dried out, it may rattle when you shake it, but it will never come apart. Incidentally, Windsor chairs were always painted—green, red, black, even yellow or white.

Shaker 1760–1800: Here is a case of an isolated society producing something new and different. The Shakers were a religious community that secluded themselves, mainly in upper New York State, and after a brief period of prosperity died out because of their rule that the members couldn't have children. New members could be brought into the group only by recruitment, but they didn't do much recruiting.

At any rate, Shaker furniture was designed and made in their own shops for the use of the community only. (Some other products were manufactured for sale to outsiders.) They believed in absolutely no frills, and in their efforts toward simplicity came up with many "modern-looking" designs. In fact, a lot of modern furniture has been inspired by Shaker designs.

American Fancy 1810–1840: In the years before the arrival of Victorian furniture, many American furniture factories sprang up to manufacture what the people called "fancy chairs" by the hundreds of thousands. In the beginning they were made in small cabinet shops, but as the demand grew with the craze, the shops quickly became factories, culminating in the first really mass-production furniture factory of Lambert Hitchcock.

Boston rockers also come from this period, as well as spool furniture. The latter, of course, was invented by some unknown genius in a spool factory, where spools for thread were turned from long wooden poles, then sawed apart.

All of this furniture was made out of whatever wood came to hand, and was then painted and decorated. (See section on DECORATION.)

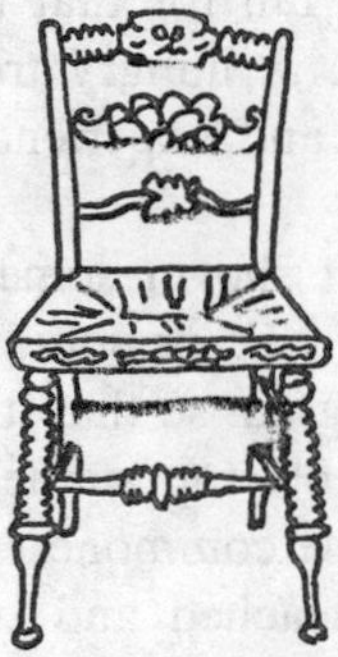

AMERICAN FANCY CHAIRS

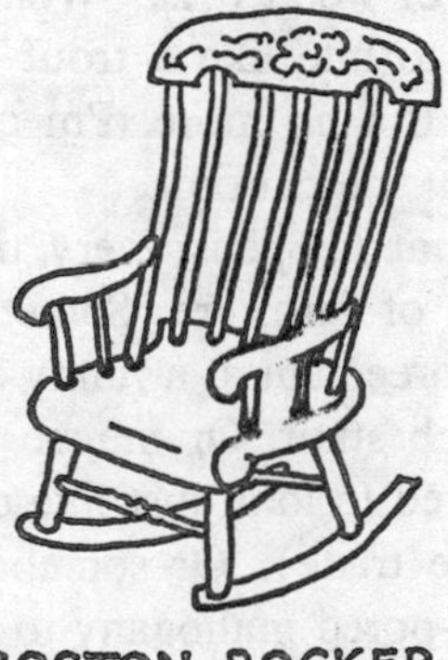

BOSTON ROCKER

Section 14

ALL ABOUT THE WOODS

Merely the first intelligent guide to cabinet woods ever printed: how to tell them apart, where and when they are used, and how they cut and stain

Every once in a while, someone says to me, "Say, I've got something I want you to look at. Maybe you can tell me what kind of wood it is." Well, once I used to fall for that bait. I used to bite like a trout in a spring rain. A hungry trout at that. But no more. I'm an old fish now, and experience has taught me caution.

What happens every time is that I get shown some trick piece of furniture. Sometimes it's swamp oak or some other rare breed cut at a funny angle across the grain so that it looks like chestnut. Or maybe it is a poplar table top stained and finished to look just like cherry (one of the commonest tricks in the trade). Or somebody will have bleached and stained large-pored mahogany to look like walnut. Don't ask me why they did it. Cabinetmakers are mostly crazy, anyway. Not to mention that they are *all* frustrated forgers at heart.

So now when anyone asks me what some wood is, I immediately figure that it has to be something else other than what it looks like. So if it looks like oak I say it's chestnut. And vice versa and et cetera. This way I manage to preserve my dignity at least a good 50 per cent of the time. Before that, I was batting zero.

However, these trick pieces come to less than 3 per cent of the furniture you are likely to see. I see a higher percentage of them of course, because everyone loves to bait a self-appointed expert. But for the average person it is not hard to learn to identify woods, especially if you have a handy guide such as the one that follows in this section.

You may ask why it wouldn't be better to have color photos or even a set of wood samples. The first reason is that even if you had a set of samples, you would need at least fifty pieces, because maple, for instance, comes plain, curly, and bird's-eye. And many of the large-pored woods can be cut in several different ways to make them look very different. You would also need pieces of each wood stained in three different colors and shades, at least. And then each of these would have to be shown finished and unfinished. So you would end with so many samples your confusion would be permanent.

Also, samples can't talk, so they can't tell you about the different hardnesses and weights of wood, their cutting characteristics, how they take stains, and where it is possible to find them in furniture and where it is not. There is no such thing, for instance, as a pine rung in a chair—unless it was made by either an idiot or a maniac. Pine is too easily broken, so maple is almost always used. And there are a lot of other clues, such as the woods used in different areas and countries, as you will see in the listings that follow.

So we make the assumption (I hope, correctly) that you have a general idea of what walnut looks like, that you know maple is a pale, poreless wood, and so on. What you are interested in are the problems: such as the difference between maple and birch and the other pale, hard woods. Well, believe me, sometimes these problems can be solved only by taking slivers of the actual wood to a laboratory where it can be examined by microscopic and chemical tests.

So anybody who says he is an expert at identifying woods is to be looked at with a little suspicion. And if a birch table looks so much like maple that no one but a scientist can tell the difference, what difference does it make. The table either has a certain characteristic beauty that both woods have, or it doesn't. Or to coin a phrase, a rose by any other name is still a rose. I certainly wouldn't mind having a three-hundred-year-old table that I had to tell people was either birch or maple. That certainly wouldn't make a bit of difference in its value, or in its beauty or usefulness.

The difference between woods really counts when someone is trying to cheat by faking an inferior wood to look like a more valuable one. Ignorance is bliss, of course, but if you buy a poplar table thinking it is cherry, sooner or later someone is sure to come along to dispel your ignorance.

So before going into the different woods, let's list the basic problems and the substitutions that are generally made.

(1) As already noted, birch and maple can be substituted for each other without it making much difference. But you want to look for pine or gumwood or poplar being substituted for them.

(2) This brings us to the central problem of faking, namely, the substitution of poplar or gum for practically anything. Both these woods are abundant and cheap, and not particularly attractive. They are "colorless." They have no distinctive grain, coloring, or figure. But they both have an even texture that makes them take stain just about perfectly. You can make them any even color, fake-grain them, or put figures into them very easily.

(3) The third major problem is distinguishing between the large-pored woods. Oak and chestnut are the most alike. Walnut and mahogany are quite different in color, but staining can confuse this issue completely. And, in fact, when walnut and mahogany are bleached, they can easily be confused with the naturally lighter oak and chestnut.

(4) Finally, we have the woods used in inlays, where almost any wood can be found. The leading ones are satinwood, holly, and tulipwood, which are used because they cut well and are so light that they can be stained. And, of course, they respond to stain in an even way. That is, they have no figure, but are evenly grained. Distinguishing between these

woods and the dark, almost black ones is not considered important. They are just grouped as "inlay woods." Where really fancy woods, such as zebra or violet wood are used, that, of course is a different matter.

The following listings are all written with these particular problems in mind.

The craftsman is also interested in the characteristics of the wood in relationship to building things with it and finishing it. Is it soft or hard, heavy or light? Is it good for carving, or does it splinter or crack easily? How well does it take stain, and can you bleach it? These questions are also covered in the following listings.

Finally, all of the listings are for specific woods, with two exceptions. These are the listings for *fruitwoods* and *inlay woods*. This is because there are so many of both that it would be foolish to list them all. Our list would run to over a thousand different kinds of wood, 90 per cent of which you will never see except on antique furniture imported from Europe. Of course, if you want to see such woods, go to 57th Street in Manhattan, between Third and Madison avenues. Also up Madison Avenue from there. The Parke-Bernet Gallery on Madison is a fine place, and admission is free. Just try to look as if you had money, and no one will bother you.

Note on the rare woods: Any listing of woods "commonly used" is an arbitrary one. How commonly do you mean? The list for furniture made in this country—whether antique or modern—could be as short as eighteen woods. To avoid argument, I've broadened the following list to twenty-four—plus variations. As to rare woods from all over the world that are found in inlays, there are over a thousand of these, a couple of hundred of which can be found in American-made furniture. For easier reference, I have grouped the more commonly used and available ones under the listing for *inlay woods*.

apple Apple ranges in color from creamy white to a pale tan. It is either plain or streaked with thin, irregularly curving lines of a medium brown. It is very like cherry except for its lighter color and these lines. It is a hard wood with a very fine, almost invisible grain, and no visible pores. It cuts without splintering, but is too hard for carving. It is good for turning on a lathe—hence is sometimes used for table and chair legs—and buttons have even been made of it. It takes stain in an even way, but usually only a pale stain is used. It was never cut as timber, but came into use mostly because old apple trees had to be cut down. So it is most often found in small tables, small wooden boxes, and other small objects, and occasionally in a drop-leaf table. In early times it was used more by the country cabinetmakers, who were taking advantage of the odd lots of wood that came their way. It is not used in modern furniture because of the supply problem.

ash (white and brown) White ash is the wood used in professional baseball bats. It has a supple, elastic strength. Oak bats, for contrast, would break all the time. It is a grayish to creamy white with a noticeable long straight grain, but no figures. It is also used for oars, boats, and tool handles, and for doors and trim inside houses. Its virtue is its strength and relative lightness and easiness to cut. On the other hand, it is not a very interesting wood, because staining doesn't bring out any depth of grain but simply colors it. The grain is so straight there isn't any depth of grain to be brought out—as opposed to cherry, for instance. It bends well when steamed, which makes for nice curved plow handles.

Brown ash has an even longer grain and is a little lighter, which makes it the wood used in splint baskets. Because it also holds its shape after being bent under steam, it was used for curved slats in Colonial chairs and for the long bent pieces in Windsor chairs. The spokes would usually be hickory, but in many cases the woods were used interchangeably. Brown ash ranges in color from a medium brown to very dark.

basswood Basswood has such an even texture that it is said to "cut like cheese." It is not, however, that soft. It is harder than pine, a little less hard than poplar, which it closely resembles. It has a pale, creamy color and, in the raw, doesn't look like anything much. But the evenness of its grain makes it take stain beautifully—either pale or dark, evenly or in streaks. Because of this you often find it in the legs of modern furniture, where it has been stained to match the rest of the piece, which is usually mahogany, walnut, or cherry. This isn't just in cheap furniture, but also up through the medium grades.

beech A moderately hard, even-grained wood without any spectacular figure, beech has been commonly used for chairs and table legs since they started making furniture in Europe. The American variety finds the same use. In its natural state it looks somewhat like maple, but its fibers are not as closely packed, making it lighter, and not as strong. In modern furniture it is usually found stained to match other woods. It will absorb more stain than maple, and it is one of the woods you can use a water-base stain on without raising the grain.

birch A hard, dense wood that is very much like maple, except that you do not find the bird's-eye figures. Nevertheless, it finishes so beautifully that many cabinetmakers prefer it to maple. The outstanding thing about birch is that it is probably the best wood of all for imitating cherry. When properly stained, it is almost impossible to tell the difference until you sand off the finish so that you can see the bare wood.

In the past, curly birch has been used as a veneer, and was also used in Early American pieces of the more primitive or "country-cabinetmaker" type. Birch takes any stain very well. In fact, stain is necessary to reveal its curly figures.

butternut This is a minor cabinet wood that is characterized by its nickname of "white walnut." In fact, it was stained to imitate walnut during Victorian times. It grows generally in the northeastern part of the United States, where it was used in Colonial furniture to some extent. It was also used as interior trim in houses.

It is a lighter, more splintery wood than walnut, and generally has larger pores. Of course, saying that it is more splintery than walnut is unfair, because walnut is such an even-grained wood. Butternut can actually be cut and worked very well, and also takes stains moderately well.

cedar Because of its use in cedar chests, few people are unfamiliar with this wood. However, they may not know that it is an easily worked wood because of its soft, even texture. It is like a good soft pine, only a little harder. The natural red color makes it hard to stain or disguise, and because of a natural oiliness, the raw wood should receive a first coat of shellac when being finished. This seals the oils in best.

cherry With their crushing inferiority complex about English furniture, the Early American cabinetmakers called cherry American mahogany—and usually stained it to look like mahogany. This is something like gilding a lily with mud. Finished either naturally or stained to bring out the figure, cherry is a more beautiful and exciting wood than mahogany ever dreamed of being. And it is also harder and stronger, if you look at these things from a practical point of view. As you may guess, cherry is my favorite wood. But I am far from alone in this. So far as one can have a favorite wood, it is a well-known fact that more cabinetmakers prefer cherry than cigarettes.

In addition to its beauty and strength (less than maple, but more than mahogany or walnut) cherry has a fine even texture that not only takes stain beautifully, but also makes it ideal for carving and turning.

It is very difficult to bleach cherry—though why anyone would want to is beyond me.

The best examples of cherry are found in Early American furniture, where it was used for larger pieces such as highboys and tables, as well as in candlestands and chairs. When Grand Rapids gets ahold of cherry, it usually fakes it up with a film of brown lacquer that does nothing for the wood except make it look dull and even-textured. More progress—in reverse.

chestnut Chestnut looks like, and has the open pores of, oak, so it was used in Victorian furniture to imitate oak or walnut. However, in modern times we have recognized its natural beauty, and use it widely in picture frames. It is also used as paneling and sometimes in "interest-catcher" tables, where it is sometimes given a pickled finish.

Because it doesn't warp, it was used in the past for drawers and as core wood for veneer panels.

Wormy chestnut—the kind most popular for picture frames—is the result of a borer that works on the standing tree. A blight hit American chestnut trees in the early 1900s, increasing the rarity and popularity of the wood.

Chestnut is tan, as opposed to oak's yellowness, and is less splintery, more even-grained, and an easier-to-cut wood.

cypress Because cypress was introduced to this country from England—where it had been brought from Cyprus, of course—this wood was only rarely used in Early American furniture, though it has been widely used for furniture in the Mediterranean countries for centuries. Today it is mainly used for garden furniture and interior trim on houses.

It is a close-grained, evenly textured wood with hardly any figure, and is an unimpressive tan color. Its outstanding characteristic is that it is quite porous, and as a result very light and strong in relation to its bulk. It will take any stain reasonably well, though not many people bother with it.

fir This wood is familiar to us through its use in fir plywood, and that is the only reason it is mentioned here. It is not considered a cabinet wood, because the surface has a very hard, raised figure running through soft wood. Shrinkage of the soft wood causes the figure to stand out, and it is almost impossible to ever sand this surface smooth. Also, the surface has a wild fiber that has to be sealed with shellac or Firzite even if you are only going to paint it. This is also necessary to stop coats of paint or varnish from checking in a year or so. Fir takes stain reasonably well if you have sealed the soft wood with shellac first. But whatever you do to it—including eight coats of paint—it still looks like fir plywood.

Plywood, of course, is excellent for unseen structural parts of furniture. And marine plywood is widely, and very successfully, used in boats.

gum This wood is often confused with poplar, the difference being that gum has a tannish core as opposed to the greenish one found in poplar. Gum is also a little denser and heavier. It has a fine grain and no figure except for black streaks, quite irregular, that only occur in some trees. When sanded, the wood looks like very pale, tannish stain.

Used in some early American furniture, it was even then used to simulate other woods, and is widely used for this purpose now (as is poplar, of course). It takes all kinds of stain perfectly, and you can make it look like anything. Works and carves beautifully, too.

Grand Rapids uses gum—as well as poplar and basswood—for legs of veneered tables, and the faking comes off so well that you can live with one for years before you notice the difference.

hickory This tannish wood is distinguished by the fact that cutting it with the grain reveals the pores of the wood as long channels. It is a splintery, hard-to-work wood something like brown ash, but not quite as pliable. It is used for the larger bent pieces in Colonial furniture such as back slats, though you can sometimes find a whole chair made out of hickory. Typical of the uses of both hickory and brown ash are the backs of Windsor chairs, which were made of either of them, or of a combination of the two, with ash being used for the more curved pieces.

holly Holly is probably the best-known of the "inlay woods." It is quite hard, even-grained, and poreless and figureless to the naked eye. It is pure white, and usually used that way, most finishes giving it a pale amber tone. Because of its whiteness it is ideal for dyeing all the colors of the rainbow, which is widely done. The odd shades of purples, pinks, and so forth that you see are usually holly. Holly was used as an inlay and veneer wood mostly during the 1700s for the best grades of furniture produced in both America and England. It was used in the largest areas in furniture of the Federal period in this country.

inlay woods Fancy woods have been collected and used in fine inlay work for many centuries. And a lot of woods common enough to be used in veneer work are also used in inlays. When you add to this the use of holly, which is dyed all the shades of the rainbow, it is almost impossible to identify a specific piece of wood used in an inlaid design.

For fifty cents you can get an illustrated catalogue of fancy woods from H. Wild, 510 East 11th Street, New York City. This third-generation firm lists 132 natural varieties, selling for an average of twenty cents a square foot, 24 varieties of butt, burl, and crotch figures, and another 32 dyed woods. They also sell preassembled borders, designs, checkerboards, and so forth. These come glued to a piece of brown paper. You glue the wood side onto your base wood, then when dry, sand the brown paper off the top of the inlay. Pretty clever, what? And all along you thought cabinetmakers cut the little pieces and fit them in by hand. Well, maybe a couple of hundred years ago, but not any more. For instance, you can buy an inlaid checkerboard that would take you three years to cut by hand for only four dollars.

mahogany The original mahogany came from the West Indies and the neighboring mainland, and is now called Honduras mahogany. It was originally called Spanish mahogany because Spain had control of this area during the 1700s. It is also called American mahogany to distinguish it from the varieties that come from Africa and the Philippines.

This Genuine Mahogany—as it is also called—is undoubtedly the king of furniture woods. It is a hard wood with a fine even grain that is ideal for structural members and carving. But the real reason for its popularity is the wide variety of rich figuring that is found in it, and the fact that these areas are large—due to the size of the tree itself. They are often ten or twelve feet in diameter just above their gnarled, rooty bases, and grow one hundred and fifty feet tall. There is also a plentiful supply.

The pores are small in genuine mahogany, often needing no filling, but the surface should be sealed first with a coat of shellac before varnish is applied. The wood stains easily, and can be bleached with the one-and-two bleaches. Of course, bleaching is only done to the uninteresting straight-grain pieces, because this destroys any figure. And the figured wood is naturally more expensive than the straight grain. In fact, bleaching is usually confined to the African and Philippine varieties because of this cost factor.

African mahogany came into use around the middle of the 1800s, and while it is used today in the finest furniture, it is considered second grade on the basis of a tendency to have a pinkish color and larger pores. It is also about 25 per cent lighter than Genuine-Honduras-American mahogany. It does, however, have the same beautiful figures in the same large areas, and it would take an expert to tell the difference after the wood has been well stained and finished.

The so-called Philippine mahoganies are of a slightly different genus from true mahogany, but they also have the size and figuring that make them a very good imitation for mass-production work. The wood is even more open-pored and lighter in color than the African mahoganies. This makes it easy to distinguish the three varieties if you can scrape down the surface on the back of a drawer or the bottom of a table: genuine mahogany is quite dark when just wet. There will be little difference between the scraped area and the finished surface. Philippine mahogany, even when wet, is a pale, pinkish wood. African mahogany falls in between the two.

maple Ranging in color from white to pale cream, maple is one of the hardest woods used in furniture—certainly the hardest and strongest commonly used. It takes stain well up to medium-brown shades, after which the wood won't take any more. You can lay or spray more coats of stain on, but you will have lost the look of maple.

It is so hard that trying to nail it will cause it to split—or, more likely, bend your nail. When screws are used (as part of an assembly technique and to hold pieces together while the glue dries) you must drill holes as big as the shank of the screw and not much smaller than the cutting edges. The wood is naturally quite difficult to cut and work without tools designed to do the job.

Light staining will bring out in maple its well-known fancy figures which give it various names: bird's-eye, fiddle-back, curly, or blister. Any stain may be used.

The extreme hardness of the wood makes it one of the few to which you can successfully apply a wax finish. Some staining is usually done first to bring out the figure, and the wood must previously have been sanded perfectly smooth.

Maple tables and cabinet furniture have been made in all styles since this country was first settled, and it still is widely used. Because of its strength, it is especially valuable for use in chairs.

When the term *maple* is used, it is understood that we are referring to the hard Northern or sugar maple that flourishes in New England. Other varieties of maple grow in warmer climates, and while these are almost as strong, they are darker in color and lack the beauty of Northern maple.

oak Around 1700, oak was used in this country to make chests in imitation of the Jacobean style popular in England—the so-called Connecticut cupboards. But being a rather dull wood, as well as hard to work, it fell into disuse until the monstrosities of the Victorian period were inflicted upon the world by the energetic but tasteless men who converted us into an industrial nation.

As everyone must have observed by now, oak is a yellowish, large-grained, open-pored wood that has no interesting figure and is hard and splintery.

The pores are so large that they are hard to fill, so they are usually left open unless the work is being done with factory equipment. Because of the pores, this wood is also the most popular for novelty finishes. (See *pickled finish* in section on FINISHES: OPAQUE.) By the use of these finishes, pieces that were originally Victorian horrors can be made into very "interesting" modern furniture.

pine This is the main soft wood that is used in furniture. In fact, the only other soft woods in this list are cedar and fir, both of which are special-purpose woods.

It was this very softness of pine that led to its wide use in Early American furniture of a primitive or "country-cabinet-maker" nature. Pine was easier to work with hand tools—and crude ones at that—than the hard woods such as cherry and maple that were popular with the big-city cabinetmakers. But the trouble with pine is twofold. First, it doesn't have the strength to stand up under use in thin members in chairs. Second, the wood is so soft that it is easily dented. This doesn't mean that some beautiful furniture wasn't made out of pine.

But it did mean that there had to be a basic bulkiness about its design.

When we speak of pine, we mean, of course, Eastern or white pine. Recently the copywriters have put the term *Punkin Pine* into the language, but it is the same thing as Eastern or white pine. The wood is poreless and grainless, and the only figures are the characteristic knots. It stains and finishes beautifully, and when knotless was often stained to imitate maple.

Pine made fine original—and now, reproduction—cobbler's benches and such pieces, but it is not good for table tops or other tops that get a lot of use, because the lack of support for the finish will cause it to crack and mar even if obvious dents do not occur.

The yellow pines are harder, splintery, and resinous, with a prominent streaky grain, and are used mainly in building houses. These come mostly from the South.

Western pine comes, believe it or not, from the Western states, and is similar to the Eastern pine, actually being a little stronger.

poplar Here we enter into a maze of conflicting names, because this wood is known with great local variation as white poplar, yellow poplar, whitewood, tulip, tulip poplar, cucumber wood, and popple. On top of this, the tree belongs to the magnolia family of trees, and is scientifically known as the American tulip tree—*Liriodendron tulipifera.* I know because I just looked it up.

At any rate, poplar is a medium-hard wood of a very even texture that works and glues well, and takes stain like a dream walking. In the old days it was widely used to imitate maple, cherry, and mahogany in tables, and today is still used for this purpose by the mass-producers of furniture the same way gumwood is used.

The distinguishing feature of this wood is a tannish or greenish heartwood, the color depending not on age, but on the moisture and other climatic and soil conditions under which the wood was grown. However, you will find many boards without any sign of this colored core, because the trees can grow to twelve feet in diameter. This has contributed to the confusion of names, and has led many people to believe that there are two kinds of poplar—or rather of the American tulip tree, which we call poplar, or whitewood, or cucumber, etc.

rosewood A really lovely if somewhat flamboyant wood, rosewood ranges from medium browns, through red to purplish-red in its base color. This is shot with very strong black figuring in well-defined streaks. In use, the browner woods are stained red—simply, I suppose, because that's what people expect rosewood to be.

The wood is very hard to work, being half again as heavy as maple, and having very large open pores that are often filled with colored plaster of Paris due to the oiliness of the wood, which tends to prevent other fillers from drying. The wood stains best with aniline dyes dissolved in alcohol.

Rosewood has been used in fine English furniture since the 1700s, but didn't occur often in American work until the Empire period, when it was used both solid and in veneers, the latter being very popular in melodeons. As Empire blended into the Victorian era, rosewood was still used, and was even more widely imitated by staining pine red and then irregularly streaking it with black stain applied with a ragged sponge.

Almost all rosewood used in American furniture both now and in the past comes from South America, especially Brazil, and hence is called Brazilian rosewood. There is a very similar variety that comes from the East Indies, but this has usually gone into European furniture.

tulipwood This wood comes from South America and is a cousin of Brazilian rosewood. Its physical characteristics are the same, the difference being that its coloring and figuration are more moderate. Instead of reds, we have pinks and tans with dark-brown streaks. It's nice.

This is the *real* tulipwood, as opposed to the loose use of the term for what we all should agree to call American poplar. I don't want to go over all that again, so see listing above for *poplar*.

walnut A very nice wood. Somehow a man's wood. And certainly a cabinetmaker's wood. Browner than mahogany—in fact, cocoa-colored when sanded—walnut is similar to mahogany in its even, easily-carved and worked texture as well as in the size and richness of its figuration. There is also considerable variation in the color of walnut—from light tan to dark brown, and sometimes alternating streaks of this in the same tree. This is a result of the conditions of moisture and soil in which the tree grew.

Although a lot of inferior walnut was used in Victorian furniture, the better kinds are recognized as the equal of the finest mahogany, which it is so like. Therefore, for the kind of figures that occur and for its working and staining characteristics, see listing for *mahogany*, above.

whitewood (basswood and "poplar") A common name for the American tulip tree or *poplar*, for which see listing above.

Section 15

SUPPLIES: OUR OWN "YELLOW PAGES"

A craftsman's directory of sources for hard-to-find items

I'll admit that it's not often that you need a sheet of ground cork, a bed-bolt cover, the works for a music box, or an unfilled paint tube. Still, it's nice to know where you can find them just in case. It gives you a feeling of security. At least, it does me. So in the following pages I have listed sources of supply for every possible item even the most professional cabinet shop or interior decorator could use.

Of course, the basic idea of this book has been to tell you how you can repair and refinish your furniture with *commonly available* materials. And I guess we can all agree this means things that can be bought at local paint and hardware stores. Well, that is true. You *can* do 90 per cent of the jobs that come up with such materials. So don't let this list scare you. Just think of these sources as your reserve forces—to be called on only in case of emergency.

Incidentally, I have dealt with all of these firms, and can recommend both their products and their ethics—though a few of them are a little slow in answering their mail. None of them have paid to get their names on the list, and couldn't get them on that way if they wanted to. They are there because I have found over the years that they had the things I needed.

brasses Send thirty-five cents for photo-illustrated catalogue to: Horton Brasses, Berlin, Connecticut. This is a complete line of reproductions, solid brass, struck from steel dies exactly the way the originals were made. (That is, not cast.) They are widely accepted as the standard of quality in the field. In addition to escutcheons and many styles of pulls, they have bed-bolt covers, casters, bellows nozzles, tip-table catches, porcelain knobs in white and brown, even snipe hinges, and all sorts of other specialties.

bronze powders See *stenciling supplies,* below.

cane Get free instruction sheet and price list from: Gocart Shop, P.O. Box 52, New Bedford, Massachusetts. The best instruction booklet is *Cane Seats for Chairs,* Bulletin 681, issued by the Cornell Extension Service. Send twenty-five cents to: Home Economics Department, Extension Service Publications, Cornell University, Ithaca, New York.

captains' chairs These are made in a number of mills in northern New England, and you can get them at very low prices by buying direct. For instance, at the time this was written, you could get one unfinished for fifteen dollars from: Colonial Reproductions, Georgetown, Massachusetts. They also have decorated ones for twenty-eight dollars. Send for folder.

carving Send for brochure from: J. L. Lacey, R.F.D. 1, Ridgefield, Connecticut. For very special jobs write: Clark Vorhies, Old Lyme, Connecticut.

clock paintings See listing, below, for *paintings on glass.*

clock works and faces Write: Mason and Sullivan Company, Noroton, Connecticut. They have a catalogue that also includes plans for reproduction clocks, molding, barometers, music boxes, etc., a good selection of the works and faces, and also kits.

containers The Baehm Paper Company, 219 Fulton Street, New York City, has everything you could think of and a lot you never expected existed. Jars and cans in all sizes and shapes, empty oil-paint tubes, pillboxes, tin boxes, round and square cardboard containers, plastic boxes and vials. They have no catalogue, but will serve you well if you make drawings of what you want.

cork sheets Cork runs from twelve cents to thirty cents a square foot depending on thickness, from: J. L. Hammett Company, Kendall Square, Cambridge, Massachusetts. Send twenty-five cents for catalogue of all sorts of craft supplies.

eagles Send for free brochure of finished and unfinished wooden carved eagles to: J. L. Lacey, R.F.D. 1, Ridgefield, Connecticut.

felt Get free price list from: Eastern Mills, Box 154, Chelsea, Massachusetts.

finishing supplies For the most complete line of finishing supplies and cabinet woods, send twenty-five cents for a catalogue to: A. Constantine, 2050 Eastchester Road, Bronx, New York 10461. This is a terrific catalogue of all kinds of finishes, stains, colors, chemicals, cabinet hardware, shellac sticks, padding lacquer—everything you could think of. Good service, too. Be sure to tell him I sent you, and maybe I can get a free can of varnish out of him someday.

There is another great place in New York City, but you have to go there as they do not run a mail-order department. This is H. Behlen & Brothers, Inc., at 10 Christopher Street,

New York, New York. That's down around Eighth Street near Sixth Avenue (Avenue of the Americas), which is the old Greenwich Village area and full of lots of good little restaurants for lunch. Thousands of items on display so you can read the labels and think about what you want.

gold leaf H. Behlen & Brothers, Inc. See listing for finishing supplies, above.

hardware All kinds of metal fittings for furniture are supplied by: Albert Constantine & Son, Inc., 2050 Eastchester Road, New York, New York. They have everything from invisible hinges to spring fixtures for typewriter desks. Send thirty-five cents for catalogue.

knobs For wooden, brass, and brown or white porcelain knobs, send twenty-five cents for catalogue to: Horton Brasses, Berlin, Connecticut. (See listing above for *brasses.*)

For limited quantities of authentic wood and fancy knobs (circa 1880s), write: Andy Elder, Dublin, New Hampshire. Some teardrop knobs available.

leather Good variety of kinds and thicknesses from J. L. Hammett Company, Kendall Square, Cambridge, Massachusetts. Send twenty-five cents for catalogue of craft supplies.

marble Vermont Marble Company, 101 Park Avenue, New York City.

music boxes Movements that play many standard tunes. Write: Mason and Sullivan Company, Noroton, Connecticut.

painting on glass These are the primitive-style paintings of scenes on the back of glass that are found in old clocks and mirrors. Write for free pamphlet from John F. Williams, R.F.D. 3, Great Barrington, Massachusetts.

reproductions (finished) Probably the biggest mail-order supplier of this kind of furniture is: The Old Guilford Forge, Guilford, Connecticut. Send twenty-five cents for catalogue.

reproductions (unfinished) A beautiful and ever-growing selection of these is offered by Cohasset Colonials, Cohasset, Massachusetts. See also listing, above, for *captains' chairs.*

rush Flat green rush, imitation rush, and caning are sold by: J. L. Hammett Company, Kendall Square, Cambridge, Massachusetts.

shellac sticks From Behlen in full range of colors. See listing above for *finishing supplies.*

stains See listing above for *finishing supplies.*

stenciling supplies Although not a mail-order house, a basic source for bronze powders is: B. F. Drakenfield and Company, 45 Park Place, New York City. For a good general line of supplies write: The Workshop, 122 Main Street, Penn Yann, New York. Also see any dealer in artist's supplies who is listed in the Yellow Pages of your telephone book.

stencils and patterns For a very wide selection of these—including custom-cut stencils from any design—write: The Peg Hall Studios, Brookville, Massachusetts.

tinware For trays, write: The Peg Hall Studios, Brookville, Massachusetts.

tools Good selections of woodworking tools are widely available through hardware stores. But for the specialized and rarer tools, the names Stanley and Millers Falls stand out. Dealers carrying these lines may not have everything in stock, but they have catalogue sheets, and can order from them for you. For instance, let's say you want a dowel-making machine. I know it's pretty unlikely, but in case you do, Stanley makes one. And the Millers Falls group of attachments for their hand drill is the best-thought-out line ever made. Both firms produce only top-quality products.

veneers and inlays For about a hundred and sixty varieties of veneer in all patterns and colors from all over the world, send twenty-five cents for catalogue to: H. L. Wild, 510 East 11th Street, New York City. They also have all kinds of precut inlays, and tools for doing veneer and inlay work. (See listings for *veneers* and *inlays* in section on REPAIRING.)

wooden boxes In assorted small sizes, with and without hinges. J. L. Hammett Company, Kendall Square, Cambridge, Massachusetts. Send twenty-five cents for catalogue.

woods For fine cabinet woods, planed and cut to exact dimensions, send twenty-five cents for catalogue to: H. L. Wild, 510 East 11th Street, New York City. This is an old, reliable family firm (as is Behlen, for that matter) that knows all there is to know about wood, and has everything. (See also listing for *veneers*, above.)

For the New England woods such as cherry, pine, maple, and birch, you can get larger pieces and better prices on any sizable amount by going to the original sources. Two of these are: N. W. Fellows & Son, Pittsfield, Vermont; and John Rowell, Tunbridge, Vermont. (Tunbridge, of course, is the home of that Vermont wonder, The Tunbridge World's Fair—the only permanently located annual world's fair there is.)

INDEX

Page numbers in italics indicate illustrations.

T2

HOW TO UNDERSTAND
(Or, Exploding the Myth

Being a chronology of furniture styles in England, France, and the United States which demonstrates how truly new styles of furniture originate only as new societies are born . . . and demonstrating how there have been

ENGLISH

Tudor - 1485-1585
Elizabethan - 1558-1603
Jacobean - 1603-1689
William and Mary - 1689-1702

Previous to the emergence of Britain as a world power, there was a confusion of influences on a still fluid society from the rest of Old Europe.

QUEEN ANNE 1702-1742
Georgian - 1720-1749

But with the birth of the Empire came the birth of the "mother" style of English furniture, the first original concept since the Middle Ages.

Chippendale - 1749-1779
Adam - 1758-1792
Hepplewhite - 1750-1790
Sheraton - 1790-1810
Phyfe - 1800-1815
Federal - made in U.S., but actually only a remake Hepplewhite, Sheraton, and Phyfe

All these turn out to be merely the application of various Greek and Roman motifs onto the Queen Anne idea until it is lost completely in a hodgepodge of rickety, pretentious junk—each "innovation" being as commercially inspired as styles in women's clothing are today. All appeared a few years later in the U. S. (Phyfe, of course, being an English cabinetmaker who happened to live here).

VICTORIAN 1840-1900

A goulash, of course, of everything that had ever happened before in the history of the world.